Praise for Finding Ecohappiness

"As a mom, I saw first hand how connection with nature lightened everyone's mood. *Finding Ecohappiness* is a beautiful and informative guide to calming our mind and replenishing our souls in nature for ourselves as well as our children."
—**Kyra Sedgwick**, actor/director

"In a time when children are under unprecedented environmental and social stress, Sandi Schwartz makes an impassioned and practical case for focusing on nature connection as a way to build their mental health, resilience and happiness. *Finding Ecohappiness* is, in short, a prescription for reducing the loneliness of our species."
—**Richard Louv**, author of *Last Child in the Woods*, *Vitamin N*, and *Our Wild Calling*

"What a gift this book is to parents looking to improve the mental health and happiness of their children and themselves! Drawing on the growing body of research on the healing power of nature, and packed with practical activities, *Finding Ecohappiness* provides a road map for reaping nature's benefits and healing the planet at the same time."
—**Marti Erickson, PhD,** cohost of the *Mom Enough* podcast

"Sandi Schwartz offers us a rich and practical guide to finding connection between ourselves and the natural world. The practices described in this book will help you and the ones you love step through the real doorways to the world outside and through the barriers in our minds to a relationship with nature that heals and sustains."
—**John Muir Laws**, scientist, artist, educator, and author of several books including *The Laws Guide to Nature Drawing and Journaling*

"*Finding Ecohappiness* is filled with important activities that children and families need right now. This book is a huge inspiration and an essential tool in our arsenal that we will utilize again and again!"
—**Giselle Shardlow**, Kids Yoga Stories

"Now more than ever, we could all benefit from greater connection to the healing powers of nature. In *Finding Ecohappiness*, Sandi Schwartz does an amazing job of bringing together engaging stories, cutting-edge research, and practical tips on how to tap into the therapeutic benefits of the natural world. A timely and essential book!"
—**Jonah Paquette, PsyD,** author of *Awestruck: How Embracing Wonder Can Make You Happier, Healthier, and More Connected*

"I highly recommend this book to any family interested in accessing the many benefits of the natural world. The tips and activities are practical and simple to adopt, while also being assured to help any child or family gain the full health and happiness benefits nature provides."
—**Dennis Kiley**, founder, EcoPsychology Initiative

"*Finding Ecohappiness* is a welcome and needed addition for every home and classroom. Tools and tips are shared throughout, and the checklists and resources at the end of each chapter are ready made for busy parents, teachers, and caregivers. Bravo!"
—**Harriet Shugarman**, award-winning author of *How to Talk to Your Kids about Climate Change*

"Through personal experiences, expert interviews, and social science research, Sandi Schwartz provides a comprehensive, accessible guide to using the natural environment to boost your family's mental health. If you struggle with anxiety or just want to find a bit more ecohappiness, you should definitely check out this book!"
—**Shannon Brescher Shea**, author of *Growing Sustainable Together: Practical Resources for Raising Kind, Engaged, Resilient Children*

"With compelling scientific research, concise storytelling, and actionable tips, *Finding Ecohappiness* will help families harness the awesome power of nature to stay connected, reduce stress, and increase happiness."
—**Natalie Silverstein, MPH**, author of *Simple Acts: The Busy Family's Guide to Giving Back*

Finding
Ecohappiness

FUN NATURE ACTIVITIES
TO HELP YOUR KIDS FEEL
HAPPIER AND CALMER

SANDI SCHWARTZ

Fresno, California

Published by Quill Driver Books
An imprint of Linden Publishing
2006 South Mary Street, Fresno, California 93721
(559) 233-6633 / (800) 345-4447
QuillDriverBooks.com

Quill Driver Books and Colophon are trademarks of
Linden Publishing, Inc.

The content of this book is for informational purposes only and is not intended to diagnose, treat, cure, or prevent any condition or disease. You understand that this book is not intended as a substitute for consultation with a licensed practitioner. Please consult with your own physician or healthcare specialist regarding the suggestions and recommendations made in this book. The use of this book implies your acceptance of this disclaimer.

ISBN 978-0-941936-50-7
135798642

Printed in the United States of America on acid-free paper.

Library of Congress Cataloging-in-Publication Data

Names: Schwartz, Sandi, author.
Title: Finding ecohappiness : fun nature activities to help your kids feel
    happier and calmer / Sandi Schwartz.
Description: Fresno, California : Quill Driver Books, [2022] | Includes
    bibliographical references and index.
Identifiers: LCCN 2021043429 | ISBN 9780941936507 (paperback) | ISBN
    9781610353878 (epub)
Subjects: LCSH: Nature--Psychological aspects. | Children and the
    environment. | Outdoor recreation for children. | Nature study--Activity
    programs. | Anxiety in children--Treatment.
Classification: LCC BF353.5.N37 S355 2022 | DDC
    155.4/1891--dc23/eng/20211109
LC record available at https://lccn.loc.gov/2021043429

Contents

Introduction vii

Chapter 1: How Nature Heals. 1

Chapter 2: Mindfulness. 27

Chapter 3: Awe and Gratitude 63

Chapter 4: Outdoor Play and Adventure 91

Chapter 5: Creative Arts 127

Chapter 6: Animals 163

Chapter 7: Food 193

Chapter 8: Volunteering 233

Conclusion: How Your Nature Habit Can Heal Your Family
and the Planet 265

Notes. 269

Index 289

Acknowledgments. 303

About the Author 305

To my dear children, who bring a tremendous
amount of joy and awe to my life every day.

To my loving husband, my rock, who encourages
and supports me to follow my dreams.

Introduction

ORTUROUS headaches, stomach pain, dizziness, tingling fingers, feeling like the floor is moving up and down, zaps throughout my body, a metallic taste in my mouth, brain fog. And I cannot forget the many times I was so dizzy and breathless that I was convinced I was going to collapse right then and there. These irritating, painful, troublesome symptoms of anxiety and panic have disturbed my life in profound ways.

I remember as a young child being so nervous before leaving for school in the morning that I felt nauseous. For many years, I refused to eat breakfast because of this agonizing sensation. I also have a clear memory of being at a friend's birthday party in third grade where I did not know anyone attending except for the birthday girl. I was so sick to my stomach that I passed on the pizza placed in front of me and ran off to the bathroom to collect myself. Middle school math class brought sweaty palms and a racing heart as I feared that the teacher would call on me to provide the answer to a complicated equation. Fast-forward to the end of my first semester at college when I suffered unbearable and frightening chest pains after receiving a poor grade and dealing with roommate conflicts. I guess you could say that anxiety was an unwelcome guest that accompanied me throughout my youth and into adulthood.

For too long, my battle with stress and anxiety remained undiagnosed and unmitigated. It was not until my own motherhood journey dealing with infertility and a high-risk pregnancy that I realized what was going on. The intense anxiety and panic attacks that appeared postpartum were the tipping point that pushed me to seek answers. All I wanted was to feel better so that I could take care of my baby and be the best mom possible. After numerous trips to doctors over the years with bizarre symptoms that turned out to be psychosomatic, many hours of cognitive behavioral therapy, and my own science-based research, I discovered ways to manage my stress and anxiety and return to a balanced state of mind, body, and spirit (at least most of the time). I have come a very long way. I am now aware of what is happening and how to tap into some powerful tools to reset and relax so I can enjoy life to its fullest, especially with my son and daughter, now in eighth and fourth grades.

Upon reflection, I found important lessons during some of these most challenging moments in my life that led to a positive path filled with inspiration and passion. These struggles gave me the desire to help others who are battling stress and anxiety, especially children. For nearly six years, I blogged under the name Happy Science Mom to help parents guide their children to better manage stress and improve well-being through a tool kit based on the science of positive psychology. I recently relaunched my website and blog under the new name, Ecohappiness Project, to highlight many of these same tools—including mindfulness, volunteering, nutrition, exercise, awe, gratitude, and creativity—through a nature lens. This is the tool kit that I wish I had growing up. My goal is to give my children—and all children—the ability to turn to some simple, natural tools when they feel distraught. The last thing I want is for anyone to get stuck in the anxiety quicksand as I did.

Throughout my journey, I discovered many ways to feel calmer and happier and noticed that nature is the common denominator in many of these practices. I have found solace in nature to relieve stress and anxiety through activities like walks in my neighborhood, bike rides by the water, painting nature scenes, and environmental volunteer projects. When I was having a meltdown my senior year of college because law school no longer seemed to be in the cards, a good friend took me on a walk to enjoy the beauty of the cherry blossoms in Washington, DC. Those pink-and-white flowers were so spectacular that I quickly forgot about my postgraduation worries for the afternoon. When I was nervously anticipating fertility treatments, I went for long strolls and bike rides on the boardwalk by the breathtaking ocean. When I felt glum about turning forty, I chose a weeklong Alaskan cruise and was pleasantly surprised how healing it was to be immersed in nature and to experience so much awe. I am thrilled to have discovered the incredible power of nature to help me feel happier and calmer, and I want your family to tap into it, too.

Our Children Are Struggling

Sadly, my story is not unique.

Many children are super stressed in this always-on pressure-cooker culture. From too much screen time to navigating social media to obsessing over grades and extracurricular activity overload, kids face a number of challenges that can trigger emotional issues at times. Many cultural themes also put a strain on our children's sense of safety and security, whether it be bullying; school shootings; both personal and global-scale health issues like COVID-19; climate change; politics; and being accepted for who they are no matter their race, religion, gender, appearance, and otherwise.

We know that all these stressors are taking a toll on our children, even at a young age. In fact, child and adolescent mental health disorders are the most common illnesses that children will experience under the age of eighteen.[1] In addition, each year one in five American children ages three through seventeen (approximately fifteen million children) are diagnosed with a mental, emotional, or behavioral disorder, according to the Centers for Disease Control and Prevention (CDC).[2]

It is clear that many parents are concerned about their children maintaining a healthy balance in life. The 2020 National Poll on Children's Health from C.S. Mott Children's Hospital presented parents' top ten health concerns for their children. Depression and suicide ranked at number five on the list and stress and anxiety were at number seven.[3] To help their children, parents often turn to quick fixes like medication without considering natural science-backed stress reduction techniques like mindfulness, gratitude, exercise, nutrition, art, and spending time in nature. This book focuses on how nature, specifically, can play a highly beneficial role in helping children feel happier and calmer so they can thrive.

How Nature Can Help

Have you ever gone on a walk just to clear your mind or taken a "mental health day" from your job to visit the beach, woods, mountains, or even a local park? What we all suspected intuitively, science has confirmed: spending time connecting to nature is a safe, effective tool to help minimize the effects of stress and boost mood. It also reduces our response to stress and allows us to recover from tense situations more quickly. Additionally, nature has been shown to improve focus and attention; lower the production of stress hormones like cortisol; and reduce stress-related physical symptoms like high blood pressure, increased heart rate, and muscle tension.

A growing number of studies over the past few decades from around the world have shown the importance of nature in improving our health and happiness. Examples cover a broad scope, including recreation activities in the wilderness, community gardens, nature art, views of nature, outdoor exercise, nature-related mindfulness and meditation, and contact with animals. You will read about many of these studies in the pages to come.

Richard Louv, author, recipient of the Audubon Medal, and cofounder and chairman emeritus of the Children & Nature Network, has been talking about the need for children to spend more time in nature since 2005 with the publication of his landmark book *Last Child in the Woods: Saving Our Children from Nature-Deficit Disorder*. While Louv and others have explored the topic of children and nature from a variety of perspectives, this book dives deeply into the intersection of nature and mental health, what I like to refer to as "ecohappiness." In the following chapters, you will discover a comprehensive collection of nature-based stress reduction tools to help your children thrive by living a happy, balanced life. You will learn why nature helps children feel happier and calmer, how to incorporate nature into your family's current lifestyle, ways to discover new nature activities to love, and the most effective way to build a consistent nature habit for your family.

Who This Book Is For

Whether you want to prevent your children from feeling stressed and overwhelmed; manage their current issues regarding stress, anxiety, and mood; enhance their treatment plan with some simple nature tools; or simply expand your time enjoying nature as a family, this book is for you.

My goal is to make the concept of nature for stress reduction accessible to all families, no matter the location, socioeconomic status, or even interest in the environment. Whether you already consider yourself outdoorsy and an avid environmentalist or have never even given nature much thought, this book will guide you to incorporate nature into your family's routine to help you and your children feel happier and calmer. It is filled with simple, practical, fun tips for bringing nature into your life, from creating a backyard garden to visiting nature centers and science museums to working on nature-related art and volunteer projects.

You do not have to commit to anything huge like hiking up a mountain or organizing a camping trip. In fact, while I consider myself to be a longtime environmentalist, I have never been camping! By slowly trying out different nature activities as a family and exploring the many tools highlighted throughout this book, you will be able to build a positive, beneficial nature habit that works for your family. Even if it is just taking care of a plant in your home or watching awe-inspiring nature videos, you will enhance your children's well-being as they connect with nature.

I understand that not all parents have the time or financial means to provide nature activities for their children. Therefore, I am committed to donating a portion of the proceeds from this book to help those children access nature through organizations such as the Children & Nature Network and National Wildlife Federation. These groups offer exceptional programs to ensure that all children have access to outdoor spaces and activities.

Although written with parents in mind, this book can also be helpful if you are a child psychologist who wants to share the ideas and resources with your patients and their parents; a pediatrician interested in giving out nature prescriptions to your patients to address their stress level; a school principal, teacher, camp director, yoga instructor, or other type of educator looking to include more calming nature-related activities into your curriculum; or another type of caretaker like a grandparent or child-care provider.

And while this is a parenting book focused on helping children feel happier and calmer, when we do these activities alongside our children, *our* well-being improves tremendously as well!

Important note: There are a number of ways to address stress and anxiety in children, including therapy, medication, and natural remedies. If your child is suffering from a serious anxiety or depression disorder, I recommend that you seek help from a trained medical professional. These mental health issues are very different from the stress we typically face on a daily basis and need to be addressed. While nature can have a profound positive effect on our mood and stress level, it is not a substitute for professional guidance and medication if needed. The goal of this book is to help manage stress before it gets too serious, and nature is a scientifically proven tool to do just that. When I was really struggling with prolonged anxiety, I saw a cognitive behavioral therapist who guided me so I could learn how to manage my stress and anxiety primarily on my own. He pointed me to important tools like positive self-talk, mindset shifting, breathing techniques, mindfulness, and enjoying life interests like art and nature. Some children will need to go through that process with a therapist, while others can learn to prevent and manage their mental health by using tools like spending time outdoors in nature.

How to Use This Book

This book is organized by nature tool, with the exception of chapter 1, which provides a general overview of the science behind how nature reduces stress and boosts mood. The rest of the chapters each explore one tool in depth that your family can use to tap into nature to feel happier and calmer. You will find scientific background supporting the effectiveness of the tool and multiple activities for your family to enjoy. The book concludes with a call to action about the critical need to recognize nature's role in supporting all our mental health.

Throughout each chapter, you will find inspiring success stories, specific activities to try, and tips to overcome typical barriers related to the specific tool. At the end of each chapter there is a list of resources and a sample activity checklist to help you build your nature habit.

While you are certainly welcome to read the book straight through from start to finish, feel free to skip around to the tools that initially pique your interest. As you read each chapter, you may notice some slight overlap. Mindful eating and gardening, for example, are covered in the food chapter, but meditation gardens are addressed in the chapter about mindfulness. While a broad topic may be repeated, the specific aspect of how it relates to the tool will be unique to the chapter where it appears.

I am thrilled to embark on this journey with you and hope that you and your family will find a tremendous amount of ecohappiness as you discover new and exciting ways to tap into the incredible healing power of nature.

❧ 1 ❧

How Nature Heals

Just being surrounded by
bountiful nature, rejuvenates
and inspires us.

E. O. Wilson

S POTTING a rainbow after a storm. Breathing in the sweet scent of a flower. Exploring a hiking trail while being surrounded by the tree canopy above and wildlife all around. Nature provides endless magical moments. Have you ever felt joyful, relaxed, and energized after connecting with nature in this way? These experiences can be therapeutic, helping to lighten our mood and ease the stress we may be feeling. While cultures around the world have tapped into the healing power of nature for generations, it was not until recently that science began to back up this notion.

There are now hundreds of studies confirming that spending time in nature can improve mental health, so we no longer need to rely on stories, anecdotes, or even a gut feeling. A groundbreaking 2019 study published in *Scientific Reports* found that spending at least 120 minutes a week in nature is associated with good health and well-being.[4] *The Nature of Americans* report, a collaborative effort involving federal and state agencies, nongovernmental institutions, and corporations, including Disney Conservation Fund, U.S. Fish & Wildlife Service, and Yale University, revealed that nearly all the children surveyed felt happier and healthier as a result of nature, which promoted their physical, psychological, and social well-being.[5] The catchy Mappiness study involved an app that beeped throughout the day to ask people how they felt and where they were at the time. It showed that most people are happier when engaging in outdoor activities—such as playing sports, hiking, birdwatching, and gardening—than when spending time indoors.[6] In addition, a study out of Denmark determined that the more time children spend outside, the happier they are as adults. Being raised surrounded by nature meant a fifty-five percent lower rate of developing mental health issues later in life.[7]

Before we dive into the individual tools that your family can use to connect to nature, let's examine the science behind how nature reduces stress and boosts mood. I will summarize the disciplines focusing on the intersection of nature and mental health, including ecopsychology, environmental psychology, and ecotherapy, and share the main theories about why nature is so healing for us. The rest of the chapter will explore specific sensory benefits of nature and elements of nature, such as light, water, negative ions, and scents, and how they improve mental health. While the rest of the book focuses on tools that can help children feel happier and calmer, the information covered in this introductory chapter is more general and may appear again later as it relates to specific tools.

Studying the Psychology of Nature

Several disciplines have sprouted up at the juncture of nature and mental health. Environmental psychology explores the dynamic connections between people and our surroundings. Our interaction with the natural environment can lead to the restoration of our attention and energy. Ecopsychology studies the link between our minds and the environment.

It is a way to bring together our inner life with the outer life around us. Ecopsychology has evolved to include ecotherapy, which focuses on both what we do to the earth and what the earth does for us, like improving our emotional well-being. It involves a range of practices, such as pet therapy and horticultural therapy, that help us connect to nature in a mindful and meaningful way with the guidance of a trained professional. The premise is to get back to our roots to reconnect with nature. This can help us feel more grounded, positive, relaxed, energized, and resilient.

Instructive Metaphors from Nature

Ecotherapists often use nature metaphors to connect with their clients. These figures of speech act as a symbol of something else in order to create a teachable comparison. Using nature metaphors is a helpful way for people, especially children, to better understand what they are going through emotionally and can be a catalyst for them to communicate their feelings.

The metaphors tend to be quite visual, which can be powerful when trying to get someone to open up about their struggles. We can use these vivid comparisons to talk to our children about how they are feeling with regard to stress, anxiety, and sadness. During an ecotherapy training session, Dennis Kiley, president of the EcoPsychology Initiative, discussed how we can use nature to talk about emotional balance. He correlates air to the mind and thoughts, earth to the physical body, water to emotions, and fire to passion and anger. This paints a clear picture of how different aspects of our mind and body interact to generate our many complex feelings.

Here are some more nature metaphors to share with your children. It would be fun to see what additional metaphors they can come up with on their own.

- **Seasons.** Seasonal changes in weather can correspond to seasons in our lives. For example, we can talk about feeling cold and dark like during wintertime.

- **Trees.** A tree is strong yet flexible. Its roots keep it grounded in the earth while its branches and leaves can bend and change to help it survive storms. We can use this metaphor to talk about how we can overcome challenging times.
- **Animals.** Different animals can be used to represent feelings, such as a loud, roaring lion to show anger and a soaring eagle to indicate power and freedom.
- **Waves.** The ebb and flow of ocean waves can resemble our fluctuating emotions.
- **Leaves floating on a stream.** This is commonly used to encourage people to "go with the flow" and not get stressed out.
- **Stones and rocks.** They represent a sense of sturdiness and strength.
- **Planting seeds.** This metaphor is used to stimulate curiosity and to encourage people to work toward growth and progress.
- **Life cycle of a butterfly.** Kids love learning about how caterpillars transform into butterflies. This process offers a great way to talk about how we go through changes in life and how we can start fresh at times.

Walk and talk therapy is becoming more popular as therapists realize the many benefits of spending time outdoors with their patients. This type of ecotherapy entails meeting at an outdoor location like a park, pond, hiking trail, botanical garden, or urban greenspace to conduct the therapy session. Throughout the appointment, the therapist and the patient may sit together on a bench or walk around outside. Nature is cleverly used throughout the session as a positive distraction, to offer opportunities for mindfulness and to guide the conversation. Conducting therapy outdoors has been shown to be beneficial. Patients who participated in therapy in a forest setting (such as an arboretum) experienced outcomes with less depression and stress than those who had therapy in an office or hospital setting.[8] We will explore various types of ecotherapy in greater detail throughout the rest of the book.

Another type of ecotherapy that is really catching on is the concept of a nature prescription. As more children struggle with mental health issues, pediatricians are turning to nature as an intervention. Just like a prescription for medication, doctors prescribe time outdoors to their patients. It can be written down on a typical prescription pad or generated electronically. To be as effective as possible, each nature prescription should have a specific location, activity, frequency, and duration included, according to Dr. Robert Zarr, MD, MPH, founder of Park Rx America. Founded in 2017, Park Rx America is a nonprofit organization whose mission is to decrease chronic disease, increase health and happiness, and foster environmental stewardship as a result of health care providers prescribing nature. The organization educates health professionals about the benefits of prescribing nature and provides a website to locate and prescribe visits to parks.

Seeing the Results of Nature Prescriptions

The main goal of any nature prescription program is to observe clear results. Dr. Zarr likes to see measurable changes in the mental health of his patients, but he also wants to hear about the experience they have in nature and how it makes them feel. His patient's success story was featured in a short film produced by the Healthy US Collaborative, a nonprofit organization focused on inspiring individuals to actively participate in their health and health care.[9] This otherwise healthy fifteen-year-old girl ended up in the emergency room with chest pain and excruciating headaches. Several medical tests were done, but doctors did not find anything physically wrong with her. Her symptoms were ultimately diagnosed as stress-related.

When the teen met with Dr. Zarr after her hospital visit, he asked her if she had any place outside where she can spend time since not all families have access to safe green space. Fortunately, her father's house had a hammock in the backyard. Dr. Zarr was thrilled that she had this wonderful outdoor spot as a resource. The nature prescription he gave her to help reduce stress was very specific. He asked her to spend time relaxing outside in the hammock, observing nature around her every week for sixty minutes without any distractions, including electronics.

Because it was an actual prescription, she took the directions quite seriously. It was hard to leave her phone behind for an hour, but she did it. She carved out an hour every Wednesday to sit in the hammock. This was a completely new experience for her. She began to notice things in her environment that she never did before, such as leaves changing colors, birds chirping, the breeze blowing against her skin, and clouds moving slowly in the sky above. As a result of filling her nature prescription, her chest pain disappeared, and she learned how to better manage her strong emotions like stress and anger.

If you are looking for a doctor in the United States who already prescribes nature, you can search the Park Rx America directory at https://www.parkrx.org. There are about one hundred offices in thirty-five states, yet this list is expected to grow.

Theories on Why Nature Heals

As researchers investigated how nature impacts our health and well-being, some key theories about why nature heals us have been developed over the years. The first one is called biophilia. This is an instinct we humans have to immerse ourselves in our natural environment. Our connection to nature provides a sense of well-being and offers solace and comfort unlike what we can find in any human-made environment. Although the term was originally defined in medical books in the early twentieth century as the urge to "affiliate with other forms of life," it gained attention in the 1980s when Harvard University scientist and Pulitzer Prize–winning author Edward O. Wilson proposed that it is a key reason why humans benefit emotionally from spending time in nature. He believes that our desire to be connected to nature is based on a biological need—part of our genetics. Nature helps us thrive and feel comfortable, and is a fundamental part of our health and happiness.[10] According to Stephen R. Kellert in *Nature by Design: The Practice of Biophilic Design*, this affinity for nature developed throughout evolution as humans spent much time outdoors. He voiced concern that so much of our time now is spent indoors.[11] Without a connection to nature, we can struggle emotionally.

Attention Restoration Theory (ART) is another highly regarded theory in this space. Developed by Rachel and Stephen Kaplan in the 1980s, it says that spending time in nature provides us with the opportunity to rest, reflect, and restore ourselves, especially after hard work or being indoors for long periods. ART can also be effective in recovering from stress.

As Adam Alter explains in *Drunk Tank Pink*, "The business of every-day life is depleting, and what man-made environments take away from us, nature gives back." Busy, urban environments are draining and force us to direct our attention to specific distractions like traffic and noise. On the other hand, natural environments like forests and oceans demand very little energy from us. Alter continues, "The difference between natural and urban landscapes is how they command our attention." While human-made places overstimulate us, nature helps us replenish exhausted mental resources.[12]

How Attention Restoration Theory (ART) Works

The Kaplans proposed that there are four states of attention during the restoration process as a result of being in nature: improved concentration, mental fatigue recovery, soft fascination, and reflection. First, we clear our mind of thoughts and worries. Next, our attention begins to restore to normal levels. The third state allows us to be gently distracted and engaged in a low-stimulation activity, which gives us a chance to relax. In the final state, the restorative environment allows us to more fully relax; restore our attention; and reflect on our life, including priorities, actions, and goals. According to ART, the following components characterize a restorative natural environment:[13]

- **Being away.** This is the sense of being separate and apart from our worries. We do not have to be physically away, but it is certainly helpful.
- **Soft fascination.** This occurs when our attention is held without any effort, like having to focus directly on something.
- **Extent.** This means that the quality of an environment helps us feel totally immersed and engaged.
- **Compatibility.** This is all about feeling enjoyment and comfort in our environment. To be restorative, an environment should be a place we choose that is familiar to us.

Finally, Roger Ulrich's Stress Reduction Theory (SRT) focuses on how nature can immediately lower anxiety and stress levels so we can think more clearly and feel happier. It differs from ART because it proposes a much faster shift in mood. Roger Ulrich was the first to study health consequences by observing nature. In the 1980s, he measured brain waves in people while they viewed nature slides and hypothesized that nature views could reduce patient stress. He also examined records of surgery patients over several years; some had been assigned to a room with a window view of trees while others looked out to a brick wall. He found that patients with views of nature needed fewer days in the hospital to recover, requested less pain medication, and were described by nurses as having a better attitude overall. Published in *Science* in 1984, this study has been cited by thousands of researchers.[14]

Sensory Benefits of Nature

Nature offers a soothing sensory experience like none other. Listening to birds chirping, breathing in the moist air after a rainstorm, and walking barefoot on the warm sand are natural treasures that help improve our mood. Studies show that viewing natural scenery like flowers, green plants, and woods leads to more relaxed feelings than looking at images with no nature at all.[15] Colors, patterns, textures, scents, and sounds are the primary ways we can experience nature through our senses.

Color

The most calming colors stem from nature. Creams, tans, pale blues, and pale greens help create a quiet atmosphere. According to color psychology experts, blue calms the mind and body, lowering blood pressure, heart rate, and respiration. It also minimizes feelings of anxiety and aggression and creates a sense of well-being. Interestingly enough, blue is overwhelmingly chosen as a favorite color by people around the world.[16] The color green promotes a serene and calming environment and is associated with health, healing, and well-being; soothes the body and mind; and reduces

anxiety. Neutral colors—tan, beige, ecru, cream, light brown, taupe, and gray—manifest an organic, earthy feeling. We can bring the benefits of nature's calming colors inside by using more natural hues when decorating our homes. Try using cool colors like blues and greens when choosing décor for your children's bedrooms since their calming effects help make the room feel spacious and relaxing, like the blue sky or ocean.

Patterns

Scientists have discovered that the reason nature is so soothing to us is that many patterns naturally occur in our environment. Known as fractal patterns, these repetitive, aesthetically pleasing aspects of nature help reduce stress. Physicist Richard Taylor investigated what happens when we look at fractal patterns. As a result of tracking eye movement and brain activity, he found that we are hardwired to respond to these types of patterns in nature. In fact, looking at fractals even for a short time can reduce stress by as much as sixty percent.[17]

Whether we observe the patterns outdoors or stare at a piece of nature, we can feel calmer after having viewed the images. Our vision is set up to efficiently process these patterns with ease and comfort. In fact, we develop a preference for fractals early on in life, before the age of three.[18] These patterns are found in plants, animals, and landscapes. A tree, for example, contains fractal patterns. First you see the large branches growing out of the trunk, and then you see smaller versions growing out of each big branch. As you keep zooming into the tree, you notice tinier and tinier branches all the way down to the most minute twigs. Other examples of nature's fractals include clouds, ocean waves, snowflakes, spirals of a seashell, pine cones, leaves, flowers, coastlines, and mountains.

Scents

We are all familiar with the old adage "stop and smell the roses." It helps us remember to take a moment and appreciate what we have and the beauty of simple things like a bed of flowers in our neighborhood. This saying also points to the fact that naturally occurring fragrances in our environment can help us relax and boost our mood. Indeed, our sense of smell is one tool that we can easily tap into to reduce tension and stress. Numerous scientific studies prove that plant scents impact the parts of the brain that process smell, memory, and emotion. These scents can affect us physiologically and mentally, improving mood, increasing alertness, reducing stress and anxiety, and even lowering blood pressure.[19] I often take in a big whiff of lavender essential oils right before my head hits the pillow at night since I find it so relaxing.

Relaxing Natural Scents

Here are some of the most relaxing natural scents, according to science:

- **Rain.** The scent of rain helps refresh us and improve our mood. Called petrichor, the fragrance of rain is a combination of chemicals secreted by bacteria in the soil, oils released from plants during dry spells, and ozone created when lightning splits oxygen and nitrogen molecules that then turn into nitric oxide. Going outside on a rainy day and breathing in the fresh air can be very relaxing.[20]
- **Pine.** The smell of pine trees is also known to relieve stress. In one Japanese study, participants who went on a walk through a pine forest said they felt significantly lower depression and stress.[21]
- **Citrus.** The smell of citrus fruit like lemons, oranges, and grapefruit helps to calm us down when we feel anxious and can give us a boost of energy.

- **Freshly cut grass.** Freshly cut grass tends to remind people of happy, playful days running around the yard. Scent researchers also found that chemicals (a number of plant-derived aliphatic alcohols and aldehydes termed "green odors") released by a newly mowed lawn can make us feel more joyful and relaxed.[22]
- **Lavender.** Extracted from the fresh flower of the lavender plant, the oil has been shown to have sedating effects that help our body and mind calm down. Its antioxidant components can lower the level of stress hormones in our body and soothe our nerves to relieve anxiety and depression.
- **Jasmine.** This floral scent is known to lift our mood. A study found that the smell of jasmine creates a sense of alertness and reduces sad thoughts. It is used to calm nerves and as an antidepressant because of its uplifting capabilities that produce a feeling of confidence, optimism, and revitalized energy.[23]

Sounds

Are you more soothed by the sound of traffic or the ocean? When we step outdoors and listen mindfully to nature, we can feel more relaxed due to the restorative effect of natural noises. I recall how happy and relaxed I felt while sitting on the beach and getting lost in the pattern of the crashing waves, walking through El Yunque rain forest in Puerto Rico and focusing on the gushing of the stream below, and hearing the lovely chirping birds in an arboretum we visited.

But until recently, scientists did not understand why nature sounds have such a powerful effect on our bodies and minds. A group of researchers in England recently discovered that nature sounds physically alter the connections in our brain, reducing our body's natural fight-flight-freeze instinct.[24]

Nature sounds like birdsong, wind, rain, and flowing water also help mask intrusive noises like airplanes flying overhead, leaf blowers, and construction sites, and undo the stress we feel from listening to them. In one study, the nervous system of adults who were exposed to sounds from both nature and noisy environments recovered faster after listening to nature.[25] In *Your Brain on Nature*, Eva M. Selhub and Alan C. Logan highlight research in office settings and hospitals that show how nature sounds help lower stress. Many of the studies focus on specific nature sounds; however, experts found that not all nature sounds have the same calming effect. The best sounds are those that provide a sense of natural space and mimic the biorhythms of an ecosystem like a forest. Loud screeching and croaking are just not going to result in the same calming feelings as sounds of water, for example, which are very soothing because of their slow, rhythmic whooshing noises.[26]

Textures

Another interesting aspect of nature is the variety of textures to help calm us down. From a fuzzy caterpillar to a smooth rock to a silky flower petal, different types of natural textures can be comforting as we explore them in a mindful way. Feeling a variety of surfaces with our hands can be an effective distraction that shifts our focus away from worries to something more positive and intriguing. We can enjoy an array of appealing natural textures outdoors and bring them into our homes as well. It is helpful to have several types of textures to rotate through, such as smooth, silky, squishy, fuzzy, and hard items. Try adding natural décor elements in your home wherever possible, such as bamboo, stones, wood or marble floors, and woven reed mats or sisal rugs made from earth-friendly materials.

Specific Elements of Nature

Several elements in nature are known to help make us feel better, including water, light, trees, plants, flowers, and negative ions.

Water

Have you ever lost yourself in the beauty of the ocean, a flowing waterfall, or an aquarium? You are certainly not alone. Throughout time people have been attracted to water for its many beneficial properties like tranquility, blue and emerald hues, and soothing sounds. Some believe this is because it is reminiscent of the time we spent in our mother's womb surrounded by amniotic fluid.[27] It may also be related to how the water makes us feel weightless and free.

Whatever the exact reason, science shows that being in and around water can calm our bodies and minds. In fact, less cortisol (the stress hormone) and more serotonin, oxytocin, and dopamine (hormones that boost mood) have been found in people as they spend time in, on, or around the ocean.[28] An international review of thirty-five studies found that blue spaces have a positive effect on mental health, particularly in terms of stress reduction.[29]

Marine biologist Wallace J. Nichols dove into this topic in his book *Blue Mind: The Surprising Science That Shows How Being Near, In, On, or Under Water Can Make You Happier, Healthier, More Connected, and Better at What You Do*. He believes that we all have a "blue mind," which he describes as "a mildly meditative state characterized by calm, peacefulness, unity, and a sense of general happiness and satisfaction with life in the moment" that is triggered when we are exposed to water. He writes, "Near water, but especially in water, our bodily senses—touch, pressure, temperature, motion, position, balance, weight, vibration—are truly alive."[30]

When we are around water, our brain becomes engaged in our environment and we enjoy staring out into the vast ocean or at the gentle movement of waves or ripples. We are naturally attracted to the blue color, shininess, sparkles and reflection of light, and motion of the water.

We become so focused on the water that we enter a mindful state like what Rachel and Stephen Kaplan talked about in their Attention Restoration Theory. During this time, our brain is interested and engaged in the water, taking in sensory input but not distracted and overloaded by it. When we are immersed in water, such as swimming or floating, we feel lighter and more relaxed. As a result, we enjoy lower stress levels; relief from anxiety, pain, and depression; improved mental clarity and focus; and better sleep.

Water also provides soothing sounds that help us feel calm, as evidenced by all the relaxation and sleep aids that use sounds of water—whether they be crashing waves, the pitter-patter of rainfall, or the rush of a flowing river. Why does the sound of water cause this reaction? Studies show that it is based on how our brain interprets different noises. These slow, rhythmic whooshing sounds are nonthreatening, which is why they calm us down. Also, the sound of water is a type of white noise that helps drown out other sounds that might cause us concern.[31]

Light

Natural sunlight can have a huge impact on our well-being. According to Stephen R. Kellert in *Nature by Design: The Practice of Biophilic Design*, "Light is among the most basic aspects of life and human existence. Fluctuations in light and dark help people orient themselves within an environment, move across spaces with relative ease and familiarity, experience comfort and good health, and be productive." This is due to the interaction between environmental light and light-sensitive cells in the retina of our eyes that can impact our sleep, alertness, mood, and cognitive performance.[32]

Inadequate exposure to natural light can lead to health problems. We often hear the term "seasonal affective disorder," or SAD, to describe when someone is unhappy during the cold, dark time of year. It is a form of depression that follows a seasonal pattern. As winter approaches and the days get shorter, ten to twenty percent of people experience mild symptoms of SAD and about six percent have considerably worse symptoms. Experts are not sure what triggers SAD, but some theories include environmental factors like the change in the amount and intensity of light exposure.[33] We can remedy this situation by spending time outside and allowing more natural light inside through windows, glass doors, and skylights.

Trees

You do not have to hug a tree to feel better. As Dr. Qing Li states in *Forest Bathing: How Trees Can Help You Find Health and Happiness*, "The sounds of the forest, the scent of the trees, the sunlight playing through the leaves, the fresh, clean air—these things give us a sense of comfort. They ease our stress and worry, help us to relax and to think more clearly."[34] Trees are the essence of connecting to the outdoors and a major symbol of nature. As we are taught as children, trees can provide us with shade, fruit, flowers, colorful leaves, a sturdy seat to relax and get lost in a good book, and the perfect place to hang a swing.

Trees help us feel happier and calmer in numerous ways. One extensive study in the United Kingdom found that people who live around trees and green space are less anxious and depressed, and that the positive effects of trees on people's mental well-being last a long time.[35] Over five hundred young adults in Japan felt more energetic and less anxious and depressed after walking for fifteen minutes in the forest compared to walking in an urban area.[36] In another study, participants in Poland spent fifteen minutes gazing at either a wintertime urban forest or an urban landscape lined with buildings. The trees in the forest had no leaves because of winter and there was no other shrubbery below the trees. Still, those who spent time looking at the winter forest reported significantly better moods, more positive emotions, higher energy, and a greater sense of personal restoration compared to those who looked at the urban scene.[37]

A well-known reason why trees are positive for our health is that they produce oxygen, which invigorates us. Another reason that trees can boost our mood is that they give off aromatic chemicals called phytoncides that have been found to uplift and relax our brain. These natural oils are part of the tree's defense system to help it stay alive. A tree

releases phytoncides to protect itself from bacteria, fungi, and insects. The concentration of phytoncides in the air depends on the temperature and other seasonal fluctuations that occur throughout the year, and the type and amount varies depending on the tree species. Also, the different chemicals have unique scents mimicking lemon, pine, and herb-like smells such as basil and dill. Phytoncides can reduce the production of stress hormones, and therefore anxiety. Dr. Li's groundbreaking research in Japan found that on days when phytoncides from Japanese Hinoki cypress trees were sprayed in hotel rooms, study participants had lower levels of stress hormones.[38]

Additionally, green, leafy trees can provide sensory relief in urban areas dominated by hard surfaces, right angles, glass, concrete, metal, and distractions like billboards. The vibrant colors, natural shapes, intriguing textures, fresh aromas, and soothing sounds of leaves rustling in the breeze provide a positive, restorative distraction from the stresses in our lives.[39] Tree-filled spaces also provide a welcoming area to gather and interact with friends and family and to connect to wildlife like birds and squirrels.

Plants and Flowers

Whether we enjoy the beauty and scents of flowers and plants outdoors or inside our homes, they can boost our family's mood and help us feel more relaxed. Simply adding plants in even a windowless room can improve our mental health. We can bring flowers and plants into our lives by gardening, visiting botanical gardens, adding attractive landscaping to our yard, buying freshly cut flower bouquets, and taking care of plants.

The therapeutic benefits of plants and flowers have been recognized for many years. Research done in hospitals, offices, and schools proves that even a simple plant in a room can have a significant impact on reducing stress and anxiety. It is believed that this is the result of natural stimuli affecting our senses of vision, hearing, touch, and smell.

Plants boost healing. Viewing plants during recovery from surgery can lead to a significant improvement in physiologic responses. Patients with plants in their room had lower blood pressure and less pain, anxiety, and fatigue compared to patients who did not have plants in their room.[40] In addition, a study involving elementary school students viewing an actual plant, an artificial plant, a photograph of a plant, and no plant determined that looking at the living plant led to a more positive mood, improved attention and concentration, and feelings of comfort.[41]

Negative Ions

Why do we feel so relaxed and refreshed walking in the rain or standing by a waterfall? It may be something invisible in the air boosting our mood. Scientists are finding that negative ions can help reduce stress, anxiety, and depression. Negative ions are charged molecules that we cannot feel, see, smell, or taste. Yet, breathing them in can help improve our well-being. In nature, you can find them where discharges of electricity are in the air after thunder or a lightning strike, where water collides with itself like a waterfall or at the beach, and in forests. They are also abundant during and right after a rainfall.[42] Overall, water and plants create over fifty percent of the negative ions produced naturally.[43]

As Florence Williams points out in *The Nature Fix*, negative ions can be easily inhaled into our lungs and absorbed into the bloodstream. They increase levels of serotonin, creating an overall happiness and calming effect.[44] In one study, researchers treated patients who had SAD with different concentrations of negative ions and found that a high concentration reduced some of the patient's depressive effects.[45] Another study showed that patients prone to panic attacks were less likely to experience an episode after a rainfall, when negative ion count is high.[46] I would be remiss if I did not point out that although several studies have suggested mental health benefits from negative ions, other studies have showed inconclusive results or no significant impact at all.

Capturing the Benefits of Nature from Indoors

Being outside is one of the best activities for our kids, but sometimes it is too cold or rainy to go outside. Is it possible to experience the benefits of nature from indoors? Nothing beats actually immersing ourselves outside in the natural environment, but science finds that we can still capture the essence of what nature has to offer through things like photographs, artwork, textures, plants, and sounds inside our home. Amazingly, just looking at pictures of nature scenes can make us feel similar to actually spending time outdoors. A recent study found that you can reduce stress by simply viewing images of nature. When participants looked at pictures of natural scenes, their stress level decreased because their parasympathetic nervous system (which helps us calm down) was activated.[47]

Here are some ideas on how to expose your children to nature from indoors:

- Visit indoor sanctuaries of nature such as an arboretum, butterfly garden, botanical garden, greenhouse, science museum, or aquarium.
- Decorate your home with awe-inspiring images of nature. Collect gorgeous pieces from famous photographers like Ansel Adams or take your own pictures to display.
- Add a variety of plants to your home.
- Start an indoor garden of herbs and flowers.
- Watch nature shows, movies, and documentaries as a family.
- Include pictures and objects of nature that are green and blue in your house since they are particularly calming.
- Play nature sounds in your home, especially at bedtime.

Exploring the Healing Benefits of Virtual Nature

Can nature on a screen be as healing as the real thing? Scientists are working hard to answer this question. So far, there is very good news if you enjoy virtual reality (VR) and nature videos. VR is a technology that combines multisensory stimuli to provide the perception of being "present" within computer-generated environments. It also allows us to interact in a 3-D world, resembling real-life events. What is also intriguing is that it can give us the chance to enjoy experiences that we otherwise would not have access to, such as flying or walking on the bottom of the sea floor.

In *Your Brain on Nature*, Eva M. Selhub and Alan C. Logan conclude that "we have no doubt that simulated nature can have medicinal effects, and while these may not be as strong as nature in its complete form, the scientific evidence supporting isolated elements of nature does exist. Sitting in a virtual forest has been shown to reduce stress, although in head-to-head duals, actual nature experience appears to have the edge on mental energy, vitality, and restoration."[48]

So, although I encourage you to always choose authentic nature when you can for your family, it is exciting that virtual nature can also provide key health benefits. In an analysis of over thirty studies that reviewed the effects of spending time in nature versus urban environments, researchers found that being exposed to nature led to people feeling happier whether they were outdoors or viewing nature on a screen. They also discovered that simulated environments with realistic images of nature, such as interactive VR, led to greater psychological benefits than less immersive choices like photographs.[49]

In 2020, researchers found that watching nature programs on television can uplift people's moods and reduce negative emotions. Experiencing nature with VR could have even larger benefits, boosting positive feelings and increasing people's connection to the natural world. During the experiment, individuals viewed scenes of an underwater coral reef in one of the following ways: on television, using a 360-degree VR video, and via VR using computer-generated interactive graphics. All three viewing methods minimized negative feelings such as sadness; however, only the interactive VR experience led to increases in positive emotions like happiness.[50]

This tells us that we can use virtual nature to boost our mood. Also, the more interactive your virtual nature experience is, the better you will feel.

As you can see, nature is filled with extraordinary attributes that can help your family feel happier and calmer. In the upcoming chapters, you will learn how to connect with all that nature has to offer by exploring these gifts through the lens of mindfulness, awe and gratitude, outdoor play and adventure, creative arts, animals, food, and volunteering. By the end of this journey, you will probably never look at a leaf, rock, pond, vegetable, or living creature in the same way again. This is my intent. I want your family to embrace the incredible healing power of nature so you and your children can flourish in mind, body, and spirit. Nature is waiting for us. We just need to open up our senses and dive right in to embody the tremendous benefits it generously offers.

Resources

Organizations

EcoPsychology Initiative: https://www.ecopsychologyinitiative.com
National ParkRx Initiative: https://www.parkrx.org
Nature Therapy Online: https://naturetherapyonline.net
Park Rx America: https://parkrxamerica.org
Walk with a Doc: https://walkwithadoc.org

Books

Nature by Design: The Practice of Biophilic Design by Stephen R. Kellert
The Nature Fix: Why Nature Makes Us Happier, Healthier, and More Creative by Florence Williams
Your Brain on Nature by Eva M. Selhub and Alan C. Logan

❧ 2 ❧

Mindfulness

Being outside and exploring the natural world support a calm and alert state of mind—and learning to deepen and stabilize that state through breathing practices, meditation, and other techniques that connect you with nature can make your experience even more rewarding.

Micah Mortali

A S I lay nervously on the acupuncture table once again, I closed my eyes and tried to relax. Needles frightened me, and I was so concerned that I would never get pregnant even after going through all this. I felt alone, angry, and scared. After a few appointments, I finally started to try to enjoy the silence and calming energy that followed my treatments. I eventually learned how to calm my mind and often ended up with the same overpowering image: a vision of me, my husband, and my future child holding hands and dancing on the beach. This became a meditative practice that helped me get through one of the most stressful times in my life: when I was trying to overcome infertility issues to finally have a baby.

We often turn to mindfulness and meditation to help calm us down. As it turns out, images of nature seem to be where the mind automatically goes to when we try to unwind. It is often rainbows, ocean waves, trees, flowers, and lovable animals that we envision when we want a soothing image, not concrete buildings or the many inanimate objects that fill our homes.

A thread of mindfulness is woven through this book. All aspects of nature require us to have some level of mindfulness to reap the benefits. The most important thing to remember is that when we connect to nature, whether it be while swimming, volunteering outdoors, gardening, birdwatching, going for a hike, or painting a nature scene, mindfulness is essential. In this chapter, we will explore what mindfulness is, its benefits to our mental health and well-being, and a number of specific ways to practice nature-related mindfulness. At the juncture of mindfulness and nature, our children can find a tremendous sense of calm when they need it most. Through a variety of mindfulness techniques, we can help our children harness the calming aspects of nature during stressful times they face now and far into the future.

What Is Mindfulness?

Mindfulness is the act of being fully present in the moment in a non-judgmental way, according to Jon Kabat-Zinn, the leading expert on mindfulness and creator of the Stress Reduction Clinic and the Center for Mindfulness in Medicine, Health Care, and Society at the University of Massachusetts Medical School.[51] As we practice mindfulness, we begin to understand our bodies and minds better and learn how to be less reactive to thoughts, emotions, and physical sensations.

With mindfulness, we develop a quality of attention that can be present no matter what is happening around us. This helps us have more peace, ease, and balance in our lives. It also helps us accept what is happening without thinking about whether it is right or wrong, good or bad. It allows us to quiet the endless distracting chatter in our minds so we can focus on the current moment. Furthermore, when we experience mindfulness, we connect with our inner thoughts and feelings so we can make calm, positive decisions. It helps us stay in the present moment rather than dwelling on the past or worrying about the future. Essentially, this act of focus frees us from the many distractions that cause stress and anxiety.

Now that mindfulness is practiced widely in schools and recommended by therapists, it is hard to believe how unknown it was in the United States just a decade or so ago. During my own cognitive behavioral therapy for anxiety, my doctor recommended mindfulness as one of the most important and effective ways to calm my mind. Although I do not meditate ritually every morning, I find mindful nature walks and bike rides, meditating outside in my backyard looking at the palm trees, and listening to a nature sound app to be extremely soothing.

While the idea of mindfulness and meditation can conjure up images of intensely focused Master Buddhas and monks, it is actually a pretty simple concept that has been proven to change our bodies and minds for the better. Numerous studies over the years have shown the incredible impact mindfulness can have on our lives by helping to reduce stress and anxiety and increase attention and focus. Scientists have actually witnessed people's brains thicken in areas in charge of decision making, emotional flexibility, and empathy during meditative practices.[52]

The brain constantly evolves during our lifetime, most quickly during childhood. By helping children develop a mindfulness practice, we can equip them with an exceptional tool that will help them make better decisions, regulate emotions, and improve their understanding of the world throughout their lives. As it turns out, scientists have discovered over the past several years the incredible power we have within ourselves to transform our brain and, therefore, our thought. In *The Whole-Brain Child*, authors Daniel J. Siegel, MD, and Tina Payne Bryson, PhD, explain how the brain physically changes in response to new experiences, a process called neuroplasticity. Because our brain can change based on what we experience and focus on, we can alter the way we respond to and interact with the world around us.[53] We can even reduce negative patterns like fear and form new, healthier ones. We do this by redirecting our attention toward something that relaxes us.

Fortunately, we have many effective tools to help our children practice mindfulness, including meditation, yoga, breathing techniques, and guided imagery. All these approaches involve directing attention to an object, image, sound, mantra, or our breath. In this chapter, we will discover a number of ways for your children to practice mindfulness using nature.

Linking Mindfulness and Nature

Nature innately induces mindfulness, according to Cortney Cameron and Natalia Clarke, authors of *Nature Therapy Walks: 22 Sensory Activities to Enjoy in Nature for Wellbeing*.[54] Staring out at the immense ocean, watching a gorgeous sunset, and standing in awe next to a giant redwood tree are moments involving nature that spur mindfulness. It is so easy to get lost in the present moment when we are witnessing the beauty of nature.

During his presentation at the March 2020 Mindful Living Summit, Mark Coleman, author of *Awake in the Wild: Mindfulness in Nature as a Path to Self-Discovery*, talked about how the sensory world of nature is an easy place to be in the present moment because of the numerous sights, sounds, and scents. Breathing outdoors, for example, helps us notice natural fragrances and the temperature and also take in fresh oxygen as we connect with the greenery. We also feel the warmth of the sun and cool breeze on our skin. He explained that when we are outside, our physical sensations awaken and we become more mindful of our environment—including the wider rhythm of life like the seasons and migrating birds. We also tend to be less self-absorbed when we are outside in nature, allowing our minds to settle down. This helps us feel a deep sense of peace through the stillness and pleasurable sensory experiences of nature. He mentioned, "Through the power of mindfulness people can cultivate a receptive, open quality of awareness that allows a rich sensitivity and connection to the natural world. Unlike being indoors, meditating in the wild allows you to utilize all of your senses and the sensory environment."[55]

Teaching our children this special trick of focused, mindful attention can help them in so many ways throughout their lives. By being aware of their emotions and learning how to shift their concentration, they will feel empowered and in control of their thoughts, emotions, and bodily sensations. From an early age, we can start to introduce some fun ways for kids to build up their mindfulness muscle. Focusing on awe-inspiring scenes of nature—whether in person or through pictures and videos—can engage children's attention and help them feel more mindful and relaxed. Schedule some outdoor time, sit down and watch a nature show, or enjoy gorgeous photographs of our natural environment. Teach your children that just sitting quietly and staring at these images is relaxing and a helpful way to focus. Here are some additional ways for kids to feel mindful from looking at nature:

- Visit zoos, mountains, forests, hiking trails, beaches, waterfalls, botanical gardens, canyons, and caves, and enjoy clear starry nights, rainbows, sunsets, and sunrises.
- Observe nature using various media tools such as videos, photographs, slide shows, and even 3-D or 4-D movies at an IMAX theater.
- Get a packet of national park postcards or nature-themed photicular books that use a special technology so each image is like a 3-D movie on the page.

- Practice meditations that tap into nature scenes. For example, the Over the Rainbow Breathing meditation instructs children to breathe in each color as they visualize a rainbow and then say a positive affirmation either silently or out loud.[56]

Another way children can feel more mindful is by listening to soothing sounds of nature. Ask them to sit back and close their eyes while they listen to the relaxing noises they hear. Teach them how to use visualization techniques and their own imagination to feel the full effect of the nature sounds they hear. We can bring the serene sounds of nature into our daily lives by taking the following steps:

- Invest in some nature meditation CDs and apps. Try out a few different kinds to see what your children prefer. Some have music along with nature sounds and others are just the natural sound of rushing water or chirping birds.
- Record your own nature sounds. Take along a recording device during a nature walk, trip to the beach, or other outdoor excursion. Capture those relaxing sounds to play again later.
- Install an indoor water fountain. One of the local spas by my home has a relaxation room with the most soothing waterfall on a rock-covered wall. Consider adding a small waterfall to your home to enjoy.

Finally, using the sense of touch can also help children be more mindful in nature. In fact, feeling different textures can be an effective distraction tool and is one trick that I use whenever I start to feel panicky. By touching one element at a time slowly and mindfully, we become more focused on the present and stop heading down a path of worry. Doing this out in nature can be very effective. Look for different types of textures. Some ideas include tree bark, grass, leaves, flower petals, stones, and friendly animals to pet.

How Sit Spots Help Children Find
Silence and Serenity

Being able to sit in silence may be challenging for some children. If they are able to do it—especially outdoors surrounded by nature—this practice can be incredibly beneficial to them. Silence has a profound calming effect. It settles the many emotions we experience that are activated by talking and listening. As our mental and emotional lives calm down in a quiet space, our bodies can relax as well. We need silence to bring us back to the present moment, helping us to calm down and not worry about what happened in the past or what may happen in the future. It is a wonderful way for us to take a step back, find peace, and recharge. Silence also helps us more effectively connect to the world around us. Essentially, all our senses are heightened when we are silent. We may notice sounds that we never did before and view our surroundings with a fresh perspective.

In the world of nature meditation, it is recommended that we choose a sit spot to both savor the silence and absorb all that nature has to offer. A sit spot is a favorite place in nature that we visit regularly to cultivate awareness of our surroundings as we expand our senses and observe local plants, birds, trees, animals, and so on. By choosing one place outside that we visit over and over again, we can develop an enhanced sensitivity to nature and the ability to be more mindful.

Encourage your children to choose their own sit spot. If they are too young or need some guidance, you can identify a place where you can sit together. A sit spot can be anywhere that connects you to nature. If you have a backyard, each member of your family can find their own sit spot. This could be on a tree stump, small bench, chair, or even a blanket or towel you bring outside with you. If you do not have a backyard, you can choose a spot in a nearby park, in a schoolyard, by a community garden, or on an apartment balcony. Another fabulous sit spot idea for children is a treehouse or part of their swing set where they can sit for a few minutes.

The best part of having a sit spot is that children learn to go to that special, peaceful place when they are feeling stressed or uneasy. It helps them quiet their mind and focus on nature as opposed to other distractions like schoolwork and technology. The amount of time they visit their sit spot can vary. Children can benefit from just five minutes. As they get older and more used to it, they can work their way up to sitting for thirty minutes or more at a time. This is a great way for them to practice mindfulness skills like deep breathing, listening to nature sounds, and other nature-related meditation activities like looking for certain colors or shapes.

Nature Meditation

Meditation can come in many different forms that target one or more of our senses and emotions to help us feel still and relaxed. Nature is ripe with opportunities for our children to meditate, whether they be through visualizations, sounds, smells, or textures. Mellisa Dormoy is a best-selling author, guided imagery expert, and founder of ShambalaKids. Her meditation audios help children and teens relieve stress and anxiety by offering therapeutic messages and engaging their imagination. "Nature teaches us so much, heals us, and grounds us," Mellisa comments. When she envisions a meditation for children, it is usually outside because they can easily feel the beauty and peace of nature. "Children connect with nature because it is all around us. Nature has so many tools and examples that can serve as an analogy to life's experiences. Mountains represent how we can overcome challenges, a butterfly or bird flying helps us feel light and free, and ocean waves resemble our emotions rolling in and out." Her guided meditations teach children in ways they can understand and help them get to a calm place within when they are feeling unsettled.[57]

The best part is that nature meditation does not always have to be performed outdoors; from visualizations to nature sound apps, there are so many ways to experience mindfulness using nature even from inside the comfort of your home. The best advice I can give is to play around with different types of nature meditations with your kids and see what speaks to them. Here are a few examples for your family to try.

Color Meditation

An easy way to get started, especially with young children, is to focus on color since it is a simple concept for them to grasp and a big part of their world. Color is all around and provides the perfect opportunity to tap into our children's wonder and to encourage them to be more mindful of their surroundings. At first, we can guide them to be more mindful of the colors in their environment. You can do this by going on a slow walk and taking time to look at and discuss the vibrant colors you spot, observing the many colorful fruits and vegetables at the grocery store or farmer's

Crown   Sahasrara

Third Eye   Ajna

Throat   Vishuddha

Heart   Anahata

Solar Plexus   Manipura

Sacrum   Svadhisthana

Root   Muladhara

market, or visiting a garden or flower shop and soaking in the beauty of the flowers and plants.

We can also use color as part of meditation to help our children visualize the beauty of nature. I once took a restorative yoga class in which the teacher led us in a lovely, serene color meditation. She asked us to envision dust in different shades that coordinated with our chakras, the wheels of energy throughout our body according to Hindu and Buddhist traditions.

There are seven chakras from the base of the spine to the crown of the head. To give you a sense, purple is for the top of our head, green is for our heart, and red is for our root or the bottom of our body. During that meditation, I became totally lost in the images within my mind. She asked us to sense the smell and temperature of each color. Red felt warm to me and yellow smelled like lemons. You can get very creative with color meditation for children as they are learning about their senses. Here are some other ways to bring color into your children's meditation time:

- Ask them to link each color to a fruit and to think about how that fruit tastes, smells, and feels.
- Have them visually paint or draw a picture in their mind using each color. You can guide them in painting a rainbow or a nature scene with a yellow sun, green tree, blue pond, and so on.
- Link each color to a flower and have them imagine smelling each one. What does a red rose or a yellow sunflower smell like?

Flower-Gazing Meditation

Flowers can be powerful items to use during meditation because of their intriguing shapes, colors, textures, and edges that help soothe us. Examining a flower up close to see what it actually looks like can be a wonderful way to get our children interested in nature meditation. By focusing on this one beautiful object, we can tune out the rest of the stimuli around us. Your family can practice flower-gazing meditation by taking the following steps:

1. Have your children choose a flower that is attractive to them. You can buy a bouquet from the grocery store or local flower shop or pick a flower from your own garden or a friend's garden (just be sure to ask first).
2. Your children can either hold the flower or set it down about a foot in front of them, preferably at eye level.
3. Direct them to gaze at it with soft, relaxed eyes. They should blink normally and try to relax their face and body.
4. Invite them to look at the flower in fresh ways and at different angles. They can first focus on the petals for a few minutes, then shift to the pollen, and later the stem.
5. Besides making this a visual experience, they can also use other senses by feeling the flower's textures and smelling its scent.
6. Let them know that if they get distracted by thoughts or noises, they should bring their attention back to the flower.
7. At the end of the session, which can last ten or more minutes, have them thank the flower and offer gratitude to it.

8. You may also want to extend this mindful moment with a creative project, such as asking your kids to write a poem about the flower or draw a picture of it.[58]

Loving-kindness Meditation for Nature

Also called Metta or compassion meditation, loving-kindness meditation is one of the most commonly practiced types of meditations. Quite simply, it involves directing positive thoughts and well wishes to ourselves and others. Practicing loving-kindness meditation helps us feel less isolated and more connected to the world around us. It leads to positive changes in the brain, bringing benefits to our lives such as reducing stress and anxiety and lifting our mood. We can tweak this practice by sending love and kindness to nature. Ask your children to sit comfortably with their eyes closed, imagining what they wish for in that moment. The four phrases that they can either say out loud or think silently during the practice are typically:

> May I/you be safe.
> May I/you be healthy and strong.
> May I/you be happy.
> May I/you be peaceful and at ease.

Have them repeat these wishes, first directing the words to themselves and then toward different aspects of nature like a tree, butterfly, or animal. Here are the steps to follow:

1. Start by directing the phrases to yourself.
2. Next, direct the Metta toward something in nature you feel thankful for. (Example: rainbows)
3. Now visualize something in nature you feel neutral about—you neither like nor dislike it. Direct the thoughts to that object. (Example: grass)
4. Next, direct the thoughts to something in nature you do not like. (Example: spiders)
5. Finally, direct the Metta toward the entire planet: *May all beings everywhere be happy.*

Guided Relaxation: Peaceful Butterfly

Please enjoy this guided meditation for bedtime provided by Mellisa Dormoy. Simply read the following words in a loving, soothing voice with a gentle pace, pausing often. Watch how your child visibly relaxes and engages the imagination in this meditative story:

Close your eyes and take in a nice deep breath. Allow your tummy to fill up like a balloon, and then exhale slowly. Do this five times to really relax your whole body completely.

Your body begins to feel deeply relaxed and sinks down farther and farther into your nice, soft bed. Your legs begin to feel very heavy. Your arms begin to feel heavy and relaxed. You enjoy every moment as your body continues to relax with each word I say.

Now as your body relaxes, imagine you are a beautiful butterfly fluttering high in the sky. You see the lovely green valley below you with lots of colorful flowers, just waiting for you to enjoy. You feel the wind blow against your delicate wings. As the wind touches you, it gently blows away any worries, any stress you feel. Notice how wonderful it is to be so free. Your mind is clear and calm. You have left any worries far behind now. You are completely peaceful. You are beautiful as you allow your true happiness to shine through.

The sun touches your body and warms you. The big, puffy clouds floating in the sky remind you how relaxed and calm you can be whenever you want, just by thinking about it. The earth is a patchwork of color and you enjoy each moment here, gliding along feeling so joyful and peaceful. You spread your wings far and stretch. It feels so good. Your body is calm and your mind is peaceful. You are ready for a wonderful, peaceful sleep tonight.

Take in a deep breath now and exhale slowly. When you are ready, give your body a big stretch. With a clear, calm mind, say these words to yourself: I am peaceful and I am calm, ready for a wonderful adventure in dreamland.[59]

Mindful Breathing

A common symptom of stress and anxiety is feeling like we cannot breathe. It can be very frightening and lead to more panic. On the other hand, the breath is central to a mindfulness practice and can instantly help calm us down. Having a breathing practice has been scientifically proven to minimize stress and anxiety, and is a simple tool to teach our children to use in times of stress.[60] Best of all, it is portable, so they can access it whenever they need.

Fortunately, there are a multitude of breathing exercises that can slow our breathing and mitigate unsettling emotions. Some involve breathing in a particular pattern while others are all about visualization. The most important thing is to teach children how to breathe from their diaphragm; this is when the belly expands and fills up with air. Small, shallow chest breathing only exacerbates anxiety. It is also recommended to breathe in through the nose and out through the mouth for the most relaxing effect.

We can pass along this important instrument to our kids by using some fun, playful approaches that relate to nature:

- **Dandelion breath.** Either get a real dandelion or ask your children to use their imagination. While holding it about an arm's length out in front, have them take in a big inhalation through their nose, hold for a few seconds, and then slowly blow the dandelion so the seeds disperse through the air.
- **Wave breath.** If you have access to a beach nearby, you can have your kids breathe in and out to the rhythm of the waves cresting and crashing. You can also use a video to create the same effect.
- **Flower breath.** Find a flower or have your children visualize their favorite flower. As they breathe in deeply, ask them to take in a big whiff of the flower's scent. They can hold their breath to the count of three and then exhale slowly.
- **Sunrise breath.** Invite your children to stand up tall with their arms by their sides. Tell them to raise both arms high above their head until their fingers touch and their arms are in a round shape

like the sun. Hold for a few seconds and then exhale strongly, allowing the arms to gently fall back down.

- **Hand breath.** Invite children to create a heart shape with their hands by touching their fingertips together. As they breathe in, they expand their hands to a heart shape. As they breathe out, their hands collapse into two fists side by side. Have them imagine this is a jellyfish floating around, fish gills, or a flower blooming.

Yoga

Yoga is another type of mindfulness practice that offers so many incredible benefits to our children, including a time for inner focus, a way to connect to their bodies, a retreat from the pressures and stress of daily life, and even an opportunity to enjoy a bit of silliness to lighten the moment. Various studies in recent years have shown how yoga can reduce stress and anxiety and boost mood.[61] Children need relaxing breaks like yoga to help keep them happy and balanced. Outdoor yoga, nature-themed yoga, and yoga with animals are all intriguing ways to intertwine the benefits of both nature and a yoga practice to help kids unwind and feel at peace.

Just by simply taking a yoga practice outdoors to the woods, the beach, or even your own backyard, you can enhance your children's mindfulness experience. One of the most powerful poses to do outside is tree pose. There is something so special about standing tall and strong while looking at a real tree. If you are not familiar with how to do tree pose, then follow these simple steps:

1. Stand upright on one foot only while the other foot rests on the inside of the standing leg either above or below the knee. The higher up the foot rests, the more challenging it is to stay balanced.
2. Bring your hands together at the heart or above your head, opened to the sky (this requires more balance). If these positions are too challenging, it may be helpful to extend both arms out to the side to find your balance.
3. Focus on rooting your foot into the ground and keeping the body straight and strong.
4. Try shifting your gaze from straight ahead to up to the blue sky to see how your body feels differently. It becomes harder to stay balanced on one foot as you look up high.
5. Carefully release the raised leg and place it on the ground.
6. Switch legs and repeat.

We can also incorporate fun nature concepts into children's yoga practice, such as asking them to pretend to be animals while doing their yoga moves. Some other creative ideas include renaming yoga poses with animal names, asking children to meow during cat pose and moo during cow pose, and pretending that a small furry animal is moving from one part of their body to another when they do a body scan.

Giselle Shardlow, children's author and founder of Kids Yoga Stories, develops books, card decks, posters, games, and teaching resources for children to explore yoga. Her materials use engaging characters and adventures to encourage kids to learn, move, and have fun through simple yoga poses. Many of her stories link to nature, and her reason for doing so involves the origin of yoga. She explains, "Yoga was invented five thousand years ago in India when a group of men went up to the mountains to sit and reflect. They started to mimic what they saw in nature and used different poses to express their feelings." Yoga means "union" and involves the union of mind, body, and spirit. "It is really in nature that we can experience deep reflections, peace, and tranquility. It is easier to practice yoga in nature than indoors."[62]

As an environmental enthusiast and former elementary school teacher and yoga instructor, Giselle often develops stories set in natural places from around the world. Examples include titles like *Rachel's Day in the Garden, Mia's Mountain Hike, Jenny's Winter Walk,* and *Maria Explores the Ocean.* To make yoga really enjoyable for the kids, she also creates yoga poses based on the movements of animals. For example, she has a set of yoga pose cards about animals with tails that include the following: stingray (warrior 3 pose), scorpion (dancer's pose), zebra (triangle forward bend), kangaroo (chair pose), and chipmunk (squat pose). She finds that kids relate more to the names and images of animals than the traditional yoga pose names. This also opens the door for children to develop their own yoga moves based on their experiences in nature, which helps them be in tune with nature through their body, senses, and breath.

Over the years, Giselle has received a tremendous amount of feedback from parents about how their children have benefited from her resources. One mom wrote to thank Giselle because her boy, who often was on the verge of exploding emotionally, learned how to control outbursts by using the Kids Yoga Stories Calm Down Yoga Cards that show fun and colorful drawings of animals in yoga poses. She was thrilled that her son now has a tool to self-regulate. A dad told her how impressed he was that his four-year-old son sat down quietly and began deep breathing completely on his own.

Practicing yoga with animals has become a trend in recent years, and people are getting quite creative about it. In the United Kingdom, yoga classes alongside lemurs are offered. The "lemoga" classes blend nature and mindfulness outside in a wildlife park. The lemurs enjoy the play time while the participants enjoy the laughs.[63] People are also doing horse

yoga, which entails great skill to balance on top of a horse in various positions. You can try some alpaca yoga on Martha's Vineyard at Island Alpaca Farm. At the Butterfly Pavilion near Denver, there is an hour-long rainforest yoga class where you can surround yourself with exotic plants and gorgeous butterflies.

Jenn Jones is a fitness instructor in Minneapolis, Minnesota. The gym where she worked held a bunny yoga session for the staff as part of their annual meeting. A bunny rescue organization brought in about twenty-five rabbits of all shapes, sizes, and colors. "It was like any gentle yoga class, but most poses kept us on the floor or close to the floor and we were reminded to look out for the animals before getting into the next pose." Participants were encouraged to engage with the rabbits if they joined them on the mat. "Yoga is about slowing down and centering, which the bunnies really helped us do. Everyone in the class was smiling from start to finish. We all walked out refreshed, relaxed, and happy."[64]

Finally, goat yoga is becoming more popular and is accessible to children. It is yoga practiced in the presence of—and in tandem with—live goats. The goal is to allow the goats to come up right beside you and even climb on you while you are in a yoga position. Have you ever had a goat on your back while you were doing a plank? Because goats are used as therapy animals, they create a calming, loving environment for a peaceful

ANIMAL YOGA

I am a giraffe.
EXTENDED MOUNTAIN POSE

I am an elephant.
STANDING WIDE-LEGGED POSE

I am a dog.
DOWNWARD-FACING DOG POSE

I am a cat.
CAT POSE

I am a butterfly.
COBBLER'S POSE

© Kids Yoga Stories

yoga session. Ashley Lopez of the Wild Roots Mini Farm in Chattanooga, Tennessee, recently started practicing yoga with her five children and their pet goats. "They love it and I love it! Doing yoga and meditating is so relaxing, and having furry, playful animals hopping around you is just the icing on the cake," she exclaimed. She recently opened up goat yoga to the public on their family farm and hopes that other families encounter the same positive results that they have had from this unique yoga practice. Catriona Sullivan of Smith Lake Farm in Montana tries to do yoga outside with her children several times a week. "I have children who really struggle with anxiety and anger. We all have better attitudes and emotional regulation when we get a chance to reconnect to nature through yoga." One of the benefits of their doing yoga on the farm is that the goats come over and interact with them. "I find that brief moments of calm, slow movement really helps children feel better."

Consider looking for animal yoga in your area by doing a quick search online. Be sure to ask about age requirements and the safety measures taken.

Meditation Gardens

Building a meditation garden is another lovely way to combine the incredible benefits of both nature and mindfulness activities to reduce stress in our lives. This can also be a super fun way for your family to work together outdoors and plan a special place for you to relax together. In addition to the general benefits of being outside while working on your meditation garden, your children will understand the importance of nature in their lives and have a chance to get creative.

The goal of a meditation garden is to provide a quiet, calm place for you and your family to find balance and reduce emotional and physical stress. A breakthrough study in 2001 found that a healing garden at a children's hospital in California had positive effects on users—about eighty-five percent reported feeling more relaxed, refreshed, or better able to cope after spending only five minutes in the garden.[65]

You can design a garden in your backyard that serves as a sanctuary for your family members. What a wonderful place to take the kids after school before they start their homework or run off to a sport practice or music lesson. They will feel so refreshed after a long, stressful day.

When you first start planning your meditation garden, gather your family together and talk about what makes each of you feel at peace and what you plan on doing in the space. Then go exploring to find examples as a model for your garden. Look online for pictures, visit gardens at museums and hotels, observe your neighbors' gardens more closely, and check out botanical gardens in your area. Research different styles of gardens from around the world, such as Japanese Zen, Chinese, Southwestern United States, Traditional English, and Middle Eastern.

Once you have a vision of your serene space, head over to your local gardening store to pick out materials or contact a landscaper for guidance. You will want to choose plants that are low maintenance to ensure that your meditation garden does not become a new source of stress.

Finally, try your best to use eco-friendly garden products to help protect the environment and your family's health. You would not want to ruin your special place by spraying nasty pesticides all over the plants!

A meditation garden typically contains elements that help make it the serene space you desire. A meditation garden should have several components that fill your senses, such as vivid colors, soothing sounds, interesting shapes and textures, comfortable places to sit or lie down, and lovely aromas. The best part is that you can choose the elements that you want for your space based on your personal preferences and goals for the garden. Once your meditation garden is complete, you can enjoy the incredible moments of peace, tranquility, and family bonding from your own backyard.

What if you do not have the space or budget to develop a meditation garden at your home? Your family can still enjoy the benefits by choosing one or a few of the traditional meditation garden elements. If you have a balcony instead of a large backyard, for example, try using potted plants to create a meditation corner. If you have a small backyard or just a bit of space in the front or side of your home, then consider sectioning off a patch of land to hold your meditation garden spot. Finally, if you are unable to add these elements to your own home, visit gardens in your community such as an arboretum. Many cities have an arboretum open to the public.

Common Elements Found in a Meditation Garden

Keep in mind that this is just a menu of options to spark your creativity, not a list of requirements. You can pick and choose what works for your space and family.

Ü **Greenery.** Besides green being a soothing color, greenery can serve as the foundation of your meditation garden. Plants, shrubs, hedges, and trees can be used to create an isolated spot separate from the rest of your backyard. They can serve as a fence or sound barrier, or they can create artistic visual interest. If you use native plants, you can even attract wildlife to your sanctuary. Be sure to pick shrubs and trees that are easy to grow and do not require much maintenance.

Ü **Colorful flowers.** You will have a blast choosing the beautiful flowers to plant throughout your garden. From tropical to herbal to desert style, the hardest part will be narrowing down your options. Look for shapes, lines, patterns, and colors that make you feel calm. Consider including some potted plants throughout your space and even planting an herb or vegetable garden there as well. Flowers such as aloe, jasmine, rose, chamomile, or lavender can also bring soothing aromas to your garden.

Ü **Water.** Water is known to give us a sense of peace and serenity. We tend to become so focused on water that we enter a mindful state, which is why adding water elements to your meditation garden is a must-have. The calming sound of running water can mask traffic and other distracting noises. Some ideas for incorporating water into your garden include fish ponds, water bowls, birdbaths, a fountain, a garden waterfall, or other trickling water features.

Ü **Shade.** It is important to design your garden with some shade so you and your kids stay cool and out of the sun. You can incorporate shade into your garden by adding a canopy, umbrella, pergola, or greenery.

Ü **Seating.** Although not required, many people prefer to have a place to sit or lie down in their meditation garden. Consider how you plan on spending your time in the garden. If you intend to read a book, then a comfortable meditation bench or chair is a good choice. If you plan to lie down to meditate or take a nap, then consider a hammock or waterproof outdoor sofa. If you plan to stretch or practice yoga, then leave a clear, flat space large enough for a yoga mat or two.

Ü **Stones, pebbles, and sand.** As a contrast to plush elements like grasses, plants, and bushes, these solid materials provide a sense of strength to your meditation garden. Japanese Zen gardens, also known as Japanese rock gardens, include these simple elements to help soothe and heal us. Raked sand, for example, can be used as a calming element since it looks like water ripples or waves.

Ü **Pavers.** Most meditation gardens contain some type of pavers. You can get as creative as you want by making patterns or spiral paths.

Ü **Statues and sculptures.** Some people like to include different types of statues or sculptures that have meaning to them. There are many possibilities such as animals, Buddha images, or small pagodas.

Earthing

Sometimes all we need to do to feel better is to go back to the basics. Earthing, also known as grounding, involves standing or walking barefoot on the ground. This can be done on the grass in your yard, soil or mud in a nearby park or forest, or sand at the beach. The goal is to walk barefoot while paying close attention to the soles of your feet as they connect with the earth's surface. This practice provides several benefits for our kids. First, it feels good to them. It is freeing to walk around without feeling constrained by shoes all the time. Next, it improves their senses as the bottom of their feet touch different types of textures, sometimes for the first time.

Standing on cool grass or warm sand can be quite comforting. Earthing also helps them learn to be more mindful of and in tune with their natural surroundings. Overall, giving kids more opportunities to feel different sensations allows them to experience their world in brand-new ways.

As a practice done by indigenous cultures for millennia, some experts have found that earthing can also result in some health benefits like reducing pain and inflammation, lowering stress, and improving sleep. It is believed that the electrical charge from the earth neutralizes free radicals in the body to improve health. The electrons, in a sense, act as antioxidants to improve how the body functions. One study of fifty-eight healthy adults found that nearly half of them felt a decrease in stress after earthing.[66]

Over time, humans have become more distant from the earth. Our ancestors walked more and even slept outside, which meant they were in closer contact with the ground. In order to encourage this practice again,

proponents of earthing recommend that people stand, walk, or lie on the grass, soil, or sand for about thirty minutes every day.[67] This can be a fun activity to try with your children, such as part of their after-school routine, so they can relax between school and homework time. You can bring some music or a nature-related book or poetry outside with you to help make the time more enjoyable. During my family's one hundred–day ecohappiness challenge during the COVID-19 quarantine, my daughter and I practiced earthing in our backyard for the first time and felt relaxed as a result.

Mindful Nature Walks and Forest Bathing

When we think of meditation, we often assume that we need to be sitting cross-legged with our eyes closed. However, we can also find mindfulness by walking or hiking outdoors in a quiet, scenic place like a forest, around a lake, or on the grass in your backyard.

Walking meditation is simply walking while being aware of each step and breath. The goal is to move slowly without having a specific destination in mind. This can be done with or without shoes on. Mindful

walking is a wonderful way for children to learn how to stay focused in the present moment by tuning into their body's sensations, which will help reduce stress. Ask your children to feel the ground beneath them with every step they take and to pay attention to all the sounds they hear and visuals they see. Remind them to come back to focusing on their feet and legs if their mind begins to wander. This rhythmic movement of lifting each foot slowly and purposefully, while also taking in the environment with all their senses, can help them reach a calm, mindful state.

Outdoor labyrinths can be a helpful instrument for a mindful walking practice that your kids will love. Dating back about four thousand years ago in a variety of cultures around the world, labyrinths are circular or spiral paths that have a single path that leads in and out of the center. Unlike a maze in which you have to work to find your way, there are no tricks to a labyrinth and no dead ends. Labyrinth walking is a practice used for meditation. Some people believe that it represents the journey to the inner self. There is no right or wrong way to walk the path, and you can make it special for your family. Consider the following ideas:

- Choose a peaceful word or phrase as a mantra to repeat as you meander the path. Some ideas include *I am peaceful, I feel happy, om, chill out, this too shall pass,* or have your children pick something that resonates with them.
- Write down an intention on a card and then walk the labyrinth while holding your card and focusing on your intention.
- Walk the path while listening to relaxing music or recorded nature sounds.
- Pay attention to the different emotions you feel when you enter, as you twist and turn along the winding path, as you reach the center, and as you exit. Journal about these feelings once you finish your walk.

Forest bathing takes the idea of a nature hike to a whole new level. In fact, forest bathing experts do not even want it referred to as a hike. Instead, it is an immersive sensory experience in nature that allows one to reach the pinnacle of mindfulness by focusing on seeing, hearing, touching, smelling, and even tasting the elements of the surrounding natural environment. Forest bathing originated in Japan in the late 1990s to help citizens reduce stress and disconnect from their hectic city lives. In Japanese, it is called shinrin-yoku (shinrin means "forest" and yoku means "bath"). But it is not to be taken literally (make sure your kids know this!). Instead, it means to bathe in the forest by taking in nature gently and mindfully.

Over the past two decades, the practice of forest bathing has spread, and now hundreds of certified forest-bathing guides around the world are leading individuals and groups on mindful healing experiences in the woods. The main reason it has taken off so well is the documented health benefits that result from this practice, including reducing stress, decreasing stress hormones like cortisol, lowering blood pressure, suppressing the fight-flight-freeze system, and improving mood. In his book *Forest Bathing: How Trees Can Help You Find Health and Happiness*, Qing Li talks about a study he did that measured people's moods before and after walking in the woods or in an urban environment. While other studies have shown that walking anywhere outdoors reduces depression, anxiety, and anger, Li found that only the experience of walking in a forest improves people's vigor and reduces fatigue.[68] A recent study, focused on school-aged children, found a significant decrease in depressive symptoms after the kids participated in a forest therapy program that included walking and playing in the forest.[69]

I was fortunate to try out forest bathing recently in Pennsylvania. When the guide showed up with a giant wicker basket tied to his back, I was not sure what I was getting into. He led me and a few others in our group into the woods beyond the main building of the hotel where we were staying. After taking a few steps along the path, he stopped and asked us to gather around in a circle and close our eyes. He wanted us to focus on the sounds that we heard for a few minutes. This was a great way to kick off the venture since it forced us to be mindful from the start. He then asked us to open our eyes and look up to the top of the trees to get a sense of the vastness of the nature we were immersed in at that moment. Part of the experience was to share our thoughts, feelings, and observations. The guide passed around a talking stick so we could express how we felt from that first mindful exercise.

We then proceeded to walk very slowly, with the intent to feel our toes and heels touch the ground with each new step. It was fascinating to see how different people walked at varying speeds. Some had more trouble slowing down than others. We were free to play around with how we walked; I tried raising my knees really high and even walked backward for a bit. I then remember entering the edge of the forest where we saw a wide-open field. It presented such a contrasting tone to the tree-covered area. It was lighter in color and we caught a glimpse of a few birds flying overhead. More mosquitoes were in that area, which distracted me quite a bit.

Then we proceeded back into a woody area along a path and our guide directed us to disperse and find a sit spot to be in silence for about twenty minutes. The goal was to sit quietly so we could fully engage with nature, including hearing the birds chirping, observing any wildlife nearby, inhaling the fragrances, tasting the fresh air, and touching whatever we chose to explore. I found a tree stump to relax on for a while and thoroughly enjoyed the mindful time alone in this plush natural environment. I did cheat a little and brought my phone with me to snap a few pictures, and am grateful that I did because I often gaze at those photos to remind me of that serene moment. Finally, in keeping with Japanese tradition, we sipped a cup of tea to conclude our forest bathing. Now I know what was in that big basket!

Taking your kids forest bathing, whether with a guide or on your own, can be an especially momentous experience to help them mindfully engage outdoors. Look for a nice quiet wooded area, such as a local or state park. Take your time and let your feet be your guide. Children will learn a tremendous amount from this unique mindful time that will help them slow down and connect with nature. Be sure to let them choose their own sit spot and just be still for a while. You can also add to the experience in the woods with some yoga, tai chi, nature journaling, and even a healthy picnic.

Tree-Hugging Activity

In the late 1960s, legendary Zen Buddhist teacher Thich Nhat Hanh developed a hugging meditation practice that entailed the core Zen principles of interconnectedness and interbeing. He found that hugging with mindfulness can bring reconciliation, healing, understanding, and happiness.

More recently, Stone Kraushaar, PhD, a clinical psychologist known as the "Hug Doctor" and author of the book A 21-Day Journey to Embracing Yourself, Your Life, and Everyone Around You, advises, "A good embrace—a hug—squeezes every ounce of fear, worry, and negativity out of your spirit, leaving you with nothing but warmth, inner peace, and a feeling of connection." Dr. Stone's prescription is for a twenty-one-second hug (at minimum) since that is when oxytocin is released in our body and the many benefits of hugging kick in—improved immune system, reduced stress, lower blood pressure, better sleep patterns, and more. But it is not just about a number; it is about flow and getting lost in the moment.[70]

Having a meditative hugging experience with a loved one, pet, or even a tree can help us feel happier, calmer, and more connected. Consider sharing the following tree-hugging activity with your kids:

On today's walk, connect with a tree that most catches your attention right this moment. For now, do not worry too much about why you find yourself drawn to a particular tree—just follow your instincts.

Approach your chosen tree, noting its characteristics. Is it expansive and stately, a wise elder with many years of experience? Or is it a youth, sprightly with great potential? Is its foliage sparse or bushy? What is the overall color? Note whether, in today's wind, it sways or makes a sound. Is this tree different from those nearby in some manner? Is it a loner, off by itself, or social, within a group?

As you arrive, place your hand on the bark. What color is it? Is it smooth or rough? Is it deeply creviced, so that your fingertips can probe the cracks? Do you see any other organisms, such as lichens or ants? Is there an aroma? Turn your gaze upward, observing how high its canopy reaches. Does your impression of the tree change now that you are up close?

Next wrap your arms around the tree. How does the tree feel on your chest and as you breathe? If the tree's size warrants it, lean your body against the tree, letting it support you. Observe the sensations passing through you. How does it feel to share your weight with the tree?

Sit at the tree's base, letting your back rest on its trunk. For a moment, imagine that you, too, are rooting in this place. Envision your roots snaking down through the earth, connecting with the tree's roots. How does this feel? If you imagine that you can exchange nutrients and information, what does the tree share with you? What do you share with the tree? Ponder this for some time. When you are ready to leave, tell the tree farewell and thank it for its time, providing one final embrace before you part.[71]

Float Therapy

Water is also a natural element that can evoke mindfulness. In the book *Blue Mind*, author Wallace J. Nichols surmises, "This is a huge advantage of water: you don't need to meditate to take advantage of its healing effects because it meditates you."[72] Baths and showers have been used as ways to escape daily stress for ages. By practicing some mindfulness during a bath or shower, we can really focus on the sensations on our skin and the sounds of the trickling water. This helps us be in the moment and forget our worries. Floating in water has also been shown to change brain waves and reduce cortisol levels, therefore making us feel more relaxed. One experiment showed that a one-hour session of floating reduced anxiety and improved the mood of fifty anxious and depressed participants.[73]

Float therapy, a form of hydrotherapy, is becoming more popular, with hundreds of float centers popping up across North America and Europe. You can pay to float in a tank for about forty-five to ninety minutes per session. It involves relaxing in water that is about ten inches deep in a dark, private room. You are able to easily float because of the high concentrations of Epsom salt in the water. It provides a relaxing experience because of the weightlessness and sensory deprivation.

By removing sound, light, and other outside stimuli, float therapy can be very meditative. Experts believe that float therapy allows the brain to transition from a waking state to a state of deep meditative consciousness similar to the moment between waking and sleeping. In this altered state, the mind settles and we can experience a blissful feeling.[74]

Children can do float therapy, but just be sure to ask what the age requirements are at the center near you. Some have a minimum age and require a parent or guardian to sign a release form or be in the room with the child. Although float centers indicate that the therapy poses little danger of children drowning in the tank because of the salt and minimal depth of the water, it is still a good idea to monitor your children while they are in the tank so that you can be there to help them if needed.

You can look for other opportunities for your children to spend mindful time in water:

- Turn bath time into a mindfulness moment by asking them questions about how the water feels and sounds.
- Encourage them to practice floating on their back in the swimming pool.
- Take trips to visit rivers, lakes, and the ocean.

Activity Checklist

ü Visit nature-filled spots that will help your children be more mindful, such as forests, hiking trails, beaches, waterfalls, and botanical gardens.

ü Practice meditations that focus on nature scenes.

ü Invest in some nature meditation CDs and apps to play at bedtime or whenever your kids are feeling stressed.

ü Have fun with playful, mindful breathing exercises.

ü Practice yoga outside and try some animal- and nature-type poses to engage your kids.

ü Get adventurous and sign up for an animal yoga session as a family.

ü Test out a variety of natural scents by either purchasing essential oils, sprays, and other products or searching for the scents outside in your neighborhood or in a local park.

ü Transform your backyard into a serene meditation garden with the help of your kids.

ü Find some time to try earthing and see how it makes your children feel.

ü Immerse yourself in the woods by going on a mindful walk or even trying some forest bathing.

ü Experiment with floating in your pool or in a natural body of water, and look into float therapy for your family.

Resources

Organizations

Association of Nature and Forest Therapy: https://www.natureandforest therapy.earth

Calm: https://www.calm.com

Forest Bathing Central: https://www.forestbathingcentral.com

Kids Yoga Stories: https://www.kidsyogastories.com

Noisy by Nature Podcast by ABC Kids: https://www.abc.net.au/kids listen/noisy-by-nature

Piku Calm Kids App

ShambalaKids: https://shambalakids.com

Books

Awake in the Wild: Mindfulness in Nature as a Path to Self-Discovery by Mark Coleman

Gardening for Mindfulness by Holly Farrell

Nature Therapy Walks: 22 Sensory Activities to Enjoy in Nature for Wellbeing by Cortney Cameron and Natalia Clarke

Planting Seeds: Practicing Mindfulness with Children by Thich Nhat Hanh
Rewilding: Meditations, Practices, and Skills for Awakening in Nature by
    Micah Mortali

Children's Books

A Handful of Quiet: Happiness in Four Pebbles by Thich Nhat Hanh
Mindful Monkey, Happy Panda by Lauren Alderfer
Mindful Wonders: A Book about Mindfulness Using the Wonders of Nature by
    Michelle Zivkov
The Other Way to Listen by Byrd Baylor
Peaceful Piggy Meditation by Kerry MacLean
A Walk in the Wood: Meditations on Mindfulness with a Bear Named Pooh by
    Dr. Joseph Parent and Nancy Parent
What Does It Mean to Be Present? by Rana DiOrio
Wild Mindfulness by Laura Larson
Yoga Animals: A Wild Introduction to Kid-Friendly Poses by Paige Towler

❧ 3 ❧

Awe and Gratitude

The moments that make us go "wow!" are the very same moments that can change our lives.

Jonah Paquette

SOME moments in life leave a tremendous impact. They are imprinted on our brain as absolutely exhilarating. In high school, I stood over the edge of the Grand Canyon looking out and wondering if this was really planet Earth. The amber, orange, and golden colors were exquisite; the power of what nature created blew my mind. *That is awe.* During my honeymoon trip to Hawaii, I mustered up the courage to get into a tiny helicopter to fly over the most gorgeous nature scenes I have ever witnessed. As we approached an immense waterfall painted into the side of a mountain, I felt overcome by the power of nature and was truly humbled by it. *That is awe.* And when my husband and I ventured off on an Alaskan cruise, I was overtaken by the moment when we woke up in the morning and an immense glacier was in full view. It was so close. I wanted to reach out and touch it. I could feel the icy air on my skin and smell its freshness. The color of the ice, a bright turquoise in parts mixed with white and other hues of blue, was not what I expected. It literally took my breath away and tears filled my eyes. *That is awe.*

Awe is so powerful that you can probably look back over your lifetime and identify similar transformative experiences. We now know through science that awe is a unique emotion that can help us feel happier and calmer. Teaching our children how to experience awe, particularly of nature, can instill in them profound benefits for their health and happiness.

Nature provides so many opportunities for our children to notice the surrounding beauty, soak it in mindfully, and then express gratitude for it. We can introduce ways to incorporate awe and gratitude of nature into their daily lives to provide another tool to help them reduce stress, boost their mood, and stay balanced. There are so many options from inside our home, in our backyard, and through more in-depth adventures like visiting museums, exploring natural areas, and taking vacations.

In this chapter, we will define awe, explore the benefits it provides, and point out the many activities we can do with our children to help them experience more awe through nature. We will also look at the connection between awe and gratitude and why it is important to express gratitude following a moment of awe. These concepts are covered together since they are closely linked. Part of experiencing awe is having a sense of gratitude for inspiring moments. For example, it is wonderful to point out a rainbow on the drive to school, but even more impactful if we spend some time talking about it with our children and expressing why we are grateful for seeing it. We can even take it another step further by implementing more of the tools in this book. Take creativity, for example. Ask your children to sit down and paint or draw a picture of the rainbow. This action will produce even more happy thoughts and feelings and keep that awe alive in their hearts and minds for a longer period.

Opportunities to feel awe are all around us. Try not to miss them. We are all very busy and looking more at our phones than out the window, but if we make that extra effort to seek out awe and share our gratitude for it with our children, we will all be better for it.

What Is Awe?

We sometimes have special moments in life that are so profound we do not even know how to describe them. Maybe you just learned about a new, fascinating animal species; watched a video about the expansive universe; or witnessed the birth of your own child. The emotion you feel is hard to grasp—an overwhelming mix of wonder, joy, and sometimes even a speckle of fear.

These moments are so intoxicating that we get goose bumps on our arms and feel a tingling up and down our spine. Tears flood our eyes, and our jaw drops. *We call this awe.*

Awe is an emotion that has a powerful effect on our body and mind yet is hard to put into words. David Delgado, a visual strategist at NASA's Jet Propulsion Laboratory (JPL) and cofounder of the Museum of Awe, when speaking at the Greater Good Science Center's Art and Science of Awe conference in 2016, described awe as an instant when you cannot quite grasp something. "It feels like magic, amazement, mystery, reverence. It's the moment when we realize it's a gift and privilege to be alive."[75]

Awe has been addressed throughout history by the profound works of writers and scientists like Charles Darwin, Albert Einstein, and John Muir. However, researchers have only recently started to study how awe affects our well-being. In a key 2003 paper, psychologists Dacher Keltner and Jonathan Haidt described awe as "a moral, spiritual, and aesthetic emotion" found at "the upper reaches of pleasure and the boundary of fear." They then presented how awe works and the effects it has on us. Their research showed that awe consists of two core qualities:

- ü perceived vastness—something we think to be greater than ourselves in number, scope, or complexity; and
- ü a challenge to or alteration of our understanding of the world.[76]

A perfect example is our reaction to space. As I often gaze up at the immense night sky, I get lost in thought and emotion. I wonder who and

what is up there and if we will ever find out. Space is larger than we are. We cannot touch it, hear it, smell it, or see it up close to fully understand what it entails. There is so much mystery in the twinkling stars, planets, and seemingly endless dark sky that it truly alters my perception of the world and my place in it. That is how awe works.

Awe is a pro-social emotion that is part of positive psychology, similar to other mental states like mindfulness and flow (during creativity). It allows us to transcend the ordinary, tests our concept of time and scale, gives us the sense of being small in a grand universe, and helps us to truly be present in the moment. It shifts our attention away from our inner thoughts and worries so we feel like we are part of something greater than ourselves. In doing so, it has a powerful effect on our nervous system and helps us feel happier and calmer.

People, on average, feel the emotion of awe a couple of times each week.[77] Different experiences can trigger this feeling for different people. It can result from seeing profound beauty; spending time in nature; feeling connected to others; observing remarkable human accomplishments or scientific discoveries; or admiring impressive works of architecture, art, and music.

The Fine Line Between Awe and Fear

In their original definition of awe, Dacher Keltner and Jonathan Haidt mention that awe is at the cusp of fear. Dr. Jonah Paquette explains this quandary in his book *Awestruck: How Embracing Wonder Can Make You Happier, Healthier, and More Connected*. He points to examples when awe can also terrify us, such as a bear approaching our campsite, the *Challenger* space shuttle explosion, fire, and natural disasters like hurricanes and tornadoes. While we seek the positive benefits of awe, he suggests that "we must also acknowledge that there are two sides of the coin with awe." Additionally, there is evidence through a study by Dr. Paul Piff of the University of California, Irvine, that threat-based moments of awe lead to lower rates of positive emotions and higher levels of anxiety.[78] Not exactly our goal here.

On the other hand, Richard Louv points out in his book *Our Wild Calling: How Connecting with Animals Can Transform Our Lives—and*

Save Theirs, that sometimes we are so struck by awe in the presence of a wild animal we can feel an "exhilaration of wonder" and even a sense of comfort.

How do we make sure our kids enjoy awe without feeling scared? My suggestion is to start slowly and keep the nature-related awe experiences age-appropriate and benign at first. Think rainbows, butterflies, and visits to the ocean. As your family gets more daring, then you can consider swimming with dolphins or going on a safari to get closer to wild animals. It is also important to realize that weather events like hurricanes may fascinate children, but we should monitor the video footage our children absorb to make sure it is not too jarring.

Benefits of Awe

Why should we care about our children experiencing more awe, anyway? Awe provides several important health benefits. It is an amazing tool to instill a deeper sense of worldliness, kindness, and peace in our children. Here are some key positives of experiencing awe.

Broadens Social Connection

Awe changes our perspective of the world. We feel smaller and as though we are in the presence of something greater than ourselves. Awe can help us lose our awareness of "self" and feel more connected to the world around us. This helps minimize dangerous "us versus them" thinking.

Additionally, when we witness a remarkable moment like a waterfall or shooting star, we want to share it with other people, causing us to bond with family, friends, and even strangers.[79]

Stimulates Curiosity

When we observe something awesome—like images of Earth from space, a fascinating science experiment, or an animal in the wild—we want to learn more about how it is all possible.

Curiosity is so critical to children's growth and success. Even though their constant questions may be irritating at times, it is ultimately reflective of their desire for new knowledge.

Expands Creativity

Awe inspires us to act more creatively because we view the world in a broader sense. This expansive thinking helps us consider fresh perspectives and see beyond our present situation. In a 2012 study, one group of children reviewed a series of photos, starting with basic everyday objects and then shifting to vast or faraway things, like the Milky Way galaxy. The other group looked at the same images but in the opposite order. The children who saw the objects from small to expansive performed significantly better on subsequent creativity tests.[80]

Leads to Kindness and Generosity

Paul Piff found that "awe boosts a person's generosity, willingness to help others, willingness to behave in ethical ways, to take on needs of others, and de-prioritize their own needs. Awe connects us to things larger than ourselves and motivates us to care for others and the collective good."[81] His experiments prove that when people experience a moment of awe, they tend to be more generous. He had participants first look up either into tall, beautiful trees or at a large building. They then came across a person who needed assistance. Those in the tree-viewing group were more apt to help the person in need.[82]

Changes Our Perception of Time

In our hectic 24/7 lifestyle, do you wish you had more time? Awe can give us the illusion that we have more time and no longer need to rush. People who watched awe-inspiring videos featuring whales, waterfalls, and other nature scenes were more likely to report feeling like they had more time.[83]

Guides Us to Find Our Purpose in Life

By being connected to something larger than ourselves through awe, we are more likely to be inspired and motivated to face new challenges and reach our goals. Positive psychology experts have discovered that people who have a clear purpose in life experience less pain, anxiety, and depression. Additionally, children who grow up with a sense of purpose are typically happier, have more successful careers, and build stronger relationships later in life.[84]

Makes Us Grateful

Awe gives us a sense of hope and the ability to see the bigger picture. It teaches us that there might be something magical in everyday life that we can be grateful for. Louie Schwartzberg is an award-winning producer, director, and cinematographer known for his exquisite nature photography and films that use time-lapse, high-speed, and macro cinematography. Referencing his *Gratitude Revealed* video series, he said that "wonder inspires us to open our hearts and minds to engender gratitude."[85]

Improves Physical Health

Distinct physical changes result from experiencing an awe-filled moment. When we feel positive emotions like awe or love, our vagus nerve, which is linked to the parasympathetic nervous system that helps calm us down, is soothed. This leads to physical improvements like decreased heart rate, the ability to focus better, and a calmer sense overall.[86] Additionally, researchers discovered that awe reduces the level of pro-inflammatory proteins (called cytokines) that cause our immune system to work harder. This is important because high levels of cytokines can cause illness.[87]

Reduces Anxiety and Depression

Our nervous system reacts in the opposite way to awe than anxiety. Instead of the fight-flight-freeze response kicking in, awe keeps us still and relaxed. Awe seems to pull us out of our stuck mode of worrying and helps us feel more immersed in our surroundings and the larger world in an uplifting way as meditation and creativity do.[88] In one study, participants watched a slide show of either basic, everyday images of nature or more awe-inspiring nature scenes. Those who watched the awe-inspiring scenes reported more positive feelings.[89] In a second study, students recorded their emotions after each nature experience over a two-week period. The students who reported having awe experiences in nature (e.g., watching the sunset or reading a book under a tree) felt the highest levels of satisfaction and well-being.

Even more amazingly, the participants felt happier and calmer several weeks after these experiences, which shows that awe may have lasting effects on our mental health.[90]

As you can see, each of these benefits plays a role in helping us feel more relaxed and positive.

How Gratitude Enhances the Experience of Awe

We often hear a lot about gratitude in November around Thanksgiving in the United States. All of us would be better off if it was a focus during the rest of the year, too, since the practice of gratitude is a key aspect of positive psychology that can help us feel more joyful. By practicing gratitude in combination with awe of nature, we can give our children an incredible tool to use throughout their lives.

In his book *Awestruck*, Dr. Jonah Paquette eloquently connects awe and gratitude: "Gratitude is an incredibly powerful emotion, one that's been linked to a host of physical and psychological benefits. But beyond its ability to heal our mind and body, the deliberate cultivation of gratitude can also be a powerful path to feeling more awe in our everyday lives. Indeed, studies have shown that the practice of gratitude is closely linked to our ability to feel awestruck."[91] Awe and gratitude are intricately linked since we can absorb a moment of awe by expressing gratitude for it. This also helps to ensure that we reap even more benefits. Therefore, by seeking out more awe experiences in nature and then expressing gratitude for them, our children can feel better.

So, what exactly is gratitude? Dr. Robert Emmons, the world's foremost researcher on gratitude, defines it as the acknowledgment of goodness in one's life and recognizing that the source of this goodness lies at least partially outside ourself.[92] According to science, gratitude is one of the most important ways for us to feel happier and provides many incredible benefits. It improves our health, reduces stress, and helps us focus on the positive. Stepping back and being thankful for what we have gives us energy, inspires us, and transforms us. It helps us realize that life is truly a gift. Although over a decade has passed since my infertility struggles, I still take time almost every day to look into my children's eyes and be grateful that they are part of my life.

Gratitude is a powerful tool for boosting our mental health because when we are grateful, it is hard to dwell in a negative frame of mind. When we count our blessings, we interrupt the cycle of pessimistic and fearful thoughts, which allows the stress management system in our body to recover. Research shows that when we are grateful, we love our lives and want to make sure we stick around long enough to enjoy them. Expressing gratitude for the fantastic aspects of life provides us with a sense of wonder and appreciation. It elevates happiness because it allows us to savor positive experiences and keeps us from taking them for granted. In her book *10 Mindful Minutes: Giving Our Children—and Ourselves—the Social and Emotional Skills to Reduce Stress and Anxiety for Healthier, Happy Lives*, Goldie Hawn writes, "Gratitude is the elixir to bring us back to a kinder, gentler state of mind. Stopping to count our blessings is actually a blessing in itself."[93]

Being grateful also makes it more likely that we will want to give to others. It is a gut instinct that we hope to share these incredible moments of awe and gratitude with those around us. Later in this chapter, we will discuss some creative ways for children to express their gratitude for nature awe so they can share and connect with others, which will help boost their mood even more.

The Magic of Experiencing Awe Through Our Children's Eyes

Children are filled with innocent wonder, a characteristic that allows them to appreciate nature automatically. We as parents can harness our children's capacity to experience awe in even the tiniest aspects of life that would otherwise take us a bit more effort. Kassy Eichele, who blogs at *Making Time for Giggles*, realizes how special it is for her to experience the awe of nature through her children. She started her blog to share tips with other parents on how to simplify the challenges of parenthood. She wants to help other parents be able to spend more time on the things that matter most, such as being outside together in nature.

"In our family, we prioritize spending time outdoors in nature. We love taking the kids hiking with us." These family hikes have become more than just a way to get out of the house. They are awe-filled experiences that Kassy treasures. "Some of my most favorite memories have been watching my youngest daughter take her first wobbly steps on a hiking trail and observing my girls watch a waterfall for the first time. Seeing their excitement as they pick dandelions or eagerly jump into every puddle they can find has been so meaningful to me."

Kassy has also found that her daughters notice so much more than she does, which has helped her find more awe in her daily routine. "We just went on a walk specifically to see a waterfall, but the girls noticed every detail along the way, like the tiny tributaries, the creek, puddles to splash in, a log, and bugs. Children see all of the minutia while adults just pass them by. They feel awe by experiencing nature in every way possible, and I feel awe by watching them."

She is passionate about encouraging other parents to spend time outdoors in nature with their children. "Watching your children grow up with nature and experience it is so powerful. Nature engages all of our senses without overwhelming them. I love to see how they grow with nature and what they notice that I take for granted."

Her biggest advice to parents is to slow down, because being in a rush takes away the deeper meaning of our connection to nature and the ability to experience awe and gratitude for our environment.

"It's so easy to be all just about the destination, such as finishing that hike. The goal for the kids is to experience and learn, and they don't care about the time. My kids have taught me that there is so much joy in soaking it all in. Sometimes it's okay to forget about schedules and naps just to enjoy being in the moment."[94]

Activities to Help Children Experience Awe

The world offers so many opportunities for us to feel awe, but we often pass them by because of our hectic lives. While children are more prone to have a sense of wonder and amazement, it is our job as parents to provide some direction by pointing out awe to them and giving them opportunities to experience more awe.

So, how can we capture these extraordinary occasions for our children? The key is to find activities that involve a sense of vastness and alter their perspective. It is important to weave awe into our everyday routine and notice it in ordinary places, whether during the drive to school or while hanging out in the backyard. By visiting, viewing, and listening, our children will be exposed to many potential awe moments that they will treasure. Of course, nature is one of the best ways to do this.

Visit

In order for children to understand awe, they need to experience it. Professor Andy Tix wrote about awe on his blog, *Reflections on Mystery and Awe*. He believes that travel provides endless opportunities for awe because it exposes us to stimuli typically out of our routine. He suggests families take "awecations," instead of just vacations, to places that can inspire awe.[95] Take trips—whether it is an hour away from home or halfway across the world—to see natural wonders like waterfalls, volcanoes, caves, beaches, and more. If you cannot get away, look for local spots to explore.

Plane rides in and of themselves are ripe with the potential for our kids to be in awe. Encourage them to peer out the window and discuss what it looks and feels like to be flying high in the sky among the clouds. It is such a special moment when children realize how massive the world is and that there is much more beyond their house, neighborhood, and school. I often get so overwhelmed with deep thoughts while gazing out an airplane window that my eyes become tear-filled. That is awe in action.

By planning creative trips with awe in mind, we can make these powerful instances part of our family events that our children will never forget. There are endless options when it comes to incorporating awe into your travel plans. From museums to nature landmarks to walks on the beach, you can give your children so many ways to get chills up and down their spines (in a good way).

Here are a few ideas for your next nature awe adventure:

- Outdoor: zoos, mountains, forests, farmland, hiking trails, beaches, lakes, rivers, waterfalls, boat rides, clear starry nights, sunsets, sunrises, botanical gardens, canyons, caves, butterfly gardens
- Indoor: art, science, and history museums; planetariums; aquariums; aviaries

Our Awecation to the Pacific Northwest

A few years ago my family traveled throughout the Pacific Northwest for a weeklong vacation that has a special place in my heart. It is truly astonishing how many awe moments we recall from that time. We began our trip in Portland, Oregon. We first visited the International Rose Test Garden and enjoyed the abundance of flowers in every shade you could imagine. We walked slowly, meandering down paths lined with different types of roses. Every few steps we bent over and brushed our noses against the flower petals to inhale their incredible fragrances. We learned that different species have unique scents, which made it all the more enjoyable to compare and contrast them. Just seeing endless roses in one place gave us a sense of awe, and smelling the fresh flowers was also an experience that we will always treasure.

Next on the list was the Oregon Zoo. I have been to my fair share of zoos, but this time we were fortunate to see something quite remarkable. There was an orangutan who completely got our attention. We stood there staring at him for nearly an hour, watching his every move. We could not believe how much he mimicked a human.

He was playful and acted like a comedian for the audience watching him. He used a blanket to swing on the branches in his pen and looked right at us as though he was trying to have a conversation. I spoke to my children about evolution, and this hands-on educational moment definitely triggered awe in them when they realized how closely related we are to other primates. Watching animals and other people closely, in a mindful way, can be quite awe-inspiring and open our eyes to new behaviors and cultures.

We then made our way north to Mount St. Helens National Volcanic Monument, which really blew us away (not literally, thank goodness). We watched a powerful film about the volcanic eruption in 1980. We learned about the instantaneous devastation in the area but also how nature miraculously revived itself over time. My kids were very excited to be that close to a real volcano, something they definitely do not see every day. We all felt a sense of awe and wonder about how powerful nature can be, and how delicate life is when faced with a major event.

View

Whether you are traveling halfway around the globe or looking out your own window, the key to experiencing awe of nature is to view it mindfully. Several key aspects of nature bring us awe. Rainbows are probably the first thing that comes to mind when we think of awe and nature. Children especially are enthralled by a rainbow that appears in the sky after a rainstorm. The next time you are fortunate to cross paths with a rainbow, stop and fully absorb that rainbow in your mind. I love trying to figure out where the various colors begin and end. Rainbows are so beyond comprehension that they are difficult to capture through art. I once tried to paint a rainbow using a photograph I had taken, but it was impossible to replicate the natural beauty of the colors in the sky. I have also spent many hours online in awe of those full-circle rainbows.

Clouds are also pretty mesmerizing. Children can spend a long time watching the ever-evolving sky to figure out what pictures they see. Spend some time playing the cloud imagination game by asking them what they

see in the clouds, such as animals, shapes, people, or other objects. Take it one step further and challenge them to create a story about the cloud images or to draw a picture of what they see.

Watching animals in their natural habitat can also be fascinating. If we were so awestruck by the orangutan in the zoo, imagine our reactions during an African safari! Observing how animals behave in the wild gives us a peek into a place that we rarely see. It makes us feel smaller, in a way, because we realize that a whole other world is out there filled with wildlife that we do not interact with on a daily basis. I will never forget a moment during our Alaskan cruise when we took a smaller boat to get really close to a glacier. I did not expect to see the hundreds of black, wet seals lying on the mini-icebergs between our boat and the glacier. It was magnificent to observe them relaxing in their natural habitat.

There truly are so many ways for your family to capture the sensation of awe by looking at nature. Gaze at the stars and planets in the evening sky, take in a sunrise or sunset, absorb the vibrant colors around you, or look for fractal patterns in trees and leaves. Whatever way your family views nature, you will certainly feel awe and the resulting happiness from doing so.

Listen

We can also experience awe by listening to what nature is saying. Whether it be the songlike chirps of birds or the crashing of ocean waves, we can get lost in those dynamic sounds. We can provide experiences to our children that allow them to listen to nature and feel that sense of wonder. Besides visiting places in person and mindfully focusing on what we hear, we can play nature music. It can be calming at bedtime or whenever your children feel stressed out if they listen to the soothing sounds of nature. There are some incredible apps and downloadable music available with nature sounds such as waterfalls, rainstorms, blowing wind, cats purring, birds chirping, a campfire, and even the Amazon jungle. Have fun exploring unique nature sounds with your kids and let them choose their favorite ones.

Another way to listen to nature and experience a sense of awe is through reading inspiring books, poetry, and short stories to your children that include vivid descriptions of nature. Throughout history, poetry has fascinated readers and inspired them to understand the world in a deeper way. Many nature lovers have used poetry to communicate their connection to the environment. Some of the most famous nature poets include Robert Frost, Alfred Lord Tennyson, William Wordsworth, Percy Bysshe Shelley, and John Keats. Have your kids close their eyes while you read poetry to them so they can picture the nature in their minds. You can also enjoy nature poetry on their level by reading children's books together.

Virtual Experiences

But what if we cannot travel to experience the awe of nature? Sometimes we face challenges that prevent us from leaving our home or town, whether they be financial constraints, scheduling concerns, health issues, or even a pandemic like COVID-19. Fortunately, we do not necessarily even have to go outside to experience the awe of nature. We can view many incredible videos or movies to stimulate a sense of awe. If you are unable to visit a place in person, the next best thing is to observe it using various media tools such as videos, photographs, slideshows, 3-D or 4-D movies at an IMAX theater, and virtual reality (VR).

Watching science in action is one way to capture these special moments. Observing the incredible ways science works can be powerful for a young child and pique his or her interest to learn more. Try watching a time-lapse video of a flower blooming or a caterpillar exiting its cocoon. Seeing nature from this new perspective can be especially moving.

During his interview for Earth Day Live 2020, nature cinematographer Louie Schwartzberg explained how his work helps people better understand nature. He believes that his films and videos help all of us reconnect to nature in the present time. And because not everyone can travel to see the wonders of nature, he provides a special service to the world through his art. He offers his audience an intimate and unprecedented glimpse into the hidden world of plants and animals through innovative art and technology.[96]

Another way for your family to view nature is to be an electronic wildlife watcher. There are numerous live nature cams online for you to observe animals around the world in real time. The U.S. Fish & Wildlife Service and the National Conservation Training Center, for example, broadcast a bald eagle nest so you can see the eagles coming and going. The Cornell Lab of Ornithology invites the public to join the Celebrate Urban Birds project, which provides links to bird cams. Finally, Explore.org has all kinds of live animal cams to enjoy.

Using Virtual Reality to Experience Nature-Related Awe

Virtual reality (VR) offers a cutting-edge method for producing and studying awe. Researchers tested four types of virtual environments: three designed to spark awe and the fourth, a neutral one. They found that the nature-filled environments, including mountains and a forest, led to significantly higher levels of awe and positive feelings than the neutral one.[97]

My family and I had the pleasure of feeling awe in a nature-themed VR experience a few years ago at the Franklin Institute in Philadelphia, Pennsylvania. I had never tried VR and was feeling a bit nervous that I would fall over or bump into a wall. But once I put on the VR headgear I was transported to a gorgeous underwater world. I remember feeling like I was actually floating through the water among the colorful fish. I was smiling and oohing and ahhing the entire time. The best part was when a giant virtual whale swam by me, and I tried to reach out my hand to touch it.

Using VR to connect to nature is a fun, unique activity for children. I can envision a future in which we visit these virtual places to de-stress on days when we may not be able to get outside. While VR may not completely replicate being in nature, it offers an opportunity to connect with images of nature. I walked away from that exhibit at the museum feeling happier than when I entered. The thrill of my underwater adventure stayed with me for days, and I even love reminiscing about it years later.

Capturing Awe to Stay Grateful

To make the most of these awe-filled encounters, it is helpful to record them. By doing so, we have a way to go back and express gratitude for our experiences and to relish in those moments that brought us so much joy and calm. It also provides more time for reflection, which can extend the positive energy in our children. There are several creative ways to record awe moments.

First, children can write about their awe experiences. Writing allows them to sit with their thoughts for a while, which can lead to increased positive emotions. This process can take many forms depending on the age and skills of the child. A young child might write a one-paragraph memory of the nature that filled them with wonder, while an older child might try to capture their awe moment with a poem or song lyrics. Still, a more developed writer may want to compose a longer, more in-depth story.

Next, artwork can be a wonderful way for your kids to capture the awe they feel toward nature. Ask your children to create their own masterpiece to reflect something in nature that brought them awe. Tap into their talents using drawing, photography, painting, sculpture, or collage.

Finally, your children can create a nature gratitude journal. Keeping a gratitude journal is the backbone of gratitude scientific research, shown to increase our sense of happiness by forcing us to acknowledge the positive moments in our day. Parents who teach their children to write in a gratitude journal notice multiple benefits, including stress reduction and increased optimism. Some kids, however, may find gratitude journals cumbersome. It is important that we keep it fun for them so it does not feel like a chore. Here are several creative ways for your children to express gratitude stories about nature.

Books

Grab some construction paper, crayons, markers, old magazines, stickers, glue, and scissors to get started. Ask your children to develop a book in which they dedicate each page to one aspect of nature or a special memory related to nature that they are thankful for. They can sketch pictures of nature or use photographs from your nature hikes and vacations and describe the experience, including how it made them feel. You can then put the pages together into a book organized by month, year, or event.

Blogs

Writing down the aspects of nature that we are grateful for in a list on paper can get mundane for many people, probably because it does not feel like you are telling a story or sharing your experiences with others. A much more interesting way to approach gratitude is to have your children write a story around it by creating a blog so they can easily share the experiences with friends and family online.

Collages

Not all gratitude journals have to be filled with flowing prose. Another approach, especially if you have a more visual child, is to use collages to capture special awe moments. Try to find images from magazines or your own photographs to convey a message of gratitude. They may also want to include elements of nature that they found, like a flower petal or stick. They can then hang their nature collage in their room to help them feel calmer before bedtime.

Audio Recording

Children love to hear their own voices. You can have them record their gratitude journal on a phone or iPad. Once you have the recording, you can get really creative by posting it online for others to listen to or you can even put it to music and create a song or rap using highlights of what they said.

Videos

You can take it one step further by encouraging them to record a nature gratitude video log (a.k.a. vlog). This can be as simple as standing in front of the camera and reading off a script, or it can be more creative than that. Maybe have them pretend to be reporters and their gratitude is the news of the day, or they can act out scenes from the pleasant moments they had. They will have a blast talking about what they are thankful for and watching it over and over again.

You can also mix and match these media, such as posting videos on your gratitude blog.

A Family Overcome by Emotion in the Florida Springs

Linda Wampler, a freelance writer who spends much of her time enjoying the outdoors, knows what it means to experience awe of nature with her family. She recalls a momentous vacation to the springs in Homosassa, Florida. Along with her daughter and husband, Linda ventured off to camp in one of the state parks surrounding the springs. The main attraction was being able to snorkel in the crystal clear water to see the beautiful fish, rock formations, vegetation, and manatees that abound in these springs.

"There is nothing more exhilarating, peaceful, and astounding than hovering above a deep, crystal clear spring, often holding hands with my family and taking underwater pictures," she exclaims. The three of them spent hours together underwater. They could access some springs by swimming in through narrow gaps between rocks, while they reached others by walking down white sandy beaches, getting into the water, and allowing the current to take them down the river until they arrived at other springs. When they came out of the water, her daughter excitedly described every beautiful hue and detail of the fish, caves, wading grasses, and the bubbling origins of the springs called seeps.

But the most inspiring moment was yet to come. They rented a small boat to explore the clear water seeping out of the springhead.

On their travels, they saw a group of kayakers peering into the water and wondered what was attracting their attention. Then they spotted some large, dark shapes moving underwater and were thrilled to cross paths with a group of manatees!

One of the park rangers told them that if they promised to not agitate the beautiful creatures, they were free to snorkel with them in the shallow water. Needless to say, they quietly slipped from their boat and swam timidly toward the animals. "It was startling and novel to actually be in the water with the manatees because you usually are not allowed to get too close to them." Then the truly most unforgettable part of the trip happened. A trusting mama manatee and her calf swam right alongside them and they reached out to pet these gorgeous creatures. "My daughter and I were so overcome that we cried with our masks and snorkels on! They were so friendly that we worried they would get hurt by approaching people in unmonitored locations. For the moment, though, stroking their leathery skin and whiskered faces and heads was such a thrilling, moving experience."

The Wampler family will always cherish this miraculous occasion. To see such huge creatures be so kind and trusting of humans and to glide next to them definitely left the three of them awestruck!

Activity Checklist

ü Introduce the concept of awe to your children by providing them with some simple examples like how they feel when they see a rainbow.

ü On a cold or rainy day, spend some time online looking for incredible photos and videos of nature to bring your children awe.

ü Choose a few nature documentaries to watch as a family, such as *The Greatest Places, Planet Earth, Life of Birds, Turtle: The Incredible Journey,* and *The Blue Planet.*

ü Consider picking a new place each month to explore in your area where you can feel awe of nature.

ü The next time you plan a family vacation, add some nature awe experiences to your itinerary like visiting a state or national park, science museum, or garden.

ü After an awe-related adventure, take a moment to ask your children what they are thankful for and encourage them to create a gratitude journal.

ü Have your children creatively capture their awe experiences by painting, drawing, writing, singing, or other art forms.

ü Choose your next nature awe adventure activity and invite friends along.

Resources

Organizations

Greater Good Science Center: https://ggsc.berkeley.edu
Moving Art by Louie Schwartzberg: https://movingart.com
365 Gratitude: https://365gratitudejournal.com

Books

The Awe Factor: How a Little Bit of Wonder Can Make a Big Difference in Your Life by Allen Klein

Awestruck: How Embracing Wonder Can Make You Happier, Healthier, and More Connected by Jonah Paquette, PsyD

The Gratitude Project: How the Science of Thankfulness Can Rewire Our Brains for Resilience, Optimism, and the Greater Good by Jeremy Adam Smith

The Sense of Wonder: A Celebration of Nature for Parents and Children by Rachel Carson

Thanks! How the New Science of Gratitude Can Make You Happier by Robert A. Emmons, PhD

Children's Books

Apple Cake: A Gratitude by Dawn Casey

The Curious Nature Guide: Explore the Natural Wonders All Around You by Clare Walker Leslie

Giving Thanks: A Native American Good Morning Message by Chief Jake Swamp

My Grateful Book by Diana Smith

National Geographic Book of Nature Poetry by J. Patrick Lewis

The Thankful Book by Todd Parr

Thank You, Earth: A Love Letter to Our Planet by April Pulley Sayre

We All Live on This Planet Together by June Rousso, PhD

❧ 4 ❧

Outdoor Play and Adventure

Restore balance. Most kids have technology, school and extracurricular activities covered. It's time to add a pinch of adventure, a sprinkle of sunshine and a big handful of outdoor play.

Penny Whitehouse

A T the heart of a child's relationship with nature is outdoor play. So much pure joy and lightheartedness come from frolicking around outside surrounded by trees, flowers, butterflies, birds, and other gems of our natural environment. The opening scene for the television show *Little House on the Prairie,* in which Melissa Gilbert's character Laura Ingalls Wilder and her two sisters gallop joyfully in the meadow with giant smiles on their faces, is engrained in my head from my childhood. The scene exemplifies what it means for children to be free playing outside in nature and the happiness that it brings.

This chapter will focus on the importance of outdoor play and adventure for balanced mental health. It will look at the science behind the benefits of free play and outdoor play, green exercise, and outdoor travel and adventure. You will also find a sampling of engaging outdoor activities to try with your family, but by no means is this meant to be an exhaustive list. The topic of nature play is very broad, and my intention is to hone in on how it relates to children's moods and stress levels, not to provide descriptions of every type of outdoor game, sport, and adventure for you to pursue. Finally, for children who may need a bit more help dealing with mental health issues, I review nature play therapy, adventure therapy, and wilderness therapy.

It is important to note that I will not be covering outdoor education, such as Forest Schools and Waldorf Education, since that is a much broader topic that does not necessarily focus on mental health. Numerous experts and groups are already providing extensive information on nature-related education for children. If you are interested in exploring this type of educational option for your family, feel free to check out organizations such as Free Forest School, Forest School For All, and Waldorf Education.

Outdoor Play

As a child growing up in the eighties, I remember walking to school, riding my bike to the swim club and around the neighborhood to see friends, and making up all kinds of imaginative games for hours in the woods behind my house. Unfortunately, this image of playing outdoors so freely is a distant memory and not the reality for many children growing up today.

According to Richard Louv in *Last Child in the Woods: Saving Our Children from Nature-Deficit Disorder*, children today suffer from nature-deficit disorder. This refers to having less experience with and connection to nature over the last few decades.[98] American children, for example, spend thirty-five percent less time playing outside freely than their parents did, according to a recent survey.[99] In the United Kingdom, children spend half the amount of time playing outside than their parents did.[100]

A main reason for this change is the increase in the time children spend sitting inside staring at screens. Common Sense Media's 2018 report indicates that eight- to twelve-year-olds are on electronics for about five hours each day and teens are on for about seven and a half hours. This does not include time spent using screens for school or home-work.[101] The natural world is losing the battle for our children's attention, yet their electronic devices are winning. It is up to us to take action to encourage more outdoor play, especially since less time outside has been linked to higher rates of emotional illnesses like anxiety and depression.

Free Play

One important aspect of being outside is allowing children to play freely without structure and adult intervention: no organized sports, no games with lots of rules, not even educational toys with a set purpose. The children are in control, which allows them to create, use their imagination, and explore independently without our guidance. Children need lots of free play to learn how to solve their own problems, develop their own interests, learn about the world around them, and practice many skills that are necessary for healthy development. Children also benefit from these experiences so they can learn how to regulate their emotions. Peter Gray, author of *Free to Learn* and *Psychology Today*'s blog by the same name, wrote that "in play, children learn how to regulate their fear and anger and thereby how to maintain emotional control in threatening real-life situations."[102] Over time, free play helps children feel happier, calmer, and more confident.

Parks and playgrounds are an easy way to get our children outside more, and they have been shown to help boost mood and reduce stress. One study analyzed one hundred thousand tweets of people before, during, and after they visited a park. No matter which type of park they spent time in, participants felt happier as a result. Of course, large regional parks with lots of tree cover and vegetation led to the biggest rise in happiness, followed by small neighborhood parks, and then paved urban plazas. Once happiness levels went up, they stayed that way for up to four hours.[103]

There is a movement to transform traditional playgrounds into more natural-looking spaces—less plastic, metal, and asphalt and more natural elements like grass, sand, trees, plants, boulders, stumps, ropes, treehouses, and water. Research shows that children prefer natural playgrounds since they provide more opportunities for exploration, discovery, freedom, and creativity.[104] Children & Nature Network's Green Schoolyards program works to expand the number of and access to nature-filled outdoor spaces at schools to include nature play areas, gardens, trails, and walking paths in addition to traditional playground equipment. The main impetus for this program is that green schoolyards can enhance mental health and well-being and promote social-emotional skill development.[105] The best part of green schoolyards is that they are usually available for the entire community to enjoy, not just the students who attend the school.

Nature Play

While any time spent outdoors is beneficial to our children, nature play is a specific type of activity distinct from general outdoor play that can take place in settings like a traditional playground, paved area, or driveway basketball court. Nature play, on the other hand, has three specific attributes:

- ü It happens in a natural area where kids are free to explore, play, and relax.
- ü It involves true free play in which children use their imagination to make up activities as they go along while also engaging with nature by digging, collecting, catching, building, smelling, climbing, and more.
- ü It is a regular part of a child's routine.[106]

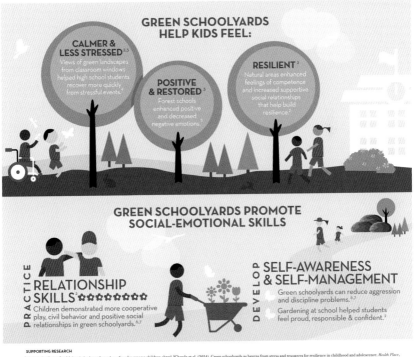

Infographic, ©2016 Children & Nature Network, provided with permission from the Children & Nature Network. Downloadable copies and additional research available at childrenandnature.org.

In *There's No Such Thing as Bad Weather: A Scandinavian Mom's Secrets for Raising Healthy, Resilient, and Confident Kids*, Linda Åkeson McGurk talks about how "children and nature work together to provide the fun and the adult provides the freedom (within limits)."[107] The essence of nature play is interacting with natural materials like plants, trees, rocks, water, dirt, logs, and many other parts of nature in an imaginative, spirited way that provides endless hours of fun and important lessons for kids.

What is it about playing outside surrounded by nature that makes it the perfect place for children to thrive? Playing actively outside provides a positive sensory experience. As pointed out in chapter 1, children can feel happier and calmer when using their five senses to interact with nature. Their senses are activated when they are romping around outside, which invigorates and relaxes them.[108]

Nature also sparks curiosity and creativity in children, who tend to play differently outdoors where there is more freedom and fewer guidelines. The objects they find in nature can turn into anything with some imagination. A stick becomes a microphone, rocks are used to build a fort, and a pile of leaves turns into a cozy bed. As Angela J. Hanscom notes in her book *Balanced and Barefoot: How Unrestricted Outdoor Play Makes for Strong, Confident, and Capable Children*, "It's a place where they can design, create, and explore. Studies show that when children have free play outdoors, they become better problem solvers and their creativity is enhanced. The outdoors challenges the mind to constantly think in new ways. There is no pressure."[109]

Children also build social-emotional skills while playing in nature because it gives them the chance to take risks and overcome fears. Perfect examples include climbing a tree or maintaining balance to walk across a log. Nature can offer opportunities for children to challenge themselves in a healthy way, and it can also offer a calm, quiet place for them to relax, feel rejuvenated, and be themselves. Being outside can provide an escape from all the loud and overstimulating distractions often found in indoor environments filled with electronics.

Encouraging our kids to engage in more nature free play may be more challenging than might be expected as our lives have trended toward a greater reliance on technology and organized activities. The Green Hearts Institute for Nature in Childhood points out that unstructured outdoor play averages only a mere thirty minutes per week for each child.[110] This is troubling, and we really need to start thinking about outdoor play as medicine for our children—an antidote to their ever-increasing screen time. The National Wildlife Federation recommends that we give our kids a daily "Green Hour" for unstructured play and interaction with the natural world. Rooted in research on creative play and health by the Centers for Disease Control and Prevention and the American Academy of Pediatrics, this program highlights how essential it is that children spend at least one hour per day engaging in unstructured free play for their physical and mental well-being.[111]

Nature free play can look like many different things depending on a child's specific interests and circumstances. If children enjoy art, they might create nature sculptures or use a stick to draw in the mud or sand. If they love sports, they might develop their own games like stickball or running a race around trees. Children engage in different types of nature play depending on whether they live in rural, suburban, or urban areas and what kind of access they have to green space. Nature play in a large open field may look different from play on a small patch of grass on a street corner, yet there are opportunities in every environment.

When it comes to specific activities, there are numerous books, magazines, blogs, and other resources you can peruse for nature play ideas. In *A Parents' Guide to Nature Play: How to Give Your Children More Outdoor Play . . . and Why You Should!*, Ken Finch recommends creating a "Kidscape" in your yard to encourage nature free play. This includes elements like a digging pit; dirt pile; plants; vegetable garden; rocks and boulders; birdhouses; trees; shrubbery; water (hose, sprinkler, rain barrel, spray bottles, buckets); somewhere to sit (swing, hammock, bench, Adirondack chair); and a play log that can be used as a table, bench, balance beam, and more. Some specific activities that he suggests include having backyard campouts, picnicking under the stars, working in the garden, dancing in the rain, building a birdhouse, organizing a scavenger hunt, and researching plants and animals using nature guides. It is also handy to have some

essential nature play tools around like shovels, rakes, hoes, buckets, collection boxes, binoculars, a compass, a magnifying glass, flashlight, tweezers, bug cages, and nets.[112] Always be ready for the next nature adventure. You can even keep a bag of these nature tools in the trunk of your car in case the perfect moment arises to go exploring.

Common Barriers to Outdoor Play

What is preventing you from spending time in nature? Many of us have excuses for why we do not spend more time outside. Believe me, I am just as guilty as anyone. It is too hot. It is too wet. I am too busy with work. It will take too much time to head over to the local park. It takes so much effort to pack up everything that the kids need. One of my biggest concerns is sun exposure since I have had a few bouts of skin cancer over the years and need to cover up when outdoors.

Here are five of the most common barriers to outdoor play. Yes, they are real concerns, and some are more challenging to overcome than others. However, nature provides so many tremendous benefits for our children's (and our) health and happiness that it is crucial we do what we can to make adjustments so we get more time outside.

Fear

In *Last Child in the Woods*, Richard Louv warned that "fear is the emotion that separates a developing child from the full, essential benefits of nature."[113] Since the 1980s, we have lived in a more fearful society hyped up by the 24/7 news cycle and now amplified by social media. We worry about many safety concerns that impact the time our children spend outside, such as traffic, crime, strangers, injury, and nature itself like wild animals, bug bites, and sun damage. However, if we check the statistics, we quickly realize that the chance of our worst fears coming true is extremely unlikely. It is all about shifting our focus and discovering truths that make us feel more comfortable. When it comes to my skin cancer worries, I always wear a hat and sun jacket and make sure the kids put on hats and sunscreen before they head outdoors. It is just part of our routine now. Being prepared and aware of our surroundings can help alleviate these common fears.

Time

Lots of children are living an overly scheduled lifestyle involving sports teams, rehearsals, indoor play and sports centers, homework, extracurricular activities, and family obligations that prevent them from enjoying free play outdoors. Many parents are also working hard at their jobs and dealing with daily chores and errands that make it difficult to find time to take their kids outside, especially during weekdays. Try to schedule in daily time for outdoor play, even if this means squeezing in a bike ride or walk before school or after dinner. You can also combine activities, such as doing homework outside in the backyard or working out with your kids or alongside them as they play outside.

Weather

No matter where you live, weather can be an issue at some point. I personally do not like being outside in the heat. Other people struggle with rainy days or long winter months. Fortunately, there are simple solutions to weather concerns. Get the right gear so your family is prepared for any type of weather. Depending on your weather challenge, stock up on raincoats, rain boots, hiking boots, umbrellas, all types of hats, sun jackets, sunscreen, gloves, and scarves. You can also schedule your outdoor time around the weather reports. On days that I know it is going to be hot and sunny, I go outside either early in the day or late in the afternoon when the sun is not as strong. You can also still enjoy being outside under covered areas like a balcony or umbrella. With a bit of creativity and flexibility, we can still fit in outside time no matter what kind of weather comes our way.

Reluctant Children

Sometimes our kids just do not want to go outside. This has become a huge concern for many parents because of the increase in technology use. Children spend so much more time focused on screens instead of nature scenes. They may also come up with excuses like they are tired or have too much homework. If this happens in your home, I encourage you to push your kids to get outside even for just a few minutes every day. It really can be part of a healthy daily routine, just

as important as brushing their teeth or taking a vitamin. One trick is to let your kids trade in "green time" for "screen time."

Access

Having access to safe parks and open green space can be a challenge for some families, especially if you live in an urban environment. Unfortunately, access to nature varies by class, education, race, and other key variables. According to a recent study, residents with higher levels of education and income are more likely to have better access to urban vegetation. On the other hand, neighborhoods with predominantly Black and Latino residents were less likely to have natural areas nearby.[114] And even if access is available, members of BIPOC (Black, Indigenous, and people of color) and LGBTQ+ communities may experience racism or discrimination during their time outdoors in nature. This is an issue that many organizations are currently working on, including the Children & Nature Network, Gateway to the Great Outdoors, Get Out Stay Out/Vamos Afuera, Latino Outdoors, Outdoor Afro, Outdoor Alliance for Kids, Soul Trak Outdoors, and Wild Diversity. If this is a challenge for your family or if you want to help others, consider reaching out to these organizations.

Green Exercise

Green exercise is another way we can enjoy the outdoors to improve how we feel. It is a term used to describe our interaction with nature while engaging in a physical fitness activity. This term was coined in 2003 by Dr. Jules Pretty and Dr. Jo Barton at the University of Essex in the United Kingdom. Their focus in this area spurred a great deal of research into how nature and exercise together can benefit our emotional well-being. They published dozens of studies on the benefits of green exercise that indicate how exercising in green spaces—no matter if they are in a city or the wilderness—has a positive effect on mood. Additional researchers from a wide background including physiology, health and well-being, environmental sustainability, community engagement, and behavioral change continue to study the link between nature, exercise, and mental health.[115] In essence, it has been found that green exercise magnifies the general benefits of exercise, reducing stress and boosting mood. This groundbreaking work can help all of us find ways to feel happier and calmer by doing something as simple as going for a walk outside.

Here are several ways in which green exercise improves mental health:

Produces endorphins. When we exercise, our body releases feel-good neurotransmitters called endorphins. These chemicals in our brain act as natural painkillers, making us feel better and less stressed. Endorphins are responsible for the natural high we get as a result of a challenging workout.

Reduces stress hormones. Exercise and being in and around nature reduce the level of stress hormones in our body like adrenaline and cortisol, helping us feel calmer.[116]

Minimizes fatigue. Exercise improves blood flow and our body's ability to use oxygen efficiently. These changes reduce fatigue and improve alertness. This helps us when we are stressed out because we are depleted and need to return to a more balanced level of energy. When we are stressed, many nerves in our brain and throughout our body are impacted. Scientists conclude, therefore, that if our body feels better, then our mind will also feel better.[117]

Provides a fun distraction. One of the best parts about exercise and spending time in nature is that these experiences give us a time to take a break from the stresses in our daily lives.

Encourages mindfulness. Exercise provides the perfect opportunity to be mindful. While we work out, we can fully engage in the present moment instead of letting our mind run wild with worries. When we combine viewing nature with physical fitness, we can get lost in the moment and experience a happiness boost.

Nature walks and hikes, water sports, and biking are just a few examples of green exercise for you to engage in as a family that have been shown to improve mental health.

Nature Walks and Hikes

Taking your children on a nature walk is one of the most convenient ways to get outside and enjoy some fresh air and relaxing scenery. Studies have found that walking in green spaces helps us feel less anxious[118] and recover from attention overload,[119] or mental fatigue. You can walk anywhere that you find calming, whether that be your neighborhood, local park, nature center, garden, farm, or near water such as around a lake or along the beach. There are thousands of hiking trails to choose from in urban, suburban, and rural areas, and many of them are free and open to the public. In *Families on Foot: Urban Hikes to Backyard Treks and National Park Adventures,* Jennifer Phare Davis and Brew Davis recommend that families start off by walking around close to home before venturing out a bit more. "Take your kids for a walk around the neighborhood and talk with them about the different things you see." These brief excursions give families some basic walking experience, they explain. "Once you are comfortable walking around the block as a family, research local parks that offer family-friendly trails. Participating in group outings with a park ranger or outdoor educator is a great way for you and your children to improve your hiking skills while acquiring fun and useful knowledge from an expert."[120]

An advantage of nature walks is that they really can be done throughout the year during any season. In autumn you can enjoy the beautiful leaves changing colors and stroll through an apple orchard or pumpkin patch. During wintertime, bundle up and take a brisk walk around a local park or flat trail. If you see snowflakes falling, head outside for a quick walk to enjoy the special winter scene. When spring arrives, visit a park, garden, or nature center to show your children the blooming flowers and trees, and try to spot some chirping birds. Finally, during summertime, enjoy a relaxing walk on the beach.

If you are concerned that your children will get antsy or bored during the walk, consider jazzing things up with a few games. Some ideas include nature bingo, a scavenger hunt, I Spy, and Simon Says. An alphabet hike is also a good idea; challenge your kids to find something in nature that starts with each letter. You can also have a nature identification challenge and see how many plants and animals they can name along your hike.

Another clever trend is that libraries are developing StoryWalk programs that combine literacy, exercise, nature, and family bonding. Story boards are set up along a walking path or hiking trail so families get exercise outdoors while reading an adorable story together. It is easily accessible and enjoyable for all ages.

Author photo.

My children and I recently discovered a StoryWalk at our local library. Behind the library is a lake with a trail circling it. On one side of the lake, there is a hidden trail that we never knew existed. The first story board is found at the entrance to this secret trail. We continued to follow the meandering path through the native sawgrass marsh to read the story that was about nature, of course. My daughter was so excited because it was like a treasure hunt. We did not know when the next page of the book would appear. As we strolled from one board to the next, we spotted birds, insects, and native plants. As soon as she saw the next page of the book, she pointed, shouted, and ran as fast as she could to find out what happened next in the story. We had such a blast during our hike. I highly recommend trying to find a StoryWalk® near you. If you cannot find any, consider recommending the idea to your local library since they are successful in many communities.

When it comes to hiking with kids, I have a few reminders. Dress in proper attire, cover up with hats, apply sunscreen, bring along bug spray and first-aid items like bandages, and take frequent breaks for water and a healthy snack. If you are looking for that extra push to get your family outside walking more, you can sign up for a family-friendly hiking challenge like Hike it Baby 30 or 52 Hike Challenge.

Water Sports

Spending time exercising in water has a tremendously soothing effect, helping us to feel more relaxed and refreshed. Experts have noted that swimming produces the same relaxation response as yoga, increasing calming chemicals, regulating our breathing, and allowing us to enter a meditative state. You can swim in a pool or engage in wild swimming, which takes place in a natural body of water like a river or lake.

In a sense, swimming is a form of meditation. When we swim laps, we can focus on our technique, the rhythm of our strokes, and the in and out of our breath, making it easy to shut out noises and other distractions going on outside the water. I can attest to this. I love how swimming laps helps me escape from the world and to be more mindful. You can even hear your own thoughts more clearly underwater. Being in the water also allows us to have a calming sensory experience. We feel the wet water on our skin and become aware of its temperature. With goggles, we can soak in all the visual stimuli around us. If you swim in clear ocean water, you can enjoy natural treasures like seashells, seaweed, and fish. Even in the pool, my vision is so crisp and clear. I love how I can see the sunlight twinkling on the surface of the water, which always lifts my spirit. Swimming also helps regulate our breathing, which is important in reducing stress and anxiety. When we are stressed, we tend to take short, shallow breaths that can lead to hyperventilation, dizziness, and a panicky feeling. Another major benefit of being in the water is feeling lighter, even weightless. There is something so blissful about this sensation that helps us feel joyful. Finally, swimming can boost dopamine, serotonin, and endorphins, hormones associated with improved mood.[121]

Additional water sports for your family to try include snorkeling, surfing, bodyboarding, diving, paddleboarding, waterskiing, water volleyball, water polo, and water aerobics.

StreetWaves: Providing Children Access to Life-Changing Water Experiences

As someone who grew up visiting the beach and hanging out at my neighborhood swim club every summer, it never occurred to me that there are children who do not have that privilege. But there are many children whose socioeconomic, historic, and/or cultural backgrounds exclude them from the water. They have never seen the ocean or dipped their toe in a pool, let alone learned how to swim.

How could this be possible? Much of this goes back to hundreds of years of systemic racism. According to the Centers for Disease Control and Prevention, this lack of access to water is a life or death issue. African American children ages five to nineteen drown in swimming pools at rates 5.5 times higher than those of whites.[122] Besides the higher risk of drowning, this is also a mental health issue. Sadly, these children are missing out on the incredible benefits of being in and around the water.

Maurice "Maui" Goodbeer, founder and executive director of the nonprofit StreetWaves Inc., has made it his life's mission to bring youth from underserved communities out to the ocean to swim, surf, and sail. The words "Waves Change Lives" are boldly displayed on StreetWaves' website. The organization's goal is to inspire and expand these children's opportunities by providing them access to get off the streets and into the ocean.

Maui and his team believe that the majesty of the sea and the mastery of the ocean cultivate courage, confidence, commitment, and character. His mother's family is from the Lipan Apache tribe near Lafayette, Louisiana, and he was taught from a very young age to honor the earth and natural bodies of water. "I grew up with nature as a priority. Our views and beliefs are that we respect the earth much like plants and animals in that we believe that we belong to the earth, it does not belong to us. We are just here to care for it as it cares for us while we are here." He has taken these experiences and embedded them into StreetWaves. "When we take the kids into the ocean, we make sure they get to have a spiritual experience with the water so they can connect deeply with nature. We include a brief ceremony in which they drink a bit of the saltwater to become one with the ocean."

Founded in 2008 in Miami Beach, StreetWaves has taught thousands of youth how to swim, surf, and sail in the south Florida area. Many of these children face tremendous hardships in their lives, including being in the foster care system. The ocean has become a place where they can escape from the chaos and accomplish new skills they never dreamed of having.

The core of StreetWaves is the free nine-week after-school Aquatics Enrichment Program. Children are bussed to the ocean or a community pool from their school every day for nine weeks to learn swimming, surfing, ocean safety skills, environmental education, social skill development, and mentorship. This consistency allows them to master swimming and surfing. Some of the children have even gone on to join swim teams and win surfing competitions. "That's the most impressive aspect of this program for me. You get kids who have never seen the ocean before and are now winning competitions because of the deep connection they have made with the ocean. To see the kids be able to shine so much and win competitions is magical for me," Maui pointed out.

StreetWaves is helping to transform the lives of these boys and girls through the healing power of the ocean. "We allow the water to do the work. We really let the water become their therapy. The negative ions in water are what people are drawn to. Just being in and around the water is so powerful," explained Maui. Children are able to deal with their stress and fears throughout the program. One child conquered the ocean and yelled out "I am not afraid anymore!" Maui also recalls a situation in which a child's mother drowned in the ocean and he was extremely afraid to go in. "Through his time with us, he was able to connect to the ocean and feel linked to his mother and her experience."

One of the main benefits of the children's time with StreetWaves is that they will bring their new experiences and skills back to their families and friends to spread positivity of nature to their community. "We try to make it a point to sow the seeds of swimming ability, surfing, and ocean exposure into the communities where we work. It's that little shift that can send things into a different direction."[123]

Courtesy Maurice "Maui" Goodbeer of StreetWaves Corp.

Biking

Grab your bikes and bike helmets and head out for a family ride in your neighborhood or through a local park. Riding together is a delightful way for your entire family to get some exercise, enjoy the fresh air, take in some natural scenery, and share special moments. My family has always enjoyed bike riding together. During a family vacation to Puerto Rico, we ventured out on the trail all around the resort property. In New Jersey during the summer, we love riding up and down the boardwalk that runs parallel to the ocean, and we often take our bikes out to ride around at a couple of local parks near our home.

Biking provides many benefits that help us feel happier and calmer, and it is a healthy, low-impact exercise that builds muscle strength and increases stamina. Whether we head to a mountain trail or city park, biking is a great way to get outside in nature to observe plants, trees, flowers, animals, and more. Next, biking gives us a healthy break from the stress in our lives.

Hopping on a bike and whizzing around with the breeze blowing on our skin can be very relaxing. It is also a magnificent way to escape

the doldrums of a normal day, blow off some steam, and experience new scenery. Additional benefits of biking linked to improving mental health include helping us sleep better, giving us a sense of pride after finishing a challenging ride, and stimulating creative thinking.

Team Sports and Other Organized Activities

Other green exercise ideas include team sports that your children can play in the open air, such as soccer, flag football, basketball, ultimate frisbee, baseball, softball, lacrosse, and beach volleyball. You can get your kids involved in orienteering, a challenging outdoor adventure sport that exercises both body and mind. Participants navigate between specific locations marked on an orienteering map and decide the best route to complete the course in the fastest way possible. It can take place anywhere outside, including a forest, countryside, or even urban parks. It is a terrific sport for runners, joggers, and walkers who love maps and the outdoors.[124] With some innovation, you can also create your own nature gym. Natural elements can provide attractive ways to exercise that supplement or replace traditional fitness equipment. Lift large rocks as weights, use strong trees for arm presses and pull-ups, find a log for balancing or stepping exercises, and do squats on a hillside for an extra challenge. Your kids will love getting creative during exercise time.

Travel and Outdoor Adventure

While we can find many amazing nature play opportunities in our own backyard and community, there is something extra special about traveling to discover exciting new places. Bringing your children on day trips, weekend getaways, or longer family vacations can play a significant role in their happiness and personal growth, not to mention all the precious memories you will build together. In fact, studies show that by just planning a vacation and getting excited about it, we can experience a boost in happiness.[125]

Why is traveling so beneficial? Getting out of our daily routines, experiencing new surroundings, and forming fresh perspectives reset our mind and body. Vacations give us something positive to look forward to and a break from the daily hustle and bustle of our hectic routines, allowing us to relax and recharge. Vacations can be inspiring, expand our knowledge, and give us the chance to build relationships and interact with new people. As a result, we feel happier and less stressed during our time away, and often that feeling lasts even after a relaxing trip.

Of course, if we choose travel adventures that encompass outdoor experiences, we can benefit from all that nature has to offer as well. Nature provides opportunities to feel mindful, grateful, and in awe, which helps boost our mood and reduce stress. The great outdoors can be an especially invigorating and peaceful place to get away.

Another aspect of outdoor family adventures is that they help our children learn how to address their fears in a healthy way. A number of experts support risky outdoor play and adventure for kids to build their confidence and resilience. In *Free to Learn*, Peter Gray writes, "In vigorous outdoor play, children deliberately dose themselves with moderate amounts of fear—as they swing, slide, or twirl on playground equipment, climb on monkey bars or trees, or skateboard down banisters—and they thereby learn how to control not only their bodies but also their fear."[126]

In *Balanced and Barefoot*, Angela J. Hanscom talks about how the outdoors forces children to assess their environment and evaluate risks. She explains that it builds their confidence, which ultimately helps them battle fears and anxiety. "They learn what they are physically and mentally capable of when they try and try again." She also talks about how challenges in nature help children learn how to adapt as needed. "When playing outdoors, children quickly learn that they can't always control the outcomes of their play. For instance, their fort may not have turned out exactly as they envisioned, and in turn they learn to be more flexible in thinking."[127]

Depending on where you live, the amount of time you have, how far you want to travel, and your budget, there are numerous outdoor adventures for your family to try. Some ideas include camping, fishing, and canoeing. When we think of outdoor adventures, the term "ecotourism" often comes to mind. According to the International Ecotourism Society, ecotourism is "responsible travel to natural areas that conserves the environment, sustains the well-being of the local people, and involves interpretation and education."[128] Ecotourism trips can include visiting parks, boating, rafting, caving, rock climbing, hiking, zip lining, exploring a natural reserve, volunteering to help the local environment, and hundreds of other experiences your family will love.

Some of my fondest ecotourism-related memories include horseback riding along the beach in Puerto Rico, taking a helicopter tour over Hawaii, hiking to see a glacier in Alaska, and a boat ride between Martha's Vineyard and Nantucket in Massachusetts during the summer. I have a friend who has checked off quite a few extraordinary bucket list family adventures, including visiting the China Conservation and Research Center for the Giant Panda, sailing in the Caribbean, rappelling in Costa Rica, and going on an African safari. You can choose the best excursions for your family, whether that means a day trip in your state or region or traveling halfway around the world. A quick Google search will give you tons of ideas and tips for your next family eco-adventure.

Taking Family Adventure to a Whole New Level

Chris Fagan is an author, speaker, trainer, business consultant, and mom. She and her husband, Marty, are also the *Guinness Book of World Records* holders for being the first American married couple to ski 570 miles from the coast of Antarctica to the South Pole, completely unassisted. This extraordinary adventure is documented in her book, *The Expedition: Two Parents Risk Life and Family in an Extraordinary Quest to the South Pole*, which is about weighing the responsibility of parenthood against fulfilling a dream for one more grand adventure.

Despite busy careers, much of the Fagans' lives have focused on outdoor adventure. They met during a twenty-five-day expedition climbing Denali, the highest mountain in North America. After their son was born, the couple continued to push the limits of endurance as ultra runners and explored mountains as a family. They traveled to many gorgeous locations around the world with their young son in tow. He could often be found playing in the dirt or woods as the family camped during these trips. "I have had many adventures with my son—from hiking for an hour on a local trail to climbing Mt. Kilimanjaro when he was ten years old," she recalls. "It seems like any time I have had an adventure with my son he is always happier and calmer after spending time outdoors with me and my husband. In fact, we have chosen to live in a place that is accessible to outdoor adventures because of the positive effect they have on us as individuals and as a family."

The Fagans integrate the outdoors into their daily lives. Hiking is convenient for them, as they live in the mountain foothills outside Seattle, Washington. There is also a river about a ten-minute walk from their home. When their son was young, they enjoyed going down to the water and watching him jump and play on the rocks. "There is a Rails to Trails near our house," Chris explains. "We brought our mountain bikes there and enjoyed riding through the large tunnel with our headlamps on. It was such a fun adventure to do as a family and I loved to see how proud our son felt when he finished the trail."

Traveling throughout the state of Washington and beyond has also brought many special memories. One of their annual traditions was to go kayaking in the Puget Sound area and camp on the islands. They enjoyed fishing; whale watching; and observing wildlife like deer, sea lions, and eagles. Mount St. Helens and Mount Rainier are within a few hours from their home, so they have explored those sites on several occasions. Outside the Northwest, family adventures have included a dinosaur-themed trip to see excavation sites in Montana, a rafting trip down the Grand Canyon in Arizona, climbing to base camp on Mount Everest in Nepal, climbing Mount Fuji in Japan, and biking through remote Tanzania.

While your family may not crave the extensive adventures the Fagans do, Chris offers the following tips to encourage all of us to add a bit more nature exploration into our lives.

ü **Decide to make adventure part of your lifestyle.** Block out time once a month to do something outside as a family and then increase the frequency over time as you see fit. Be specific and ü **Keep it simple.** At first, try not to make adventures too complicated and intense. Start with something easy that does not take a lot of time or require specialized gear, like eating dinner outside and gazing at the stars or roasting marshmallows over an open fire.

ü **Create your own micro adventures.** You do not have to go far to have a special time outdoors together. Build a fort in your garage or under an awning during bad weather; camp out in your backyard; create a treasure hunt using the five senses to discover clues; and look for nature items like rocks, leaves, and feathers.

ü **Turn everyday activities into an adventure.** Some ideas include an adventure picnic, playing games outside like an "I Spy" hike, and doing some green exercise.

ü **Plan outings around naturally occurring events.** Follow the science news to plan your family adventures around sunrises, sunsets, special moons like the harvest moon or blood moon, a solar eclipse, comets, and meteor showers. Be sure to research the events as a family beforehand.

Giving our children the gift of outdoor adventures can benefit them in so many incredible ways. Chris knows how much her family's cherished experiences have impacted her son. "He has stepped up and overcome lots of challenges. In the end, he always walks away with a great story, increased confidence, and a feeling of empowerment. I have seen my son feel happier and calmer, almost an afterglow." He was then able to come back to daily life feeling replenished. "These experiences allowed him to be really in the moment and to stop worrying. There is something that chemically changes in us and we come back reset."[129]

The Magic of Sleepaway Camp

I never thought I would be the kind of mom who would send my kids off to summer camp for several weeks away from home. I did not grow up going to camp (although my husband did), so this was a foreign concept to me. Though I spent a week crying and feeling like a huge part of me was missing after my son waved good-bye that first summer, sending both of my children to sleepaway camp turned out to be one of the best decisions I have made for my family. When I think back to my own childhood, I really could have used that type of independent living experience and positive outdoor challenges to help me learn how to deal with my fears, self-esteem, and relationship issues that led to anxiety later on.

It may be hard to believe, but letting our kids go off on their own for a while to spread their wings can help them flourish in so many ways that impact their emotional well-being. Sending children away for camp may seem daunting at first, but if you ask anyone who has spent several weeks bunking with their friends, they will tell you how it positively transformed their life and how lucky they are that their parents gave them that gift. My kids love sharing their remarkable camp experiences all year long, from accomplishing zip-line challenges to white-water rafting to fireside chats in the woods. They spend the entire year counting down the days until the camp bus departs once again.

As the owner and director of Gold Arrow Camp in Lakeshore, California, for over thirty years, Audrey Monke has worked with thousands of campers and their parents. In her book *Happy Campers: 9 Summer Camp Secrets for Raising Kids Who Become Thriving Adults*, she talks about how camp can play a huge role in helping our children thrive.

It's no wonder that—with screens safely stored at home, less focus on competition and more focus on collaboration, and lots of fresh air and outdoor fun—campers feel that camp is a haven, a safe place to relax and be themselves. Without the pressures of academics, athletics, and social media and the expectations of parents, teachers, and coaches, kids—many for the first time—experience living in the moment, enjoying each other's company, challenging themselves, and figuring out who they truly are and what they really like. Many campers feel healed, restored, or changed by their camp experience and don't want to leave. Parents, too, feel relieved to give their children the gift of a few weeks of bliss in the midst of their pressured, stressful lives.[130]

Camp provides numerous benefits to our children's growth and development, with several stemming from time in nature. As a contrast to the school year when kids spend most of the day indoors, camp allows them to have several hours outside every day playing sports, engaging in adventure activities, and freely playing with friends. This much-needed time outdoors gives them a chance to relax and soak in the natural world. Being around nature also stimulates self-reflection in some children. The school year is a busy time, but camp provides a chance for kids to slow down and listen to their own thoughts. When kids take a break from television, video games, and texting, they become more mindful of their surroundings and their own emotions.

Focusing on the simple things in life like going for a hike, watching a sunset, and singing around the campfire can be quite healing. Another major benefit of sleepaway camp is that children build confidence and self-esteem as a result of trying new activities like learning to swim and climbing rope courses, and they acquire camping skills like pitching a tent or starting a fire. When they succeed, they become empowered and are more likely to face their next challenge with confidence and ease. Finally, spending time outdoors at camp provides many opportunities for kids to conquer their fears like being afraid of the dark during a night hike or a fear of heights.

I recognize that sending a child to sleepaway camp is a luxury and not everyone has the means to afford it. Fortunately, camp scholarships are available. You can contact individual camps and the American Camp Association to learn about scholarship opportunities. Almost all camps have some sort of financial support for families in need.

Outdoor Therapy Options

When children are struggling with ongoing mental health issues like anxiety or depression, parents may need to seek out extra guidance from professional therapy programs, such as nature play therapy, adventure therapy, or wilderness therapy.

Nature Play Therapy

Nature play therapy is an innovative approach now being used to help children manage their emotions. Based on play therapy, which involves a therapist strategically using play activities to encourage children to express their feelings, modify behavior, and develop problem-solving skills, nature play therapy incorporates aspects of the natural world into this process.

Nature play therapy is a "dynamic duo that combines the therapeutic benefits of nature and play," according to Jamie Lynn Langley, licensed clinical social worker and registered play therapist supervisor, who has been a practicing child, family, and play therapist for about thirty years.

She has been using nature intentionally with her clients for over five years and now trains other therapists on the benefits of nature play therapy.

During one of her presentations, she explained, "Integrating nature-based therapeutic activities (that can often be adapted for use indoors when needed) will assist children and teens and their families to improve resiliency, overcome adversity, enhance relationship quality, and grow and thrive emotionally."[131] Nature play therapy taps into multisensory aspects of nature through tactics like storytelling, sand tray play therapy, nature art, natural sounds, and other earth-based components.

While a nature play therapy session can take place inside a therapist's office, it often involves time spent outdoors. This can look like setting up a therapeutic art table outside, the therapist and child sitting on a bench playing a game and having a conversation, or conducting the session during a nature walk. Children often feel more relaxed and free outside compared to sitting in a small, confined office. They can be loud and run around, which loosens them up and helps them feel more comfortable communicating their feelings.

Jamie Lynn loves sharing about the many ways she incorporates nature during her therapy sessions with children. "Kids often come in stressed and unregulated. I have wooden bowls filled with sand for the kids to put their hands in and sift through. This helps them relax. I use different types of sand to add colors and textures: dark brown sand, garnet sand, light purple sand, white sand, and pebble rocks, too." The children also enjoy creating "sandalas" with the sand. This is a term that she coined when referring to mandalas made of sand, which are circular designs with concentric shapes that radiate out symmetrically from the center. She has mandala and sandala stations set up in her office, and every season she puts out different color sand and nature items. In winter, for example, there is white sand to resemble snow.

She uses both structured and unstructured play to reach children. A structured nature play activity, for example, might be making characters out of rocks to resemble the emotions the children are feeling at the time like a worry or angry rock monster or creating puppets out of sticks, leaves, flower petals, and other natural items. Being creative can really

help children figure out how they are feeling. "So many kids do not get to use their imagination often. So much is already created for them. I help them get creative, which helps them emotionally," Langley explains. She also uses games like nature charades, matching games, scavenger hunts, and nature hide-and-seek to connect with the kids. A simple nature walk is an example of unstructured nature play. Langley finds that some children like to go outside and take a walk and pick up rocks and hold them. They find it very grounding. "Something so simple as holding a rock can be so effective. I once had an anxious child hold two warm rocks in her hands and then put her back up against a tree. She proceeded to do some deep breathing, and after five minutes her anxiety was reduced." She often will take clients on a sensory nature walk and ask them to slow down and absorb what is around them using their five senses. This is a very effective tool for easing stress and anxiety.

Jamie Lynn also points out the importance of nature play for perfectionist children, which is often linked to anxiety. "Getting scrapes is part of playing outside. It is good for kids to take some risk. With such challenges, kids build confidence." Allowing kids to be messy is also important. "Kids need to be able to be messy. Messiness is therapeutic and helps them deal with perfection issues. Let them paint outside, roll around in the grass, and make mud pies."[132]

Parents can also use many of these nature play tactics at home. Dr. Cheryl Fisher, author of *Mindfulness and Nature-Based Therapeutic Techniques for Children: Creative Activities for Emotion Regulation, Resilience and Connectedness*, recommends creating a nature-enhanced "time away" spot in your home or yard where children can head to when they need a place to chill out. This area could include a water table, a sand area with fossil stamps, small plants, and a tabletop Zen garden. You could also put together a movable nature kit that they can take along with them.[133] The kit can include items like a rock collection; sticks; pine cones; books and magazines about nature; animal and earth cards; index cards with nature poems; natural textures like cotton, wool, silk, bamboo, and wood; nature crafts; seashells; photos of nature; nature-mindful coloring books; nature and animal stamps; and essential oils to smell.

Adventure Therapy and Wilderness Therapy

You can also look into an outdoor therapeutic program, often referred to as outdoor adventure therapy, outdoor behavioral health care, or wilderness therapy. This type of therapy mixes traditional therapy techniques—such as talk therapy, cognitive behavioral therapy, and group therapy—with being outside in a wilderness setting. It utilizes outdoor experiences and activities to kinesthetically engage individuals on cognitive, behavioral, and physical levels.

Adventure therapy and wilderness therapy are especially effective because they involve spending time outdoors in nature, engaging in physical exercise and free play, trying new adventures, overcoming achievable challenges, practicing mindfulness, working consistently with a therapist on a daily basis, and participating in group activities that build relationship skills.[134] In *Last Child in the Woods*, Richard Louv highlights the effectiveness of these programs: "Studies of outdoor education programs geared toward troubled youth—especially those diagnosed with mental health problems—show a clear therapeutic value. Participants in

adventure therapy programs made gains in self-esteem, leadership, academics, personality, and interpersonal relations."[135]

A unique aspect of this type of therapy is that participants work through their issues in a physical way with challenging experiences that facilitate self-discovery and personal growth while learning flow, grit, growth mindset, and self-efficacy. By engaging both mind and body to address their emotions in the moment, they connect to themselves, others, and the natural world.

There is a slight distinction between the two approaches. In adventure therapy, participants engage in experiential activities that involve some level of risk that are both physically and emotionally challenging. Typical activities include backpacking expeditions, mountain biking, rock climbing, kayaking, doing a ropes course, geocaching, canoeing, skiing, river rafting, and paddleboarding. With wilderness therapy, the children are immersed in nature and sense a radical change of their environment. They learn healthy coping strategies and build confidence through a daily routine in the wilderness and basic life skills like pitching a tent, starting a fire, cooking at a campsite, building a shelter, and creating primitive art and instruments.[136] These activities and adventures help the kids feel safe and connected to their therapists, making them more open to the therapeutic process overall. Therefore, therapists are able to lead an intense therapeutic program that would otherwise take a much longer time to accomplish in an office setting.

As I have discussed throughout this book, nature is a special ingredient in our lives that helps improve our well-being, and that is especially evident in these outdoor therapy programs. Based in Utah, Second Nature provides wilderness therapy programs for struggling adolescents. On their blog, they address why nature is such a critical component of their program:

> Nature shows that nothing is wrong with us. There are no mirrors to look at and judge ourselves, which allows more time to focus on the setting and the work being done.
>
> There are no clocks so there is a return to our natural rhythms. Nature models a healthier pace of life.

It may sound unpleasant, but nature forces us to surrender comfort. This is a good thing. Our culture propagates this myth that we should strive to be as comfortable as possible at all times. But, to achieve permanent comfort and control actually leads us to dull, meaningless lives that damage the soul. Nature calls us back to reality. It rains, the sun goes down, things grow where they want, your muscles will ache if you hike or climb or swim. Nature makes us realize how little control we actually have, which frees the mind and the spirit.

The constant noise of our move-faster, get-more, keep-going culture fades with time in nature, the mind calms, and we truly experience and grow to love silence and stillness. In this stillness we're able to remember who we truly are.

Best of all, being in nature gives us a sense of awe, of being small. This helps us to stop focusing on ourselves and to consider the things and the people around us. We learn we have a place in the world of others.[137]

With over twenty-five privately run therapeutic wilderness programs and hundreds run by government or nongovernmental organizations (NGOs), there are many options for families. The majority require students to be twelve years or older, but there are some preteen wilderness programs available for younger children. For more information, contact the Outdoor Behavioral Healthcare Council, National Association of Therapeutic Schools and Programs, or Association for Experiential Education.

Activity Checklist

ü Try to ensure that your children get about one hour of outside time each day.

ü Take your children to local parks and playgrounds. Try to discover ones with natural elements.

ü Stock up on essential nature play tools like shovels, rakes, hoes, buckets, collection boxes, binoculars, a compass, a magnifying glass, a flashlight, tweezers, bug cages, and nets.

ü Keep a bag of nature tools in the trunk of your car to always be ready for the next outdoor adventure.

ü Create a nature-enhanced "time-away" spot in your home or yard where children can head to when they need a place to chill out.

ü Go on a family nature walk; look for a StoryWalk program in your community.

ü Sign up for a family hiking challenge.

ü Try new types of green exercise as a family, such as orienteering, paddleboarding, and mountain biking.

ü Plan an ecotourism vacation within your family's goals and budget. Maybe create a bucket list of your dream trips.

ü Consider sending your children to a camp program with a wide variety of outdoor activities.

ü If your children are struggling with mental health issues and need extra support, consider finding a nature play therapist or enrolling them in an adventure therapy or wilderness therapy program.

Resources

Organizations

American Camp Association: https://www.acacamps.org
Association for Experiential Education: https://www.aee.org
Association for Play Therapy: https://www.a4pt.org
Children & Nature Network: https://www.childrenandnature.org
52 Hike Challenge: https://www.52hikechallenge.com
Forest School For All: https://forestschoolforall.com
Free Forest School: https://www.freeforestschool.org
Gateway to the Great Outdoors: https://www.gatewayoutdoors.org
Get Out Stay Out/Vamos Afuera: https://vamosafuera.org

Hike it Baby: https://www.hikeitbaby.com
Latino Outdoors: https://latinooutdoors.org
Mother Natured Blog: https://mothernatured.com
National Association of Therapeutic Schools and Programs:
	https://natsap.org
1000 Hours Outside: https://www.1000hoursoutside.com
Orienteering USA: https://orienteeringusa.org
Outdoor Afro: https://outdoorafro.com
Outdoor Alliance for Kids: https://outdoorsallianceforkids.org
Outdoor Behavioral Healthcare Council: https://obhcouncil.com
Soul Trak Outdoors: https://soultrak.com
StoryWalk: https://letsmovelibraries.org/storywalk
Waldorf Education: https://www.waldorfeducation.org
Wild Diversity: https://wilddiversity.com

Books

Balanced and Barefoot: How Unrestricted Outdoor Play Makes for Strong, Confident, and Capable Children by Angela J. Hanscom
The Down and Dirty Guide to Camping with Kids: How to Plan Memorable Family Adventures and Connect Kids to Nature by Helen Olsson
Free to Learn by Peter Gray
How to Raise a Wild Child: The Art and Science of Falling in Love with Nature by Scott D. Sampson
Nature Play at Home: Creating Outdoor Spaces That Connect Children with the Natural World by Nancy Striniste
100 Parks, 5,000 Ideas: Where to Go, When to Go, What to See, What to Do by Joe Yogerst
There's No Such Thing as Bad Weather: A Scandinavian Mom's Secrets for Raising Healthy, Resilient, and Confident Kids by Linda Åkeson McGurk

Children's Books

Backpack Explorer: On the Nature Trail: What Will You Find? by Editors of Storey Publishing

Backyard Adventure: Get Messy, Get Wet, Build Cool Things, and Have Tons of Wild Fun! 51 Free-Play Activities by Amanda Thomsen

Exploring Nature Activity Book for Kids: 50 Creative Projects to Spark Curiosity in the Outdoors by Kim Andrews

Let's Play Outdoors!: Exploring Nature for Children by Catherine Ard

National Geographic Kids' Get Outside Guide by Nancy Honovich and Julie Beer

❧ 5 ❧

Creative Arts

The artist and the photographer, especially among the young people of our time, seek the mysteries and the adventures of experience in nature.

Ansel Adams

ART is healing, and every time I turn to it to ease my feelings of stress and anxiety, I immediately feel better. This is especially the case when a creative project involves nature. It is simply not as soothing to paint a building as it is to paint a flower.

A few summers ago, I was immersed in creativity and nature at a lovely nature-themed spa in Pennsylvania that offers an extensive array of art, outdoor, and mind and body classes. It is like summer camp with a calming twist for adults. During my four days there, I took as many art classes that my schedule would allow, including mindful rock painting, nature doodling, painting a forest scene, and going on a nature poetry walk. Each experience gave me a happiness boost as I learned a new skill while enjoying the moment.

While all the classes were amazing, the poetry walk was an adventure that will always have a special place in my heart. It was the first time I was ever exposed to this type of activity, so I left the hotel with the group not knowing what to expect. Our guide asked us to follow her along the winding trail, but she requested that we walk very slowly and stay silent. We meandered into an area where there were bushes and some sporadic trees. When we could no longer see the building, we spotted a large brown deer. We all stared in amazement since we were so close to wildlife. We noticed him more than he noticed us. We then kept walking, and I recall a squirrel jumping out in front of us, almost as if he were trying to say hello and usher us along our way.

We continued to walk up a slight hill and came to a tree that had a swarm of buzzing bees high above it. Although we were a bit frightened and made sure to keep our distance, this was a huge moment during our nature walk—which was later evident by all our poems mentioning the bees. After this tense moment, we entered a gorgeous, colorful garden filled with bright yellow sunflowers and neon orange flowers. Finally, we made our way to an area around an inviting, sturdy tree. A couple of women sat on the grass, one plopped down on a gray boulder, and I joined two others on a lovely tree swing. I will never forget how comforting it was to sway back and forth in the breeze while crafting my poem after the walk.

When we create in, around, or based on nature, we benefit tremendously. We feel happier, calmer, inspired, and a whole host of other positive emotions. Incorporating more creative occasions in our children's lives is a simple, pleasurable approach for improving their well-being.

Benefits of Creative Arts

Creativity is the ability to think in unusual, divergent ways. It involves using the right side of the brain from where imagination, intuition, visualization, emotions, and daydreaming originate. It does not refer only to artistic and musical expression; it is also essential for science, math, and social/emotional intelligence. Creativity has been shown to develop many positive characteristics and help children lead happy, successful lives. When children are creative, they tap into curiosity, intuition, and playfulness to help them solve complex problems.

Creativity can also be an important stress buster to help kids feel happier and more relaxed. It provides a healthy outlet for them to express and cope with their emotions in a safe, calm manner. In fact, art has been scientifically proven to reduce stress levels, so much so that an entire discipline of art therapy has been developed. It is a distinct type of therapy that allows people to express themselves through the creative arts and can help bring healing and balance to one's emotional, physical, and mental well-being. It is especially effective for children who have a hard time expressing themselves verbally.[138]

There is a great deal of evidence linking creativity to improved mental health. A 2019 World Health Organization report synthesized over three thousand studies and concluded that the arts can have a positive role in improving health and well-being by lowering stress hormones and helping people open up about their emotions. The key aspects of art that promote health include aesthetic engagement, imagination, invoking emotion, and social interaction. The research also showed how creative arts can be used to prevent mental health issues. Activities such as listening to music, dancing, making art, and visiting cultural sites are associated with stress management and prevention. Arts engagement can also help to reduce the risk of developing mental illness, such as depression in adolescence, since participating in art activities can build confidence and self-worth.[139]

When we engage in creative arts, we can experience physiological changes that reflect a reduction in stress. Our amygdala, the part of the brain that controls our fear and stress response, appears to calm, for example. Less activity in the amygdala can reduce the effect of negative emotions and allow our children to let go of their problems for a while. Stress hormones are also reduced. One study found that just forty-five minutes of creating art can significantly lower stress hormones in our body. A group of adults was given art supplies, including markers, paper, modeling clay, and collage materials. They spent forty-five minutes creating a piece of art on their own without any instruction. Cortisol levels were measured both before and after the art project. Results showed a significant decrease in cortisol levels, and participants said they found the art session to be relaxing and a chance to lose themselves in their work.[140] In addition, our breathing pattern changes while we are engaged in creativity, allowing us to take in more oxygen. This leads to an overall feeling of calm.[141]

So, why does creativity improve mental health? Here are some of the reasons art boosts mood and reduces stress and anxiety:

- **Distraction.** An important tactic in managing anxiety is to distract ourselves from what is tormenting our minds. Art is a great way to focus on something more positive, productive, and inspiring. Brain scientist Dr. Joel Pearson believes that concentrating on a creative activity like coloring can replace negative thoughts and images with pleasant ones.[142] Our kids will be so engaged in looking at the shapes, sizes, edges, and colors that they will not have time to be stressed. Basically, our worries fade away because it is almost impossible to keep ruminating about our problems when we are focused on doing something creative.

- **Flow.** Artists can become so absorbed in their work that they achieve a state of flow, the sense of being completely engaged in an activity to the point of entering a near-meditative state. When we are in a state of flow, we forget about our thoughts and lose track of time. This can calm our nerves and reduce stress.

- **Mindfulness.** When we are focused on an art project, we become completely absorbed in the present moment. This helps to quiet the mind as we engage in the task at hand instead of our worries. According to neuropsychologist Dr. Stan Rodski, art leads to a relaxed mindset similar to what we experience from meditation. It allows us to switch off our brains from other thoughts and focus on what is happening in the here and now.[143] Art takes a great deal of concentration, so we fall into almost a trance that allows us to essentially meditate without necessarily realizing it. Our attention shifts from our worries and mental chatter to the present moment. Since getting our kids to sit down and meditate may be challenging, engaging in a creative activity can be a much easier path for them to reach a meditative state.

- **Self-care.** Having a hobby that we enjoy helps us feel more balanced and allows for mental and emotional downtime. This is especially true if it involves some social interaction, such as taking an art class with other students or sharing artistic creations with family and friends.

- **Reduced stimulation.** When our children spend time focused on an art activity, they are taking a much-needed break from all the stimulation around them like their electronic gadgets and other noisy distractions.

- **Chance to slow down.** Our lives are so hectic, and our kids are not immune to the stress that all that busyness causes. Engaging in art projects can be a wonderful antidote to all the rushing around in their lives.

As you can see, creativity can have a huge impact on a child's health and well-being. If your children are feeling stressed, you can teach them how to channel their anxious energy into a creative project or hobby.

How Nature Stimulates Creativity

There is a fascinating link between nature and creativity: nature stimulates creativity. It has the ability to evoke a creative way of thinking by making us more curious, open-minded, and imaginative. This is evident by the many stories of how writers and artists retreat into a remote natural area to finish a novel or a piece of artwork. We can also see it in our own lives. If we sit for too long inside our home or office staring at a screen, we lose creative energy. But if we get up and move around outside, we can come back to our work refreshed with new ideas. It is amazing how many blog posts and articles I have outlined in my head during walks and bike rides.

We do not have to rely on anecdotes to prove this point, as the science is clear. The researcher at the forefront of linking nature to creativity is cognition and neural scientist Dr. David Strayer. His breakthrough study in 2012 was the first to show that time outdoors in nature leads to increased creativity and problem-solving ability. About sixty adult participants were given several tests to measure creative thinking; half took the test before a backpacking trip in the wilderness and the other half took the test a few days into their trip. As it turns out, those who took the creativity test during their time outdoors had a fifty percent boost in creativity and problem solving.[144]

There are several key reasons why nature increases our creativity. First, being outside in nature helps restore our attention. The Attention Restoration Theory developed by Rachel and Stephen Kaplan suggests that mental fatigue and concentration can be improved by spending time looking at nature. It is now believed that nature can restore our overstimulated brain and improve critical thinking, problem solving, focus, and our ability to think deeply and come up with new ideas. As discussed in chapter 3, nature gives us a sense of awe about the world around us. Awe is a powerful emotion that plays a vital role in creativity and well-being. Nature also activates the imagination network in our brain. When the prefrontal cortex part of our brain quiets down, such as when we are relaxing in nature and not focusing on anything specific, the brain's default mode takes over. This is a more imaginative state when our mind begins to wander to memories, ideas, and emotions. In essence, when our prefrontal cortex is able to rest, we can experience more insights and creativity. Finally, spending time in nature allows us to enter into a state known as "soft fascination." This is that calm, meditative feeling we get when our mind is completely at ease and we take in scenery and even daydream. Neuroscientists believe this to be an ideal state for activating creativity.

How to Build a Connection to Nature Through the Arts

So much of childhood is about connecting to the creative side of the brain as kids learn new skills and facts about all kinds of subjects. As

Richard Louv explains in his book *Vitamin N: The Essential Guide to a Nature-Rich Life*, children soak up what is in their environment, so it is important for them to be stimulated by natural elements to increase their creativity.[145] By the same token, the arts can also be a path for connecting children to nature. Since both art and nature are such effective (and fun!) stress reduction tools, we can seek ways for our kids to connect with nature and be inspired by it to create a masterpiece.

Nature is one of the best sources of inspiration for creative endeavors since it is filled with so many sights, sounds, smells, textures, colors, and other stimuli. "I love looking to the natural world when searching for inspiration for creative things to do, either with children or just for my own endeavors," explained Lee Foster-Wilson, author of *The Grown-Up's Guide to Making Art with Kids: 25+ Fun and Easy Projects to Inspire You and the Little Ones in Your Life.* "With children, I think doing anything creative with them that involves nature, whether that be searching outside for natural objects to incorporate into games, creating dens in trees or with sticks, or simply looking in an encyclopedia for weird and wonderful animals to draw, gets them thinking about and interacting with the environment."[146]

There are endless opportunities for us to engage our children in various forms of environmental art, including music, drawing, painting, sculpture, photography, dance, drama, and writing. Some ideas include:

- Listen to songs about the environment and then have your children write their own lyrics to familiar tunes.
- Go for a walk and ask your children to point out beautiful nature scenes. Take pictures during your adventure and then have your kids either draw or paint what they saw or put together a collage of the photos.
- Ask your children to make up a dance about nature, such as trees blowing in the wind, different animal movements, or the way the weather changes throughout the seasons.
- Read poetry about nature to your children and then challenge them to write their own.

- Make your own playdough and have your children sculpt animals, trees, flowers, and other nature elements.
- Take art projects outdoors such as sidewalk chalk, or bring an easel out in your backyard or on the balcony so they can paint.

The rest of the chapter will explore many more ways to connect children to nature through the creative arts.

Ways to Encourage Children's Creativity

Try to keep these guidelines in mind to ensure that your children get the most out of their creative experiences.

- Keep it fun and relaxed for your children. Art is personal, and they should be able to create freely and not worry about staying in the lines or comparing their artwork to others.
- Give them the time and space to be able to express their creativity. It might be helpful to set aside a place in your home where your children can make a mess.
- Encourage creative thinking in your home by asking your children for their ideas and resisting the urge to judge what they come up with. Also, let them disagree with you and encourage them to find more than one way to solve a problem.
- Allow them the freedom to explore their ideas. Avoid setting constraints, such as using certain materials, because this can reduce flexibility in thinking.
- Limit screen time in order to make room for creative activities like rehearsing a play, learning to draw, and reading a variety of genres.

Nature Art

When I refer to nature art, I am talking about using natural items to create either a craft or art supplies like paint or brushes. These items could be purchased from a store, such as a bag of shells or bottle of sand, or found outdoors. (Please note the sidebar later in this chapter about Leave No Trace Behind before you start a nature art project with your children.) Ideas for nature art are endless and go as far as your children's imagination takes them. Here are a few examples:

- Sculpture with rocks, sticks, leaves, and other items
- Shell necklace
- Grass weaving

- Making paint from walnuts, berries, or clay
- Flower press art
- Collages
- Mindful rock painting
- Painting with mud
- Make your own paint brushes with natural items like sticks and grass
- Creating musical instruments with sticks, stones, leaves, pebbles, and so on
- Trace items like leaves or flower petals

Deborah Bazer and Lahri Bond have been teaching nature-based art to children for over twenty-five years each. They run a small summer camp in Massachusetts called Kids, Art & Nature where they strive to provide a safe community in which children can experiment artistically using a wide variety of mediums while also exploring and connecting with the natural world. The nearby woods are an integral part of the camp, providing an opportunity for the children to collect clay and other natural materials to use for their creations. The campers spend a small portion of the day inside the studio making art, but most of the camp day involves exploring in the woods, collecting natural items, and creating artwork. "A lot of what we do is to help the kids connect with nature and to really ground themselves through the arts and by being outside. Nature-related art is all about looking at nature and being inspired by it, and then translating that inspiration using different mediums like paint, drawing, or sculpture," they explain.

In order to stimulate a direct connection between nature and art, they often take art materials outdoors like paints, drawing tools, and nature journals. They also like to bring portable looms outside that can be tied to a tree so the children can work on weaving projects. Another fun activity at the camp is making their own inks, paints, and brushes out of natural materials. The brushes, for example, can be made by wrapping yarn around sticks and creating a brush head from pine needles, grass, or leaves.

They also focus on certain topics during different classes to spark the kids' interest. One class is all about trees; the children compare and contrast different types of trees and explore the creatures who live in them. They even turn themselves into trees by lying down on paper, tracing their bodies, and then making that drawing into a tree. Other class topics include working with clay; creating nature journals; making fairy gardens out of clay, bark, stones, seeds, and plants; dyeing wool with plants to use for knitting or weaving; and even building Minecraft-like structures with natural items such as sticks, leaves, and grass.

Over the years, Deborah and Lahri have noticed how children's behavior and demeanor shift during their time outside in the woods. "That is when we see the kids come to life and show their personalities. Kids become a lot freer and more focused, and their energy level completely changes," they say, noting how the kids are more social, cooperative, and playful while outside. "They also seem more peaceful during this time." All these changes allow them to relax and be more creative as they work on their nature-based art projects.

One child in particular transformed during his time at the camp. He started off the week acting very cautious and nervous about being outdoors. Unlike the other kids, he did not want to get his feet wet or try anything new. Then after a few trips into the woods, he started to warm up to his new environment. After some time, he realized how much he enjoyed being outside and went from acting timid to being covered in clay and mud. By the end of the week, he was lying down in the stream and splashing around. As Deborah explains, "The boy had discomfort and anxiety about anything that was new, but nature helped him relax and overcome personal challenges."[147]

Leave No Trace Behind

One concern about nature art activities is people removing natural items, which can slowly damage the land. In the book *Organic Crafts: 75 Earth-Friendly Art Activities*, author Kimberly Monaghan reminds us to not disturb nature for art projects. "National and state park areas are set aside to preserve the scenery and the natural and historic objects for the enjoyment of all visitors. Everything in the park is protected by law. Do not pick flowers, collect rocks, take pinecones, or touch rock formations. When hiking, stay on the marked trails. This will keep these protected areas thriving for all to enjoy."[148]

This concept of leaving the natural environment untouched is the mission of Leave No Trace, an international movement, nonprofit organization, and educational program dedicated to protecting the outdoors by teaching people to enjoy it responsibly. They promote seven principles to follow for those visiting the outdoors, whether they are in wilderness areas, local parks, or even in a backyard. Each principle covers a specific topic and provides detailed information for minimizing impacts.

Principle 4, "Leave What You Find," is the one that mostly applies to nature art projects. The guidelines state the following:

- **Minimize site alterations.** Leave areas as you found them. If you clear an area of rocks, twigs, or pinecones, be sure to replace them before you leave.
- **Avoid damaging live trees and plants.** Do not carve initials into trees or hammer nails into them to hang items. Picking a few flowers may not seem like an issue, but if every visitor does this, the impact would be significant.
- **Leave natural objects and cultural artifacts.** Natural objects of beauty or interest such as antlers, petrified wood, or colored rocks add to the uniqueness of the land and should be left so others can experience them. In national parks and many other protected places, it is illegal to remove natural objects. The same rule applies to cultural artifacts found on public lands, as they are protected by the Archaeological Resources Protection Act. It is illegal to remove or disturb archeological sites, historic sites, or artifacts found on public lands.[149]

Deborah Bazer suggests that parents talk to their kids about leaving no trace behind and leaving what you find when they are exploring nature for creative projects. "It is important for children to be aware of what they are taking from the land and determine if they really need it. If you need leaves, look on the ground first," she advises. "If you need something from a plant, sit with the plant for a minute to consider taking it or not. Be aware of what you are taking, so not to remove too much. If you dig, try to put the soil and rocks back." She encourages children to learn how to be respectful of the natural world and to be cognizant of how we interact with it. "We need to recognize that many plants and animals call the woods home. We are just visiting and need to be conscious of this." By practicing gratitude for all there is in nature, children also learn to appreciate and respect it. [150]

Nature Drawing, Painting, and Coloring

A few summers ago, I enrolled in a watercolor-painting class. I remembered enjoying art as a child, but it was never a focus in my life. To my pleasant surprise, painting has become a part of who I am now. Most importantly, it helps me get lost in the moment and forget about my worries. I gravitate toward painting nature because I love how flowers, trees, and animals are so unique, colorful, and uplifting. When I focus on the intricacies of a gorgeous flower, for example, I feel more at ease.

I have enjoyed developing this hobby over the years and know that I can always turn to it when I am looking for an escape. Here is a bit about my process that you can try with your kids. First, I go for a walk and look for attractive nature in my neighborhood or I seek out nature during our travels, whether it be a trip to the beach or a science museum. Then I snap a photo of it using my phone. I have found that when I am looking for beautiful images, I learn to be more mindful of my surroundings. I actually see the world from a different perspective and notice details that I would otherwise pass right by. Later, when I am ready to sit down and paint, I scroll through my pictures and choose one as inspiration for my artwork. I can pull up the image on my phone or computer, or I can print it out the old-fashioned way to use as a reference photo. I really enjoy painting natural scenery using watercolor, and my kids have loved joining me in this creative, relaxing activity.

Besides watercolor, you can use other types of paints like oil, acrylic, gouache, and even children's paint sets. A really fun way to get your kids' creative juices flowing is to take them outside in your backyard and set them up with paper, a paint set, and an easel and ask them to paint what they see. Even if it is raining or too cold outside, you can still find a spot by a window or sliding-glass doors for them to get a direct view of nature. Imagine the gorgeous snow scene they can paint during a winter storm!

Of course, your children can also draw nature, if they prefer, using a variety of mediums like crayons, markers, regular and colored pencils, chalk, and pastels. The options are endless since our kids can find inspiration from nature all around them. The trick to stimulating their creativity is to expose them to different types of natural scenery to get inspired. If they need some guidance, grab a nature drawing book or consider signing them up for an art class.

For children who are not ready or in the mood to draw or paint from scratch, consider starting them out with some mindful nature coloring. In the last few years, coloring books for stress reduction have become all the rage. Not only are mindful coloring books flying off the shelves, but many psychologists and therapists now prescribe them to their patients for various emotional and mental health issues like stress, anxiety, depression, and anger management. As a therapeutic activity, coloring can help our kids feel calmer, happier, less anxious, and more focused. You can look

for coloring books filled with images of landscapes, flowers, trees, and animals. As noted earlier, just looking at pictures of nature scenes can make us feel similar to actually spending time in nature, so coloring these images can be an effective stress reduction tool.

Nature Journaling

Putting our thoughts and feelings down on paper can help us work through challenging times, and many experts recommend this activity to reduce stress and anxiety. Journaling can be effective in managing emotions because it helps us practice mindfulness by offering a way to stay present in the moment. As we journal, we slow down and focus, which has been shown to decrease anxiety and promote balance. Journaling also serves as a brain dump in which we can get everything out without worrying about who will read it and judge us.

One study on the benefits of journaling involved about one hundred young adults who were asked to spend fifteen minutes journaling or drawing about a stressful event, or simply writing about their plans for the day. Those who journaled experienced a large reduction in mental health issues like anxiety and depression. This was true even though most of them did not typically journal about their feelings.[151] In another study led by James W. Pennebaker, the leading researcher on the power of writing and journaling for healing purposes, students were asked to write about their deepest thoughts and feelings on an important emotional issue. The research concluded that emotional writing can reduce the level of stress hormones in our body.[152]

Nature journaling takes it one step further by starting with the idea of recording our thoughts and adding both creativity and environmental components to the process. It is the practice of drawing and/or writing in response to what we observe in our natural environment. "This fun, relaxing practice helps you to connect more closely with nature, and results in the creation of your own unique nature journal," according to Paula Peeters in *Make a Date with Nature: An Introduction to Nature Journaling.*[153]

Many kids love working on their own nature journal and sharing their reflections about animals, trees, flowers, and more. This creative activity helps children discover the natural world in their own backyard and beyond through a combination of art, writing, science, and math. They have the creative freedom to make their journal any way they wish. Journals can include pictures of what they see in nature that can be sketched in pencil, drawn or painted in color, or presented by photographs glued onto the page. Some people use icons to represent the weather and maps to show the geographic location. Written notes with observations and ideas can be included to explain the pictures, such as the noises heard at the time. The notes can be written in complete paragraphs or brief sentences or as bullet points or labels. Some children may even want to add a story that goes into more detail about their observations. They can also include numbers, such as how many objects they counted in a particular area or a map scale to get a sense of an object's size. It really becomes their own masterpiece, and they can try new ideas over time.

Nature journaling offers so many benefits for our children. In *How to Teach Nature Journaling: Curiosity, Wonder, Attention*, John Muir Laws and Emilie Lygren highlight the following benefits: relaxation, mindfulness and focus, connecting with nature, developing creativity, an opportunity to slow down and pay attention, and a chance to experience awe and wonder.[154] It is a playful and adventurous way for children to interact with the natural world, yet it also allows them to be still, calm, and quiet while they take in their surroundings.

Kelly Pfeiffer is a teacher at Dubbo School of Distance Education in Australia. Her class of twelve- and thirteen-year-olds recently engaged in an interactive nature-journaling lesson that encouraged students to take a journal along during a walk outside. The children thoroughly enjoyed the activity and shared the following feedback about how nature journaling made them feel:

- "Being in nature makes me happier because I can see more of our property. I also love to hear the stream run by. Our stream is one

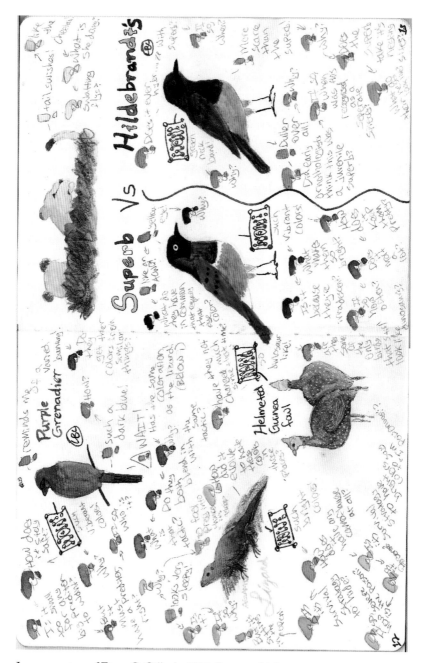

Image courtesy of Fiona C. Gillogly, 2019, fionasongbird.com.

kilometer away and I can hear it from my room which proves how powerful the outdoors can be."

- "I feel happy because I can get outside and explore."
- "I get to go outside and that makes me happy. It is good if you are stressed about school work so you can take a break."
- "This made me happy because I got to connect with nature and have a nice calming time."
- "It is really wonderful to get off the computer and get out into nature and draw it all. It makes me feel happy and calm. I feel so much better when I'm out in nature and I'm drawing!"
- "It is nice to go outside and draw or write and get things off the mind."[155]

Nature journaling can be done anywhere there is nature: beaches, parks, zoos, nature centers, waterways, gardens, farms, and your own backyard. While it is not always possible to journal outside because of issues like the weather, you can still continue with nature-journaling activities. Try bringing small natural objects, such as leaves, acorns, or pinecones, inside and write about them. You can also grow indoor plants or an herb garden to focus on in the journal. Finally, you can even set the kids up by a window and encourage them to jot down their thoughts and observations.

Once your children get the hang of it, you may want to start a nature-journaling club with their friends or classmates. This is a fun, family-friendly way to develop a closer connection with nature, build community, explore natural areas nearby, and share ideas and resources with others.

You can try contacting your school or local nature centers, zoos, museums, and other science-, nature-, or art-related venues to see if they will partner with you to host the nature-journaling club.

Tips to Get Started with Nature Journaling

Paula Peeters recommends the following materials to get started with nature journaling:

- A good-quality sketchbook with mixed-media paper or watercolor paper and a strong cover
- Waterproof-ink markers (sketches made with these pens can be painted over later without the ink smudging)
- 2B graphite pencil and eraser
- Portable watercolor paints
- Watercolor pencils
- Paintbrushes of varying sizes
- A cup of water or a paintbrush with its own water tank

She also suggests the following activities to inspire your kids when they first are learning how to journal:

Color Mapping

Head outdoors to find something you can observe closely, such as a leaf, rock, shell, or flower. Look for at least five to ten different colors in the object. Write down specific descriptions of these colors, such as sky blue or olive green. If it is helpful, you can draw a sketch of the object and label the colors you observed. This helps us get beyond preconceived ideas, such as leaves are always green or rocks are always gray. By observing more closely, your children will begin to notice new colors and details of nature.

Deep Listening

Find a place outdoors in a natural environment where you can sit or stand comfortably. Then ask your children to close their eyes and listen for about five minutes. See if they can identify as many unique sounds as possible. What direction are they coming from? Are the noises loud or soft? Are they close by or in the distance? Then have them open their eyes and write down all the sounds they heard and what they think was creating them. Ask them to draw what they heard by using their own imagination. They could even create a story from that short time just listening to their surroundings.

Word Search

This exercise helps with developing observation skills and engaging imaginatively with nature. Write a list of adjectives on a piece of paper, leaving space under each word. Some suggestions include: big, small, hard, soft, furry, prickly, rough, smooth, simple, complex, shy, bold, quiet, loud. Feel free to add your own descriptive words such as colors. Challenge your kids to find natural items that fit into each of these categories. Then have them write a sentence or two explaining why each item could be described by that word.

Other journal ideas include making a birding journal, focusing on a certain geographic area or terrain like the beach, or picking a theme like just flowers or just red objects that you find in nature. You can even change the theme monthly or each time you venture outdoors.[156]

Nature Poetry

Another way to capture creativity is through poetry. Writing colorful prose allows our children to reflect on what they experience in nature so they can hold on to those moments forever. There are many ways to use poetry to instill an appreciation for nature in your children. In addition to reading nature poetry together, you can encourage them to write down their thoughts and feelings about nature in the form of poetry after they spend time outdoors like going on a family hike, hanging at the lake, or gardening in your backyard.

An easy way to start is with haiku, a short form of poetry originally from Japan that often focuses on nature topics. It consists of just three lines and follows a specific pattern using syllables: first line has five syllables, second line has seven syllables, and third line has five syllables. The lines do not have to rhyme, but they can if you are looking for an added challenge. It is not always easy to come up with a topic and then to find the right words and syllables to fit together, but when you do, it is so rewarding. My children and I recently had a blast writing our own haiku. Here are some examples of the poetry my kids wrote:

Mountains tall and wide
They have nothing to hide here
On this sunny day.

The beach was quite fun.
I watched my quick brother run.
We jumped in water a ton.

I had a sweet pear.
Yellow sand blew in my hair.
We forgot our chair.

One of my favorite ways to inspire kids to write nature poetry is by going on a nature poetry walk. It is such a relaxing, creative, and mindful experience. The main goal is to soak in the beauty of our surrounding environment and then turn that experience into something creative that we can treasure. Writing poetry requires inspiration, and nature is the perfect backdrop for us to find that spark. The best way to do this is to use our five senses. Instead of just walking as you would on a typical hike, it is important to purposely slow down and stop occasionally to absorb what is all around. During my nature poetry walk in Pennsylvania that I mentioned earlier, our leader asked us to stop several times along the path and think about what we saw, heard, touched, smelled, and even tasted. She encouraged us to breathe in the air deeply, look all around us, and bend down and feel various items along the way. This mindful exercise forces us to really stop and absorb our environment and all that it has to offer.

A nature poetry walk provides so many incredible benefits to our children, including the following:

Teaches focus and mindfulness. According to the Poetry Foundation, poets look at the world the way scientists do, observing all the details to discover interesting concepts and patterns.[157] Going on a poetry walk is a wonderful way for your family to slow down and move mindfully through whatever environment you choose, whether it be the woods, mountains, beach, or your neighborhood park.

Reduces stress. Walking mindfully in nature is an effective stress buster. It helps our bodies and minds slow down and enjoy the moment. Plus, by tapping into our five senses, we distract ourselves from our worries.

Helps them connect with their emotions. Poetry is an excellent way to connect with and communicate our thoughts and feelings. It allows us to spend time reflecting on both our experiences and our inner thoughts. Children can use poetry to express themselves in new ways to deal with big emotions. Even young children can learn to express themselves creatively through poetry.

Gets them moving. Exercise in itself has so many benefits, so going on a family walk together gets everyone moving around a bit more.

Nature Poetry Walk Step-by-Step Instructions

1. Before you go on your first nature poetry walk, introduce your children to some nature poetry to get them interested and inspired.
2. Be sure to bring the following supplies: notebook or journal; pencils and pens; colored pencils, markers, or crayons if they want to sketch the scene they are writing about; and a phone or camera to snap some photos.
3. Choose a destination for your walk. Try different types of places each time you go.
4. Once you arrive at your spot, explain to your children that they should try to be quiet and walk slowly. Stop along the way to ask them what they are experiencing through each of their five senses. It is helpful if they start to write down these observations

in a chart sectioned off by each sense: sight, hearing, touch, smell, and taste.

5. Enjoy the walk and go with the flow as far as what you do along the way and where you end up.

6. At the end of the walk, pick a place to sit down and let your kids spend some time either writing their poetry or talking about it if they are young and need some guidance. You can also wait until you are back in the car or home for the poetry-writing time, but it is probably more effective if they at least start it outside in nature.

7. To add some more creative flair to your nature poetry experience, see if your kids want to turn the poem into song lyrics. You can also take pictures during your nature poetry walk (just be careful not to let technology be a distraction) and use those photos in a slide show or as part of a collage around the poem.

8. Finally, enjoy sharing everyone's creations with each other and talking about the experience.

Nature Photography

As I mentioned before, photography plays a major role in my nature-painting hobby. In general, photography is a fantastic art form to help reduce stress and anxiety that we can share with our children. According to sound-mind.org, "this particular stress management skill allows you to place your focus outside of yourself. Photography is a creative and fun hobby that can help distract you from the stress, anxiety, and depression you may be feeling."[158]

Photography serves as a type of mindfulness meditation in which we get lost in the moment and experience a sense of flow while snapping photos with our camera. It can be quite calming to take photographs, especially of gorgeous nature and awe-inspiring images. When I go on walks with the intention of finding some intriguing nature objects to take pictures of, I end up viewing my surroundings with an artistic eye. This can be a helpful skill to teach children, too, since it encourages them to be more mindful and curious.

In addition, research shows how effective photography can be in reducing mental health issues. A program called At Ease in the Chicago area helps veterans heal through nature photography. The veterans, often struggling with post-traumatic stress disorder (PTSD), are enrolled in a three-hour photography workshop. It enables them see things in a fresh way and shift their focus to something positive. As a result, they are better able to cope with depression and/or anxiety.[159]

Ruth Davey is the founder and director of Look Again, an organization in the United Kingdom that offers mindful photography courses that merge the creative and therapeutic benefits of photography, nature, and mindfulness to support individuals by increasing their well-being and mental health. "Mindful photography is using our sight and a camera or smartphone as an anchor to help us become more consciously aware of the present moment. It is experiencing the process of creating photographs in a non-judgmental, compassionate way," she explains. A large portion of her classes involves students going outdoors to apply this mindful approach to nature photography, such as taking a walk and focusing on all the colors they see. This practice helps them slow down, stay calm, view the world with a fresh perspective, and connect in a creative way to themselves and the beautiful natural surroundings.[160]

Since 2012, Ruth has worked with students of all ages, including youth groups and children with special needs. In 2019, the University of Gloucestershire evaluated the special methodology she applies in her courses and concluded that the Look Again approach to mindful photography is effective in increasing students' well-being and mental health, including reducing stress. Ruth reflects on the overall reaction of her students. "They slow down and notice things more clearly. They enjoy photography more and their creativity gets fired up. It gives them time to really breathe." She also pointed out how critical the aspect of community is to their well-being. "Through the nature photography classes, participants bond and inspire one another, which breaks up any feelings of loneliness they may have been experiencing."[161]

The entire process of shooting photography, from choosing subject matter to discovering new angles to manipulating the light, requires so much focus and attention. This process of observing ends up being meditative, so we feel more relaxed as a result. A large part of photography involves capturing the colors that we see with the naked eye. This can help spark imagination in children as they process what they capture through the camera lens.

In *How to Raise a Wild Child: The Art and Science of Falling in Love with Nature,* Scott D. Sampson suggests that children take photos and create a slide show or other type of art project with them. He encourages children to use the camera as a tool to heighten observation and awareness skills out in nature.[162] Children can also turn the nature photographs into a video set to relaxing music. My daughter often fills a rainy day by making videos from photos. It is a very creative activity that can help children increase awareness of patterns, colors, shadows, and other visual elements and express their feelings or views in a story-like fashion. In this regard, photography can be a jumping-off point for additional types of creative projects.

Girls Who Click: Inspiring Young Nature Photographers

Girls Who Click is a nonprofit organization based in the San Francisco area that began in 2017. The organization was founded by Suzi Eszterhas, an award-winning wildlife photographer. "Nature has always been a large part of my life and helped me feel centered. Growing up, I had a big backyard with an acre of open space where I enjoyed watching birds and squirrels. I found peace out in nature." She harnessed that passion for nature and chose a career in wildlife photography. She is best known for her work documenting newborn animals and family life in the wild. Her photographs have been published in over a hundred magazines such as *Time*, *Smithsonian*, *BBC Wildlife*, *Ranger Rick*, and *National Geographic Kids*. She is also the author of twenty-one books and has been featured on TodayShow.com and GoodMorningAmerica.com.

Suzi noticed that the nature photography field was dominated by men and wanted to do something to change that. She started Girls Who Click to inspire girls to develop a lifelong passion for capturing the nature around them and to use their work to further conservation efforts. By partnering with other female professional photographers throughout the country, they are able to offer free nature photography workshops for teen girls on topics like bird photography, butterfly photography, basics of wildlife filming, photo processing, and using photography in conservation professions.

Suzi is also very passionate about how nature impacts mental health. Although she started the group to attract more women in to the nature photography field, she has found many other benefits for the girls involved, such as a boost in happiness and reduction in stress. "As a result of the group, I see how the experience gives the girls courage and empowerment to choose a life outdoors that they enjoy. If they are able to do what they love, it is so rewarding and it gives them so much happiness."

Suzi notices with herself how she is so much calmer, less anxious, and happier on the days when she is outside taking pictures of nature compared to time spent at the computer. She sees this same type of reaction with the girls. "During a typical class, we start in the classroom and then head outside to take pictures. I watch their joy and confidence build throughout the day. They are so excited. Many of the girls are walking on air." Suzi receives lots of positive feedback from students about the classes. Some will even comment how they do not feel stressed when they are outside. It is remarkable how much just one photography class impacts and inspires them.

The sisterhood component of the program is also quite powerful. As the girls are outdoors learning and taking pictures together, they share excitement about what they capture with their camera and bond over it. Community is so important to happiness, and this type of group helps build a special connection between girls who are uniquely interested in nature photography. "Finding that support among your peers during a time when kids are more disconnected from nature is more meaningful than ever," Suzi proclaims.

Suzi hopes that the girls who participate in Girls Who Click continue to enjoy nature photography throughout their lives and even choose a career involving nature photography or something involving the outdoors like a marine biologist or conservationist. "I truly believe that choosing a life outdoors is choosing a life of peace, balance, and joy because there are so many rewards to having that type of career. I hope they all find something they love," she wishes.[163]

Nature Mandalas

Mandalas are often used in mindfulness practices as a relaxation tool. They are circular designs with concentric shapes that radiate out symmetrically from the center. Originating in India, mandalas mean "sacred circles" in Sanskrit. They have universal spiritual significance and can be found in Buddhist temples, Muslim mosques, and Christian cathedrals. In ancient Tibet, monks created intricate mandalas with colored sand made of crushed stones to use during their meditation practice. Well-known Swiss psychologist Carl Jung used the mandala for his own personal growth and also had his patients color mandalas a hundred years ago as a tool for relaxation and self-discovery.

We can use mandalas to teach our children about nature in a creative way. If we look closely, we can find patterns in nature similar to those in mandalas, such as spiderwebs, flower petals, leaves, tree bark, seashells, and of course snowflakes. Take your kids exploring outdoors and ask them to find the natural mandalas. See if they can draw their own mandala designs based on the natural objects they find. Another approach is to build mandalas outside from natural items you collect. This takes a great deal of focus and ingenuity, and your kids will be so proud of the designs they develop. Just be sure to take a picture before you leave.

Here are some simple steps to build an outdoor mandala:

1. Venture outdoors to a natural area like the woods, beach, or local park.
2. Gather natural items to make your mandala, such as leaves, flower petals, sticks, rocks, grass, pinecones, pine needles, feathers, sand, shells, soil, and so on that have fallen naturally to the ground.
3. Find an open area to work or clear one yourself.
4. Identify the center of your mandala and mark it with one of your items.
5. Create one layer of the pattern at a time by building a circular layer around your center item and radiating your design from the center point.
6. Continue to add on as many layers as you want.
7. Enjoy looking at everyone's mandalas and be sure to capture the moment with photos.
8. Return natural items to where you found them.[164]

Nature-Themed Music

Engaging in music—whether it be singing, listening, or creating—provides biological and psychological benefits. In one study, participants exhibited significant reductions in heart rate, respiratory rate, and anxiety after listening to relaxing music for just twenty minutes.[165] In another study, researchers found that music can be more effective than medication in reducing anxiety. Patients who were about to have surgery were randomly assigned to either listen to music or take antianxiety medication. Scientists tracked the patients' assessment of their own anxiety, as well as their levels of cortisol. Interestingly, the patients who listened to music had less anxiety and lower cortisol than people who took the medication.[166]

Music helps us relax by providing a healthy distraction and forcing us to be more mindful. As music draws our attention, it acts as a diversion while also helping us explore our emotions. It also keeps us focused and prevents our mind from wandering to negative thoughts. Music also allows us to lose ourselves in the moment as we enjoy the sounds we play or hear.

We can incorporate music into our children's connection with nature by either listening to meditative nature sounds that are enhanced by soothing music or creating, playing, or listening to music with nature-related content. When it comes to the first option, there are many apps available that provide nature relaxation music. This is especially an effective tool to use if your kids are having trouble falling asleep at night. On evenings when I am feeling restless, I turn on nature music to calm my mind, and before I know it, I am sound asleep.

Children also enjoy listening to music that tells a story about nature, whether it be about animals, trees, the ocean, or more. One artist to check out is Raffi, a music producer, author, and ecology advocate. He is known for his signature song "Baby Beluga" and has been producing children's music since 1976. Many of his songs have nature themes. The Laurie Berkner Band also has several nature-related songs, along with cute, engaging music videos on their website. Finally, Mister G is a Latin artist who performs bilingual songs in both Spanish and English. His album *Mundo Verde/Green World* is filled with environmental children's songs covering topics like bees, fish, and water.

If your children play a musical instrument or love to sing, they can try their hand at writing their own nature-themed music. It may be helpful for them to use other songs as inspiration, such as taking a popular song and changing the words to focus on nature. If they take piano or guitar lessons, they can easily add in their own words to the music they are already playing. Even children who have never taken a music lesson can still bang on some drums or shake a maraca to some nature lyrics they penned themselves.

Nature-Themed Dance and Movement

Creative movement of the body has been found to relieve stress and anxiety. Several notable studies in the area of movement-based creative expression and dance therapy show how these activities promote well-being.[167] We can easily connect children to nature by either performing dances outside or focusing on nature themes during movement activities, such as mimicking animals or trees blowing in the wind.

At Treehouse Learning in Florida, teachers incorporate movement into the children's day to help ground them. They often gather the children together in a circle outside to do some dancing, stomping, and Native American chanting that is all about Mother Earth. The songs and movement help the children feel uplifted and connected to nature.

In your area, you can search for creative movement and dance classes for your children that incorporate nature themes or spend some time playing around with your own activities at home. Here are a few ideas to get you started:

- Head outside and ask your children to mimic the nature that they see around them. This might be hopping like a bunny, running around like a bird flaps its wings, or swaying back and forth like the wind.
- Enjoy some fun animal dances from the past like the Pony, Bunny Hop, and Chicken Dance.
- Write down names of different animals on pieces of paper and pick one at a time. Challenge your kids to dance around like each animal.
- Play Freeze Dance only using nature-like movements.
- Have them make their own animal masks or costumes and create a dance to match that animal. If you have a group of children, they can even put on a show with all the different animals dancing around.
- Help your kids wind down with relaxing stretches using a nature theme of trees, water, and wind. This can look like swaying, bending, twisting, and rocking back and forth.

MindTravel: Merging Music, Art, Mindfulness, and Nature

Composer and pianist Murray Hidary travels the world leading groups of all ages on his MindTravel programs that combine music, art, and nature for a deeply meditative and emotional experience. His mission is to heal and enliven people through these events, many of which take place in gorgeous outdoor spaces. It is all about bringing music into people's lives to help them reflect and relax.

His signature event is called the MindTravel SilentHike. This is an immersive music and meditation experience that involves participants wearing wireless headphones while they go on a group hike. Through the headphones, they hear Murray's calming music and thoughtful commentary that helps them connect to both nature and their emotions. "A MindTravel is way more than just adding a companion soundtrack to the beauty of nature," he explains. "It evokes heightened emotions and allows us to feel like we are in a state of flow outside our normal perception of time."

Image courtesy of Murray Hidary of MindTravel.

Besides the hikes, he organizes underwater experiences involving floating meditation and creative coloring sessions set to music. Murray encourages children to choose nature-specific coloring books to enhance the experience. "The nature imagery can evoke deep connection and foster relaxation. Even better, try coloring while *in* nature, like at a park or beach."

Murray began MindTravel in 2013 and since then has conducted over five hundred experiences for over one hundred thousand people worldwide. At the end of every experience, he asks the group how they feel. "Overwhelmingly, both children and adults report feelings of peace, tranquility, and freedom," Murray notes. "One eight-year-old boy, who is typically active and easily bored, wrote down the word 'calm' on his drawing to express how he was feeling at that moment. After a SilentWalk, a ten-year-old boy shared that he was feeling relaxed and creative. These are very common reactions from children of all ages."

MindTravel is so effective because the headphones help everyone feel as if the music is being played just for them. It allows them to really stay in the moment and focus on what they are feeling as they absorb the inspiring sights and sounds around them. This is the epitome of feeling a sense of awe, which has been proven to make us feel happier and calmer.[168, 169]

Activity Checklist

ü Offer your children a variety of creative art activities at home like painting, drawing, poetry, sculpture, dance, and music to make their imagination come alive.

ü Sign them up for a variety of classes, camps, and other activities in the arts so they can discover where their talents and passions lie.

ü Listen to songs about the environment and then have your children write their own lyrics to familiar tunes.

ü Go for a walk and ask your children to point out beautiful nature scenes. Take pictures during your adventure and then have your kids either draw or paint what they saw or put together a collage of the photos.

ü Ask your children to make up a dance about nature, such as trees blowing in the wind, ocean waves, different animal movements, or the way the weather changes throughout the seasons.

ü Read poetry about the environment to your children and then challenge them to write their own.

ü Go on a family nature poetry walk and share the lovely poems you write.

ü Take art projects outdoors such as sidewalk chalk, or bring an easel out in your backyard or on the balcony so they can paint.

ü Work on some nature art projects such as grass weaving; mindful rock painting; painting with mud; and sculpture using rocks, sticks, leaves, and other items.

ü Start a family journaling habit to creatively capture your experiences outdoors.

Resources

Organizations

American Art Therapy Association: https://arttherapy.org
Girls Who Click: https://girlswhoclick.org
Leave No Trace: https://lnt.org
Look Again: https://www.look-again.org
MindTravel: https://www.mindtravel.com

Books

The Grown-Up's Guide to Making Art with Kids: 25+ Fun and Easy Projects to Inspire You and the Little Ones in Your Life by Lee Foster-Wilson
How to Teach Nature Journaling: Curiosity, Wonder, Attention by John Muir Laws and Emilie Lygren

A Little Bit of Dirt: 55+ Science and Art Activities to Reconnect Children with Nature by Asia Citro

Make a Date with Nature: An Introduction to Nature Journaling by Paula Peeters

Morning Altars: A 7-Step Practice to Nourish Your Spirit through Nature, Art, and Ritual by Day Schildkret

365 Days of Art in Nature: Find Inspiration Every Day in the Natural World by Lorna Scobie

Children's Books

Animal Poems by Valerie Worth

Handsprings: Poems & Paintings by Douglas Florian

How to Draw Things in Nature by Rob Court

Morning, Sunshine! by Keely Parrack

My Forest Is Green by Darren Lebeuf

Nature's Art Box by Laura C. Martin

Organic Crafts: 75 Earth-Friendly Art Activities by Kimberly Monaghan

Outdoor Photography by John Hamilton

❧ 6 ❧

Animals

Our relationships with other-than-human beings can have a profoundly positive impact on our health, our spirit, and our sense of inclusiveness in the world.

Richard Louv

TRUTH be told, I do not consider myself a pet person. Growing up, I brought home the occasional pet goldfish from the annual school carnival and always dreamed of having a pet turtle, but I have never snuggled up with a furry animal each night. Even so, I value how animals can help children feel happier and calmer, and I have many fond memories that involve observing and engaging with animals, both as a child and as a parent. Throughout my childhood, my family often visited zoos, aquariums, and science museums to learn about animals and their habitats. I also recall a couple of delightful pony rides at my father's company picnics that were captured in the family photo albums.

Now, with my own family, I try to incorporate animal-related activities into our experiences and vacations. When my son was still in a stroller, I pushed him around the small New Jersey beach town where we spend our summers and always stopped at the tranquil koi pond in front of our neighbor's house. Time would stand still as we gazed at the bright orange fish swimming around and listened to the trickling water. We visited many nature centers over the years, with Butterfly World in Florida being one of our favorite spots. It was meaningful to watch my children's faces light up as we tiptoed among the colorful butterflies fluttering all around us. One even landed on my son's hat, and we always giggle when we peruse the pictures from that day. During a recent trip to Niagara Falls, we stumbled upon the world's largest free-flying indoor aviary. After entering with low expectations about what we would find inside the unimpressive building, we were taken aback by the hundreds of exquisite birds that we came in close contact with that day. We even fed some lorikeets, which was a moment filled with ticklish laughter as they landed on our hands and arms to take a sip of the sweet nectar we clinched tightly.

We also connect with wildlife right in our own backyard, from vivid birds chirping to sneaky lizards hanging out on our sliding-glass doors to ducks that like to pay us a visit and paddle around our pool. And while we do not have our own pet, my daughter loves to play with our next-door neighbor's dog. They have become special friends over the years.

Even if you are not a pet family, there are still many ways to enjoy animals of all shapes and sizes. In this chapter, we will explore why animals are so calming and a variety of ways for your family to benefit from all types of animals, including pets, therapy animals, farm animals, and wildlife. We can connect with animals through a whole gamut of experiences, from watching birds in the backyard to going on an African safari, and everything in between.

Pets

Pets can have a profound impact on our children's well-being, so it is no surprise that sixty-seven percent—or about eighty-five million families in the United States—own a pet.[170] Of these, about forty percent are dogs, twenty-five percent cats, twelve percent fish, and other types of animals like birds and reptiles under four percent each.[171]

Why do so many families share their home with a pet? According to the *International Journal of Environmental Research and Public Health*, children's physical, social, emotional, and cognitive development improve when they interact with a pet. Walking, grooming, feeding, and playing with a pet are enjoyable activities for everyone in the family. Pets also push family members to slow down from their hectic lives, realize the importance of nature, communicate with one another, and spend quality time together relaxing with their animal friends.[172]

According to Lindsey Braun, program director at the Human Animal Bond Research Institute (HABRI), "Scientific research demonstrates an association between pet ownership and reduced stress. Studies have found that pets can have a buffering effect on stress, in that they can reduce the physiological reaction to stress."[173] She was referring to a study out of Yale University that had seventy-eight children ages ten to thirteen interact with a dog. They found that brief, unstructured interactions with the animal helped reduce the children's anxiety.[174]

Another study revealed that having a dog as a child makes an individual less likely to suffer from anxiety later in life. Scientists compared two groups of young children ranging in age from four to ten: 370 who were living with a dog and 273 who were not. They discovered that only twelve percent of those who grew up with a pet dog suffered from anxiety compared to twenty-one percent who did not have a dog.[175]

Other types of pets can also calm children. Nothing is more soothing than watching fish swimming around a tank. A colorful fish tank can add to the natural atmosphere in your child's bedroom and provide something tranquil to watch while trying to fall asleep at night. There is even science to back this up. One study found that people who spent a minimum of ten minutes observing an aquarium felt happier and more relaxed.[176] Even small animals like rabbits and guinea pigs are easy pets to care for and can help lower stress and anxiety in children.

Choosing the right pet for your family really depends on your family's preferences and the demeanor of the individual animal. This book is not intended to provide guidance on how to find pets, but there are endless resources available for you to explore, such as the Humane Society of the United States, Petfinder, Adoptapet.com, Petco Love, and PetSmart Charities.

Teaching Children to Respect Animals

Whether you are on a hiking trail, at a therapeutic farm, or in your own backyard, it is important that children understand how to behave around animals and treat them in a gentle, respectful manner. Here are some tips to keep in mind while interacting with animals:

- Treat pets lovingly, which means petting furry animals in the direction their hair grows and avoiding touching sensitive areas of their body. Also, no pulling tails, hitting, or taunting the animals.
- Teach your kids to ask before touching someone's pet.
- Observe wildlife from a distance without touching them to keep the animals safe and to protect your children from scratches, bites, and disease.
- When invited to interact with animals at places like zoos and nature centers, follow the instructions of the staff. Some of these animals may be hurt and in rehabilitation, so be mindful of their condition.
- Follow the rules. Sometimes disruptive behavior like quick movements, talking loudly, or using flash photography is forbidden around animals.
- Minimize your impact on the animals' precious habitat by practicing the seven principles of Leave No Trace, such as throwing away garbage, leaving behind any natural items that you find, and respecting wildlife.

Pets can provide several important emotional benefits to children:

Offer Comfort and Companionship

The companionship of a pet offers coping skills for children by alleviating loneliness and isolation, which can be part of anxiety and depression. Kids can find support and security in having a pet to always be there for them and provide unconditional love and affection. There is growing evidence that children turn to their pets for comfort, reassurance, and emotional support when feeling sad or angry.[177] One study, appropriately titled "Friends With Benefits," found that pet owners tend to be less lonely, less worried, and happier because pets help fulfill a social need related to improved well-being. In fact, just thinking about their pet boosted their mood.[178]

Provide a Healthy Distraction

Pets give children something to focus on that is positive versus the sometimes negative thoughts swirling around in their head. The magic of focused attention is that we can use it to help get over negative emotions like fear. Just petting or playing with an animal can give a child that healthy distraction they need to feel better. Psychiatrist Dr. Adam Strassberg, who wrote a poignant article in a local Palo Alto, California, newspaper on how parents can help manage their children's depression, cited owning a pet as a key step. He believes that caring for a pet can be a positive distraction for children who are struggling. "Owning a pet is behaviorally activating—you have to do things in order to take care of the animal. The animal needs you. You are responsible for the animal's well-being. So, a child taking care of a pet learns that they are needed, they have a responsibility for the animal, and that they can care for it successfully. They can gain competence and self-esteem from this experience."[179]

Boost Positive Hormones

The simple act of petting an animal releases endorphins like oxytocin into the brain. These hormones serve as powerful pain relievers and mood boosters, and are the same chemicals that give us pleasure and a natural "high" feeling. Dog owners are less likely to be depressed and have higher levels of serotonin and dopamine than non-dog owners.[180]

Increase Social Interaction

Being social boosts happiness at all ages. Having a dog provides fresh ways for children to interact with neighbors and friends. For example, when you go for a walk with your dog around the neighborhood, you will probably run into people to chat with. You can venture out with your kids to the park and see friends or make new ones. Dogs tend to also be an enjoyable topic, so having a dog helps to spark conversations with both people you know and those you want to get to know better. This is particularly helpful for children struggling with social anxiety.[181]

Encourage Exercise

We know how important exercise is for our physical and mental health. Having a dog to walk helps us get more exercise, which ultimately reduces stress. Research shows that the best companion for a walk is your dog. In one study, individuals who walked alone with a dog averaged 300 minutes a week of walking versus only 168 minutes a week if they walked with family or friends. Additionally, those who walked a dog reached the recommended level of physical activity for their age group fifty percent more often than those who walked without a dog.[182]

But what if you cannot or do not want to own your own pet? There are many reasons why having a pet is not possible: allergies, your partner or child does not want one, your apartment or neighborhood does not allow it, you travel too much, illness, financial constraints, and so on. Fortunately, there are ways that your family can still spend time with pets:

- Volunteer to walk dogs or hold and pet cats at an animal shelter.
- Offer to walk the dog of an ill or elderly friend or neighbor.
- Partner up with a friend or relative who owns a pet to volunteer to do pet therapy visits or participate in a pet-friendly charity walk or run.
- Offer to take care of a friend's pet while they are out of town.
- Foster a rescued animal temporarily or volunteer with a rescue organization.
- See if your school will start an adopt-a-pet program. Classroom pets provide significant benefits for children's social, behavioral, and academic development.[183]

Why a Mother Is Now Grateful for the Family Pet She Once Resisted

"I did not want a dog. I knew the work having a shedding, barking addition to my house would require, and I was adamantly against it," proclaimed Pearl Harris, MD. She is a physician, writer, and the mother of two school-aged children.

"But my husband and two kids had other ideas. They launched a full get-a-dog campaign complete with pictures, YouTube videos, and heart-felt pleas. I finally succumbed to my family's entreaties when my husband, making his own puppy-dog eyes at me, declared that a dog would lower his blood pressure and, as a result, he would live longer. My guilty conscience quickly flipped this to mean that if I didn't acquiesce, I might be responsible for my husband's potential untimely demise."

She finally gave in. Unlike the rest of her family who loved the little brown-and-white Cavalier King Charles spaniel at first sight, it took a while for Lily to worm her way into Pearl's heart. It was not Lily's cute, furry face or her fluffy, excited wagging tail; ultimately, it was the dog's impact on her son's mood that won Pearl over.

Pearl explained that her now-teenager has always been deeply affected by the world. "As a small child, when things did not go his way, his rage could be felt for hours. He yelled, he cried, and he

---

brought a feeling of helplessness to everyone who tried to calm him. While not entirely out of the ordinary, his reactions were definitely at the upper limit of what one would consider normal for a child." As years went by, he learned to calm himself down. As an adolescent, he replaced the rage with silence and turned inward.

This also concerned her. "It was impossible to know what was wrong, only that something was eating at my child from the inside. No one could reach him during these episodes of inward torture over a low grade or a slight from a friend. I worried for my son and what this melancholy would do to a moody teenage mind." And then Lily came into their lives.

"When something bad happens, my son will now immediately seek out Lily. Instead of descending into a funk, licks and snuggles and encouragement to throw a ball to her bring my son out of himself. Instead of hours of sadness, the few minutes of joy from a fifteen-pound Cavalier will perhaps not erase the negative emotions, but make them a lot more manageable." Pearl is grateful to see how this animal brings a pure joy to her teenager.

"So, yes, I love Lily. No human could reach my son the way Lily can. He cannot help but smile through his sadness when Lily is there with a toy in her mouth, standing patiently by while he decides that it is much better to engage in a joyful moment than to wallow in misery."

Emotional Support Animals

Beyond simply being a loving pet, animals can serve as a therapeutic tool for children struggling with emotional issues like anxiety and depression. Such pets are referred to as emotional support animals (ESAs). An ESA can be a dog, cat, or other type of pet that helps ease symptoms of an emotional or mental issue through companionship and affection. Some children have trouble connecting with adults and their peers, which is where an ESA can be beneficial. They may find it easier to bond with an animal, as they can use nonverbal (or verbal if they prefer) communication to connect with the animal. Pets are also supportive and nonjudgmental, providing a safe space for children to express themselves. ESAs are more than just pets to these children; the bond between them can be quite powerful.

A comprehensive study that reviewed sixty-nine research papers on human-animal interactions found well-documented benefits of animals, including positive mood change; reductions in stress-related physical indicators like cortisol level, heart rate, and blood pressure; and reduced feelings of fear and anxiety. In one experiment, children were put in a socially stressful environment. One group had a friendly adult with them, and the other group had a friendly dog by their side. The children with the friendly dog had lower cortisol levels and felt calmer. And the more they played with the dog, the less stressed they became.[184]

Dogs are the most popular ESA choice. They are typically energetic and enjoy lots of playtime with their companions. Both small and large dog breeds work well with children, but some breeds are known for being the best emotional support dogs and more kid-friendly than others. These include the Cavalier King Charles spaniel, Labrador retriever, bichon frisé, shih tzu, boxer, poodle, and beagle.[185]

Library dog reading programs are a popular way for children to relax and sharpen their reading skills while connecting with a lovable dog at their local library. Children are fond of reading to therapy dogs because it is less intimidating than speaking in front of their teacher or classmates. Dogs can be some of the best listeners; they are nonjudgmental and friendly and will not laugh at a child who makes a mistake. Being that the reading session takes place in a quiet library, it also offers a calm, comfortable environment for children. Typically, children pick out a book of their choice and sit down next to the dog and its handler to read. Over time, the children's reading ability and confidence improve. Reading in itself is one of the best ways to reduce stress. It is more relaxing than going for a walk, listening to music, or sipping some warm milk. Just six minutes of reading can be enough to reduce stress levels by more than two-thirds.[186] So, reading with a furry friend provides double the benefits!

As it turns out, therapy dog reading programs are sprouting up in schools and local libraries around the world. In Australia, the Delta

Society Classroom Canines Program assists children who have difficulties with literacy and/or social and emotional skills. Through the program, a trained dog and handler visit a school on a weekly basis to work with the children. As a result of the program, students improve their reading, confidence, and self-esteem. These successful outcomes are mainly due to the fact that dogs are accepting and fun to be around, allowing students to relax, gain confidence, and change their attitudes toward learning.[187]

In Westport, Connecticut, the Reading to Rover (R2R) program is thriving. Children's librarian Lynne Perrigo developed the program over fifteen years ago after reading an article about another library using therapy dogs successfully. "I have always had pets and thought this would be a fabulous way to spend more time with dogs. It was a hit from the beginning," she recalls. Over the years, R2R has included programs on Fridays when one dog visits, a summer showcase with ten to fifteen dogs, and Zoom sessions when the library was closed due to the COVID-19 pandemic. All these events provide a chance for children to read to a friendly dog for about fifteen minutes at a time. She has received tons of positive feedback and watched the program gain popularity. She has also seen children change from tense and shy to calm and comfortable enough to read to the dog when they otherwise struggled to read in public.[188]

Mom, teacher, and Count by Nature business owner Samantha Joseph was excited that her eight-year-old daughter was paired with a Labrador as part of her school's Story Dogs program. "Once a week she has the opportunity to practice her reading skills to a furry friend that does not judge or critique her. It is a wonderful opportunity each week to share some time with an animal." Besides improvements in reading, Samantha noticed other positive changes in her daughter. "Her attitude toward attending school and her happiness each week definitely is associated with the opportunity to build a relationship with her dog partner. My daughter has shown a connection to animals. She can often be found curled up beside a friend's cat or holding a friend's dog sweetly between her hands. There is definitely comfort and reassurance found in the company of animals."[189]

Next, cats are also a terrific choice for an ESA, especially for children who are intimidated by or afraid of dogs. They are a low-maintenance animal and often tender with children. They are smaller than dogs and lighter and usually enjoy sitting on laps. Additionally, they are more independent, tolerant of being left alone, and easily transportable. Cats can be an antidote to loneliness for many individuals. A study of over six hundred people found that cats improve mental health. Nearly ninety percent of those who owned a cat felt it had a positive impact on their well-being, while about seventy-five percent said they could cope with everyday life much better thanks to the company of their cat.[190] There are no specific cat breeds known to be better for emotional support; it just depends on which cat can provide comfort to those struggling with a mental or emotional issue.

Birds can also serve as pacifying companions. Parrots, in particular, are known to have a high level of empathy and provide a special type of interaction with those struggling with emotional issues. They can be taught words and phrases, which can help in therapeutic ways. Plus,

many people are fascinated by their behavior and beautiful colors, and enjoy interacting with animals that can fly.

Another group of ESAs, called "smallies," include tiny animals like rabbits, hamsters, guinea pigs, mini pigs (also called pot-bellied pigs), and even rats. When used in therapeutic ways, they can help lower stress and anxiety in children. They work well for people who find larger animals intimidating and are easy pets to have around. Rabbits come in a range of sizes up to about fifteen pounds. They are curious animals that enjoy socializing and can build bonds with humans. Hamsters are easy to care for, inexpensive, simple to transport, and calm. Guinea pigs are small enough to hold, social, inquisitive, and love to be stroked. They can bond strongly with humans. What most people do not realize is that guinea pigs are frequently vocal, whistling and purring when they are happy. Mini pigs are highly intelligent and easily trained and can be very affectionate. The most shocking of this group, of course, are the rats. Despite the obvious stigma against them, they can actually be effective ESAs since they are very social creatures with high intelligence that enjoy interacting with people in a gentle way.

Llamas and alpacas are also used for visiting those who are looking for emotional support. Although they are related species, llamas are heavier and taller with long ears and faces, and alpacas have shorter legs, more blunt faces, and small ears. Both have a natural ability to step lightly, which is helpful for visiting patients indoors. They also have a watchful nature and an ability to gauge people's emotional state, which allows them to connect with people seeking companionship.[191]

Finally, as surprising as it may sound, some types of reptiles and amphibians are now being used for therapy purposes. Caring for a lizard, frog, or turtle takes a great deal of concentration and offers individuals a reprieve from their emotional struggles. An advantage of choosing this type of ESA is that they require less care than mammals, such as not needing to be walked or groomed.[192]

If you are interested in getting an ESA for your child or registering one of your own pets as an ESA, check out ESA Registration of America for guidance. If you would like to find animal support programs in your community, contact organizations like Pet Partners, American Kennel Club, and Alliance of Therapy Dogs. You can also check with your local library for dog therapy reading events. Finally, if you are interested in volunteering with your pet to help others, contact Pet Partners or Love on a Leash and refer to chapter 8.

Therapeutic Farms and Farm Animals

A variety of domesticated farm animals are also used for therapeutic purposes, and a great deal of research has confirmed their effectiveness to help those struggling with emotional and mental health issues. While there are programs set up to help children with serious issues, referred to as Animal-Assisted Therapy (AAT), all children can benefit from time with farm animals.

Using AAT is considered beneficial since the animals have a natural tendency to create a bond with people. This approach often helps therapists overcome some of the limitations of traditional therapy that relies on talking, which may not be the most effective way for children and adolescents to address their issues. Essentially, the therapist is able to communicate with children through the animal, reducing pressure on the child to talk about their feelings the entire time.

Horses are widely recognized for the therapeutic benefits they offer, including helping children cope with emotional challenges like anxiety and depression. Equine-Assisted Psychotherapy (EAP) involves using a horse as a therapeutic tool in which a licensed therapist and a horse professional work collaboratively with the children. Many therapists recognize horses as having a nonjudgmental nature and believe this creates a relaxing environment. Having a horse around offers both emotional and physical comfort, thereby developing trust and confidence between the patient and therapist.[193]

During EAP, a variety of activities can have a positive impact on a child. Caring for the animal by feeding and brushing it can be quite soothing and builds confidence and patience in the child. Learning to ride a horse has tremendous benefits, such as figuring out how to calm

oneself down, building focus and mindfulness, and working collabora-tively with the animal. The physical contact with the horse and the rhyth-mic movement while riding can also be relaxing.

Ebony Horsewomen, Inc.: Transforming Children's Lives with Equine Therapy

At age eight, Patricia E. Kelly discovered horses as a way to escape the stress of the racism her family experienced after moving into an all-white neighborhood in Hartford, Connecticut. From the first moment she brushed her neighbor's horse, these animals became the cornerstone of her life's work. Now she serves as the founder, pres-ident, and CEO of Ebony Horsewomen, Inc., the only equine youth organization of its kind in New England and the only one in the United States led by an African American woman. Through her organization, Patricia annually helps over three hundred boys and girls ages five to seventeen to address, manage, and overcome life challenges, social and emotional concerns, and mental health issues.

Ebony Horsewomen has a team of mental health professionals and horse specialists certified in EAP. This powerful and effective therapeutic approach has had an incredible impact on the children who go through the program, many who come from challenging situations and have experienced serious trauma. The children learn about themselves and others through hands-on activities with the horses while processing and/or discussing their feelings, behaviors, and patterns.

Patricia explains why horses are such an effective therapeutic tool for children: "Kids learn that they need to control themselves in order to work with the horses. They carry a tremendous load of trauma and the horses cannot deal with them in that state, so they need to learn how to release their anxiety. They take deep breaths, practice mindfulness, and put their fears and anger aside. When they calm down, the horses calm down." The children begin to see how what goes on internally with them impacts external conditions like the horse's mood and demeanor. "That's when those horses really start to teach the children. We cannot change the conditions of what goes on in these children's lives, but we can help them manage it."

She also points out that kids who are traumatized struggle with finding the words to express their emotions. With equine therapy, they do not need to sit face to face with a therapist forced to talk about their feelings. Instead, they benefit in so many incredible ways from working with the horses. Patricia often observes children talking to the horses, which helps them feel better.

The organization has endless success stories about many children overcoming their trauma to become poised, civic-minded, and conscientious young leaders. They have participated in parades and horse shows, and have gone on to earn degrees and certifications at colleges and universities. As a result, Patricia has been recognized for her incredible work by being inducted into the National Cowgirl Hall of Fame and Museum, a CNN Top 10 Hero award recipient, and one of Aetna's Champions for Change.

Patricia reminisces about one child in particular whose life was dramatically transformed by his experience at the center. "I used to do school presentations about the barn. One day after my presentation, an eight-year-old boy asked if he could come to see the horses.

He started visiting quite often and loved helping to take care of the horses." But then one day he stopped coming, and she received a call from the psychiatry unit at the local hospital. The boy was struggling with depression but was asking to see the horses again. Once he felt up to it, he started spending more time at the center. "He came every day to the barn. His home environment was horrific and his only release was coming to visit with the horses." As time went on, he became a staple of the center for years. "He learned to be a great horse rider and knew the horses very well. This was his thing. When the blacksmith would come, he would pay close attention and learn from him." Patricia noticed his passion and encouraged him to apply to college to become a farrier, a specialist in equine hoof care. After years of struggling in an alternative school, he got accepted into Cornell University and received a full scholarship to pursue his dream. What an incredible accomplishment! "It was a horse named Chance that taught that boy all kinds of lessons. This is a kid who should not even be here anymore. He is just one of many who I have seen over the years."[194]

Besides horses, other types of equines used in therapy include donkeys, ponies, miniature horses, and camels. Several unique EAP options are offered at Green Chimneys, a world-renowned therapeutic day and residential program in New York that serves more than two hundred children annually who are facing social, emotional, and behavioral issues. Children engage in mindfulness exercises on horses through adaptive riding, groom and nurture donkeys, provide daily food and water for ponies and miniature horses, and learn about a camel's behavior and how to regulate their own by leading the animal across an outdoor pasture. Through these programs, the children gain skills essential to social-emotional learning like building trust and compassion, gaining confidence, and managing stress and anxiety.[195]

Goats are another type of animal that can help relieve stress. At her thirteen-acre farm in Dresher, Pennsylvania, Kristin Sutch offers goat snuggling to visitors. "I began using goats as my own therapy animals to help manage my anxiety and to calm me down. It is very unique to hold and feed a baby goat, and I wanted others to be able to have that experience," she explains.

She has watched many people feel calmer after their time with the goats. "They have a wonderful effect on people. I have seen visitors go from feeling miserable to happiness, bliss, and laughter after their time here." She credits this transformative experience with several conditions. First, people are stressed out and craving the quiet, simpler things in life. Most people do not live near a farm anymore, as many are closing down. By having this contact with the goats and other farm animals, people feel more energetic and better emotionally overall.

Next, there is a physical change that occurs. When they look at, hold, and snuggle with the baby goats, oxytocin is released. Finally, being in the moment with these animals allows people to be mindful, which we know improves well-being. Plus, the animals themselves love being around people and getting the attention.

About ten percent of Kristin's visitors are children. One child in particular comes to mind when she considers how children benefit emotionally from spending time with the goats. "An autistic boy was lying down with a goat. He was just staring at and petting the animal for over forty minutes. His mother was in complete shock because she has never seen him act so calmly." It was powerful to see the boy in that positive state developing a special connection with the animal.[196]

Cows are another type of farm animal used for comfort. College students at Michigan State University pay money every semester to brush the school's dairy cows to reduce stress before finals because they find the quality time with the animals very soothing.[197] Cow cuddling, which can involve milking and/or cozying up to a cow, is an innovative experience gaining traction. It might sound bizarre to think of these large farm animals being comforting, but there are some scientific reasons behind it. When cows are digesting their food, they like to lie down and become very quiet. This is the perfect time for people to snuggle up and connect with them. Plus, cows have a slightly slower heart rate than we do, so when our body is in contact with theirs, our heart rate naturally slows down as well. Their body temperature is higher than ours, which also helps us feel more relaxed.[198]

While cow cuddling is not considered a formal animal therapy session since participants are not working toward a specific goal, just sitting with the cows can be extremely therapeutic. It is done in very small groups of no more than four people at a time. Most people have never been on the other side of a fence that close to a cow. It creates an opportunity to be mindful and to try something new and interesting. Cows typically lie down in a half circle, which creates a cozy couch-like spot for someone to snuggle up in. Cow cuddlers are welcome to stroke the cow's belly as they digest their food and chew their cud, and scratch underneath their chin. The cow will literally fold into a person, almost embracing them. Some people will even start talking to the cow during this relaxing moment.[199]

Finally, care farms are a way for children to receive a therapeutic experience around farm animals. Also known as green care or therapeutic farming, they incorporate the therapeutic use of farming practices to facilitate healing in a structured, supervised way. Participants take part in ordinary farmwork tasks like feeding, cleaning, and petting the animals, in addition to milking cows. Working with farm animals can help children learn about nurturing and caring for other animals and people. In one study, children considered the farm animals to be their therapist;

they spoke to the animals and visited them when they felt sad or angry.[200] Besides connecting with the animals, the physical exercise and community building aspects of the experience also help people feel better.[201]

While several therapeutic farms like Green Chimneys focus on helping children with serious mental health issues, there are also those accessible to the general public to take your kids to for a fun, relaxing experience. Horse and Petting Pal Interaction, Inc. (HAPPI Farm) in Florida, for example, has a variety of activities for children such as therapeutic horseback riding; equine activities like feeding and grooming the horses; and a petting zoo where they can pet, feed, brush and/or hold the animals.[202] Simply do a search in your area to find goat snuggling, cow cuddling, care farms, and other similar activities for your family to enjoy together.

How Weekly Farm Sessions Supported a Child's Therapeutic Growth

With over one hundred domesticated farm animals—including cows, pigs, sheep, goats, rabbits, birds, and chickens—the Teaching Barn at Green Chimneys is one part of the campus where children engage in AAT. Interacting with farm animals gives children a unique opportunity to safely step out of their comfort zone by trying something new, gain confidence by compassionately caring for the animals, learn how to be responsible and independent, and foster meaningful connections with the animals and their therapist. In doing so, they learn how to practice coping skills, regulate their emotions, and control their behavior when stressed. During his time at Green Chimneys, one boy learned how to be compassionate, amicable, and hardworking while interacting with animals at the Teaching Barn.

This particular student spent several years visiting the Teaching Barn on a weekly basis to help care for livestock. He learned animal handling and care skills like harnessing, leading, grooming, communicating and using specific commands, and understanding each animal's behavioral signs of stress. He also became familiar with the farm equipment.

Initially, his progress in the sessions was slow. His facilitator would spend the first few minutes of each session discussing the various

---

rules of how to behave around the equipment and the animals. He was very curious and had a desire to learn more about the animals, which sometimes got him into trouble. However, a true turning point came when his facilitator and social worker created a rule book to help him understand which behaviors are acceptable at the farm.

Image courtesy of Green Chimneys.

As a result, his behavior improved. He started to act more empathetically toward the animals and to better understand their behavior. The most evident change was when he began to smile more and seemed to genuinely enjoy his time with the animals. It was clear that he had gained confidence to navigate the farm and to be more mindful of his impact on the animals' lives. With his growth, Green Chimneys honored him with the Farm Kid of the Month Award, which is inspiring to all.[203]

Wildlife

Have you ever encountered a wild animal that stopped you in your tracks? I will never forget seeing eagles flying over my head in Alaska; my mouth fell wide open and I could not take my eyes off those impressive creatures. When encountering wildlife, we often feel as though time stands still and we get lost in the moment of observing an animal's every move, its size, its color. We are intrigued and in awe.

According to Susanne Curtin's report on wildlife tourism, seeing wildlife provokes a deep sense of well-being that can lead to psychological health benefits. Our senses are heightened as we move into a state of flow where our thoughts and actions focus on spotting, watching, identifying, recording, and appreciating the wildlife around us. Being immersed in nature and among wildlife helps us step away from our day-to-day worries, making us feel more relaxed.[204]

In *Our Wild Calling: How Connecting with Animals Can Transform Our Lives—and Save Theirs*, Richard Louv suggests that the next frontier in treating mental health will be to incorporate wild animals into therapy by encouraging patients to notice the animals in their yards, neighborhoods, and beyond to improve mood. He points to a study highlighting the therapeutic value of wild animals. It found that when people detected more species in a park, they reported greater psychological well-being. Also, sharing wildlife encounters with others, such as feeding ducks, made them happier. They were able to get lost in the moment and recover from stress as a result of being around wild animals.[205]

Birdwatching is a lovely way for children to experience wildlife in a safe, captivating way. There are mental health benefits for those who can see birds around their home, no matter if they live in the city or suburbs. Lower levels of depression, anxiety, and stress are linked to the number of birds seen, no matter the type.[206] Birdsong, in particular, is especially comforting. I find chirping birds to be extremely peaceful—and I am not alone. Listening to birdsong can help restore attention and decrease stress. In fact, birdsong was found to be the natural sound most commonly linked to stress recovery.[207] Birdsong was also shown to be more relaxing than a meditation app with a human voice.[208]

In a sense, birdwatching is a form of mindfulness that can help us feel calmer as we focus on finding the birds soaring through the sky or perched up on top of a tree branch. It requires patience, stillness, silence, and slow breathing to be able to catch a glimpse of vibrant feathers.

For Joe Harkness, this hobby is immensely healing. In *Bird Therapy*, he describes his experience: "Birdwatching quickly became my escape route and I started to notice that when I was out, on my own, experiencing nature and birds in a personal and intimate way, I was more relaxed than I'd ever been before. My breathing rate slowed and I closed my mind to repetitive thoughts and worries. My only focus was observing birds and learning about them. I was losing myself in birds, in a positive way." When out birdwatching, he becomes immersed in watching the birds and feels a sense of peace as they fly around freely.[209]

For Shannon Brescher Shea's son, watching birds in their yard or during a walk helps him feel and act more peaceful. As a parenting and sustainability writer and author of *Growing Sustainable Together: Practical Resources for Raising Kind, Engaged, Resilient Children*, she is in tune with her children's connection to nature. "That is not his normal state, at least not indoors. He is an intense, sometimes emotionally volatile kid, excited one moment and angry the next. But in nature, his body and mind relax. He is calmer, gentler, and less stressed." She thinks this transformation has to do with the sensory aspects of being outside, which provide stimulation without overwhelming him. "When it comes to wildlife, he finds a reserve of patience above and beyond the usual. He is able to sit quietly without moving to watch a bird, steady his hands to lift up a worm, or drop to a whisper to not scare off a bunny. His love of animals inspires gentleness in him like nothing else can. The effect that nature has on my son's emotional state seems incredible, but I know he is not the only one."[210]

Viewing zoo animals is another option for children to connect with wildlife, although the animals are in captivity. While I recognize the concern about some zoos and similar animal exhibits, zoos tend to be accessible to a broad range of people (most major cities have a zoo) and provide educational programs for families. The Detroit Zoological Society and Michigan State University studied how viewing animals in the zoo can reduce stress. Participants were hooked up to electrodes in a lab, given a verbal math test, and then asked to deliver a speech off-the-cuff. Then they were either shown a video of a plain white screen, Detroit traffic, or animals at the Detroit Zoo. It may not come as a surprise that those who watched the animal video were the least stressed. Afterward, they went to the zoo to see otters, giraffes, and butterflies in person. As a result, their pulses slowed, heart rates decreased, and they reported feeling happier and less anxious.[211]

Observing wildlife is a special way for our children to connect to nature and feel better overall. Here are some ideas for exploring wildlife with your children:

- Take a trip to a local, state, or national park to go hiking among wildlife.
- Visit zoos, nature centers, butterfly gardens, aviaries, wildlife refuges, and animal-focused theme parks that provide a way for your kids to be in the presence of wild animals.
- Look for wildlife in your backyard or while visiting a local park and ask your kids to identify the animals they spot. Make it even more enjoyable by playing games like wildlife bingo and I Spy or creating a scavenger hunt.
- Go birdwatching as a family in different habitats, such as the beach, forest, and around a pond or lake. Bring along a bird guide

and challenge your kids to identify the different species they see. Ask them to observe the birds and notice details like their behavior, feather colors and patterns, and any unique attributes like beak size.

- Try to learn different birdsongs and ask your children which ones they like best. Some of the most uplifting birdsongs come from blackbirds, curlews, skylarks, nightingales, willow warblers, wrens, robins, and oystercatchers.
- Get involved in a citizen science project to collect data on wildlife in your area (see chapter 8).
- Plan ecotourism family vacations to get up and personal with wildlife, such as an airboat tour in the Florida Everglades or swimming with the dolphins in the Bahamas.
- Capture your wildlife experiences in creative ways and discuss them as a family. Richard Louv suggests that families relax together and tell animal stories because having encounters with animals can be very meaningful and even life-changing.[212]

Online Animal Encounters

Nothing beats holding, petting, and being up close with an animal, but sometimes that is not possible. Children can also enjoy animals through virtual encounters. When my daughter turned eight, it was during the COVID-19 pandemic lockdown and we had to think out-of-the-box for her birthday party. We already had her party booked at a local nature center, so we asked if they could do a virtual animal show for the children instead. It was a tremendous success, and the kids loved learning about turtles, snakes, owls, and sharks.

During this time, other groups began offering clever ways for people to connect with animals online. Sweet Farm, an animal sanctuary in California, started "Goat-2-Meetings" in which a goat joins a Zoom meeting for a virtual playdate or birthday party. They also give a virtual tour of their farm and introduce participants to all the resident animals.[213]

Many library dog reading programs also went online while libraries were closed. The Washington-based nonprofit group called People. Animals. Love. (PAL) hosted virtual sessions to serve hundreds of children each month. During the session, a child was paired with a dog and its volunteer handler to read a book to them. The program was a huge hit, offering a positive distraction during a stressful time.[214]

Here are some ideas for connecting with animals online:

- Look for virtual programs and tours sponsored by zoos, science centers, wildlife sanctuaries, farms, and aquariums.
- Sign up for animal-focused online classes and camps.
- Volunteer online with your pet through a therapy pet program.
- Go on a virtual "vacation" by searching for websites that have live cams of animals in the wild, including bird nests and underwater marine life.
- Connect with a relative or friend who has a pet and ask if they will do a screen call so your children can interact with the animal.

What about Animals That Elicit Fear?

Lions and tigers and bears, oh my! And what about snakes, alligators, and sharks? Whether we learn from movies, books, or our own experiences, we quickly realize that not all animals give us a warm, fuzzy feeling inside.

While many animals can help us feel happy and calm, it is also important to recognize that choosing animals that we find to be comforting is a personal decision. Some children will love cats, while others will prefer lizards and turtles. Some will be attracted to a large, strong dog while others will prefer a tiny, meek one. As we introduce our children to different types of animals, we should keep the lines of communication open and ask them how they feel and which animals they prefer.

Although I utterly fear snakes and cannot even look at them behind the glass at an exhibit without my skin crawling, there are actually people who find snakes comforting and therapeutic. Yes, there really are emotional support snakes out there!

Some experts note that otherwise scary animals can help children overcome fears and be more courageous. Birgitte Rasine is an author, publisher, and entrepreneur, and the proud mother of childhood artist Aria Luna. Her story is unique because her daughter finds joy and exhilaration from scary animals.

When my daughter was just two years old, just barely potty-trained, we whisked her off into the wild plains of the Colombian grasslands on a fishing expedition. It was my second trip there; her first. Colombia is an intensely gorgeous country, its beauty rendered all the more raw by its exuberant—and often dangerous—wildlife.

In a single week my daughter came face to face with a red-bellied piranha (really quite friendly if you hold it nice and tight), saw poisonous frogs, observed a mama caiman (an animal similar to an alligator) with her babies, and avoided a poisonous bug called a water boatman.

Today, Aria Luna much prefers the forest, mountains, and ocean to theme parks. She would rather watch birds than go shopping. Not too long ago on a hike in California, she spotted a rattlesnake just a couple feet away from her. She was thrilled and could not stop talking about it. Back home, I asked her how it felt to see a snake like that in the wild. "It gave me a lot of adrenalin," she said, her eyes widening at the recent memory. "But it's also really cool. It's a mixture of emotions, scary but awesome, and I like that feeling."

Bottom line: when it comes to feel-good animals, it is definitely a personal preference.

Activity Checklist

ü Talk to your children about their favorite animals and ways to learn more about them, such as reading books and visiting educational websites.

ü Consider if having a pet is suitable for your family. If so, research animal shelters to find your perfect pet or think about fostering a pet for a while.

ü If getting a pet is not a good fit, find activities for your children to connect with animals, like walking a neighbor's dog or taking care of a friend's pet while they are out of town.

ü Sign up to volunteer with animals, such as helping out at a nature center or walking dogs and holding and petting cats at an animal shelter.

ü Spend some time at a therapeutic farm or equine center.

ü Search for a therapy dog reading program at a local library in your community.

ü Ask your school to start an adopt-a-pet program.

ü Take your children birdwatching or sign them up for a children's bird-watching club near you. You can find birds at public gardens, nature centers, local parks, and zoos; near bodies of water like lakes, rivers, and oceans; and even in your own backyard.

ü Plan trips around animal adventures, such as visiting animal theme parks, going whale watching, or hiking to watch for wildlife.

ü Try unique animal experiences like cow cuddling or goat snuggling.

ü Explore online tools for learning about and observing animals.

Resources

Organizations

Alliance of Therapy Dogs: https://www.therapydogs.com
American Birding Association: https://www.aba.org
American Kennel Club: https://www.akc.org
eBird: https://ebird.org
Human Animal Bond Research Institute: https://habri.org
Humane Society of the United States: https://www.humanesociety.org
National Audubon Society: https://www.audubon.org
National Wildlife Federation: https://www.nwf.org/Kids-and-Family
Petfinder: https://www.petfinder.com
Pet Partners: https://petpartners.org

Books

Our Wild Calling: How Connecting with Animals Can Transform Our Lives—and Save Theirs by Richard Louv

Children's Books

Animals Helping With Healing by Ann O. Squire
Birdology: 30 Activities and Observations for Exploring the World of Birds by Monica Russo
Helping Dogs by Mary Ann Hoffman
Hero Therapy Dogs by Jon M. Fishman
National Geographic Animal Encyclopedia: 2,500 Animals with Photos, Maps, and More! by Lucy Spelman
Therapy Animals (Animals That Help Us) by Alice Boynton

❦ 7 ❦

Food

The glory of gardening: hands in the dirt, head in the sun, heart with nature. To nurture a garden is to feed not just the body, but the soul.

Alfred Austin

FOOD is an enormous part of our lives. We depend on fresh, whole foods to sustain us and to keep us healthy and flourishing. And so much of this food literally sprouts out of the earth.

Yet, choosing the right foods can be tremendously challenging. We are constantly bombarded with new messages about food—what we are supposed to eat and what we are supposed to avoid seems to change on a daily basis. We also face so many constraints when trying to stick to a healthy diet, whether it be knowledge, time, location, finances, social pressures, boredom, self-control, or personal taste. Beyond these issues, we may also need to ponder how food makes us feel, both physically and emotionally.

Have you ever considered how food may impact your children's mental health? When I first started researching how what I eat affects my anxiety level, I was in awe of all the incredible science available. The first major step I took was to completely cut caffeine out of my diet after noticing how jittery and nervous I felt from drinking caffeinated beverages like tea and soda. I saw a dramatic improvement in my anxiety almost immediately. Over the years, in an effort to continue to manage my anxiety and choose a healthy diet, I have reduced my sugar intake and slowly prioritized some of the foods in my daily meals that you will learn about later on in this chapter: berries, whole grains, beans, green leafy vegetables, and fish rich in omega-3 fatty acids. Besides eating healthy foods from the earth, spending time outside in a garden or orchard can help us feel rejuvenated, especially if we are able to enjoy the delicious produce we have picked or grown ourselves.

In this chapter, we will explore how certain properties of food are linked to improved mental health. First, we will look at choices we can make in our family's diet, including specific types of foods that are known to have a natural calming effect. We will then dive into questions regarding a plant-based diet and pesticides and their possible link to mental health. Next, we will examine the connection between gut health and mental health, including cutting-edge research about a certain bacteria found in soil known to stimulate areas of the brain that produce the feel-good hormone serotonin. We will also learn how horticultural therapy can help children who are struggling with stress, anxiety, or sadness. The rest of the chapter will explore fun, relaxing ways to connect to nature and the outdoors via food, including gardening, visiting farmer's markets, cooking, and picking seasonal produce at local farms and orchards.

Diet

We are what we eat, and this also applies to how we feel. The relationship between food, mood, and anxiety is garnering attention from the medical community. There is a growing body of evidence in the field of nutritional psychology/psychiatry, which looks at how diet can impact mental health.

According to the Center for Nutritional Psychology (CNP), this area of study examines the relationship between diet and our mood, behavior, and mental health. The organization's resource library contains more than a thousand peer-reviewed research studies demonstrating how diet plays an increasingly important role in our mental health. Much of this research looks at how essential vitamins, minerals, and nutrients found in whole, unprocessed food play a significant role in supporting our body's health, including hormone and blood sugar levels. The CNP promotes the idea that improvements in diet can support well-being and lead to more positive mental health outcomes.[215]

In 2017, the Supporting the Modification of Lifestyle in Lowered Emotional States (SMILES) study showed how making dietary changes can improve mental health. At the end of twelve weeks, individuals who ate according to the Mediterranean diet felt less depressed.[216] A Mediterranean diet is often recommended by physicians. It emphasizes healthy fats like nuts, avocado, and olive oil; whole grains and legumes instead of white flour products; filling up on plenty of fruits and vegetables; eating fatty fish like salmon and tuna instead of red meat; and avoiding processed food. This study is considered the gold standard regarding the link between the type of diet we eat and its impact on our health.

A large part of this connection between diet and emotional health has to do with our gut health. The gut microbiome is an ecosystem inside our body where good and bad bacteria, fungi, and viruses thrive. Several factors affect our gut microbiome, including our environment, genes, antibiotics, and the foods we consume. In recent years, scientists have observed the link between our gut and brain, which impacts how we feel. Stress can affect our gut and, when our gut is not balanced with the correct bacteria, can also affect our mental health.

The main reason gut bacteria have such an important impact on mental health is that they produce many of the chemicals found in our brain. If normal gut bacteria are not present, production of neurotransmitters such as dopamine, serotonin, glutamate, and gamma-aminobutyric acid (GABA)—all critically important for regulating mood—may be impacted. In essence, our brain needs the proper mix of gut bacteria in our microbiome in order to make the chemicals we need to stay healthy and balanced.[217] According to Dr. Felice Jacka, director of the Food & Mood Centre at Deakin University in Australia, the gut appears to be an engine of our immune system, which includes controlling inflammation in our body. If our immune system is not working properly, then inflammation can increase. This can impact our mental health.[218]

Diet is one of the key drivers for regulating our microbiome, according to Dr. John Cryan, chairman of the Department of Anatomy & Neuroscience at the University College Cork in Ireland. When food is broken down by the microbiota, its components may influence the level of serotonin, dopamine, and GABA in our bodies that travel to the brain and affect the way we think and feel. Some types of foods promote the growth of helpful bacteria, while others inhibit this growth.[219]

As parents, we can arm ourselves with this knowledge about which foods to choose that can benefit our child's mood. Just keep in mind that food is not going to necessarily cure anxiety or depression; it is just one tool that we can use related to nature that can help boost well-being. As Dr. Uma Naidoo, director of nutritional and lifestyle psychiatry at Massachusetts General Hospital and faculty member at Harvard Medical School, points out in her book *This Is Your Brain on Food: An Indispensable Guide to the Surprising Foods That Fight Depression, Anxiety, PTSD, OCD, ADHD, and More*, "A better diet can help, but it's only one aspect of treatment."[220] With more research, scientists hope to develop an effective treatment for mental health issues using the healthy bacteria found in our gut. Until then, we can continue to make healthy food choices.

Foods That May Improve Mental Health

Below you will find a summary of the types of foods to consider including in your family's diet to help your children feel happier and calmer.

Complex Carbohydrates

Complex carbohydrates—such as whole grains, oatmeal, quinoa, brown rice, and sweet potatoes—can boost serotonin in our brain to help calm us down.[221] Additionally, eating complex carbohydrates can help lower the levels of cortisol in our body. One study found that participants who ate a diet rich in whole, nutrient-dense carbs had significantly lower levels of cortisol than those who followed a diet high in refined carbs like white flour, white bread, white rice, pastries, pasta, and sweets.[222]

L-Tryptophan

Foods that contain the essential amino acid L-tryptophan are known to improve mood, as it is the building block used by the body to make serotonin. Good sources of L-tryptophan include spinach, watercress, soybeans, pumpkin seeds, sesame seeds, walnuts, cashews, chickpeas, bananas, and turkey.[223] However, foods containing L-tryptophan do not work alone; they should be eaten along with a carbohydrate.[224] One easy snack idea is hummus with whole grain bread or crackers.

Vitamins and Minerals

Vitamin/ Mineral	Mental Health Link	Foods
A	• Facilitates proper brain function and growth. • Deficiency may shrink parts of the brain and disrupt how our brain responds to stress.	Sweet potatoes, carrots, broccoli, cantaloupe
B1 (thiamine)	• Can help prevent depression. • Helps brain produce and synthesize neurotransmitters involved in mood regulation.	Nuts, oats, oranges, eggs, seeds, legumes, peas
B6 (pyridoxine)		Poultry, peanuts, oats, bananas

Vitamin/ Mineral	Mental Health Link	Foods
B9 (folate)	• Can help make us more resilient during stressful periods.	Spinach, broccoli, lentils
B12	• Work hand in hand with each other since deficiency in B12 can lead to folate deficiency.	Legumes, citrus fruit, bananas, avocados, leafy green and cruciferous vegetables, asparagus, nuts, seeds, fish
C	• Lowers levels of stress hormones while strengthening body's immune system. • Found to fight brain cell damage due to cortisol. • Helps repair body by controlling free radicals released during stress. • Deficiency can lead to depression.	Oranges, blueberries, cantaloupe, mangos, cranberries, strawberries, Brussels sprouts, cauliflower, leafy greens, broccoli, red and green peppers
D	• Deficiency linked to depression and other mood disorders.	Almond milk, oatmeal, fortified tofu, orange juice, wild salmon, canned fish
E	• Shown to fight free radicals associated with stress. • Acts as a powerful antioxidant. • Deficiency can alter mood, possibly leading to depression.	Sunflower seeds and almonds

Vitamin/ Mineral	Mental Health Link	Foods
Iron	• Deficiency shown to contribute to depression and brain fatigue, which can also lead to anxiety.	Shellfish, lean red meats, organ meats, legumes, pumpkin seeds, broccoli, dark chocolate
Magnesium	• Deficiency associated with both anxiety and depression. • Helps reduce anxiety because of the way it eases stress response, changing levels of harmful stress chemicals in the brain.	Legumes, nuts, seeds, avocados, black beans, edamame, salmon, leafy greens like spinach
Zinc	• Zinc may help raise GABA levels to improve anxiety symptoms. • Deficiency is possibly associated with lower GABA and glutamate, which can lead to anxiety.	Oysters, cashews, liver, lean beef, beans, nuts, egg yolks

Sources:
Vitamin B, C, and D: Blue Zones: "Are You Heart-Hungry? 5 Power Foods to Boost Your Mood," https://www.bluezones.com/2012/07/are-you-heart-hungry/.
Vitamin E: *Healthline*, "18 Foods to Help Relieve Stress," June 13, 2020, https://www.ecowatch.com/stress-relieving-foods-2646171995.html/.
Magnesium: Uma Naidoo. "Nutritional Strategies to Ease Anxiety." *Harvard Health* (blog), August 29, 2019, https://www.health.harvard.edu/blog/nutritional-strategies-to-ease-anxiety-201604139441.
Zinc: Anthony Russo, "Decreased Zinc and Increased Copper in Individuals with Anxiety," *Nutrition and Metabolic Insights* 4 (2011): 1–5.

Omega-3s

The omega-3 fatty acids found in fatty fish can boost mental health. Researchers note that omega-3s appear to lower anxiety by preventing a surge in stress hormones.[225] In one study, individuals given an omega-3 fatty acid supplement showed a twenty percent reduction in anxiety. Experts recommend that we incorporate more fatty fish into our diet instead of just taking a supplement. According to Dr. Uma Naidoo in *This Is Your Brain on Food*, omega-3 fatty acids are crucial to mental health and instrumental in fighting against depression. They promote brain health by protecting neurons from excessive inflammation. Good food sources include oily fish like salmon, tuna, sardines, anchovies, lake trout, herring, and mackerel. Other choices include walnuts and chia seeds.[226]

Fermented Foods

Fermented foods contain probiotics that can help improve our gut health. Probiotics are a combination of live beneficial bacteria and/or yeasts that naturally live in our body. During digestion, certain strains of good bacteria, such as *Lactobacillus* and *Bifidobacterium*, are introduced into the gut.

These live bacteria have a soothing effect on the nervous system and prevent inflammation.[227] *Lactobacillus reuteri*, for example, signals the brain to release oxytocin, a natural stress reliever. Research shows that restoring balance in the gut can reduce anxiety.

Probiotic-rich foods include pickles, pickled fruits and vegetables, sauerkraut, kimchi (Korean cabbage), live-cultured yogurt, miso, kefir (fermented dairy product similar to yogurt), tempeh (fermented soybeans), and kombucha tea (fermented black tea).[228]

In order for probiotics to be effective, it is helpful for them to have prebiotic foods in the gut to digest. Prebiotics are types of fiber digested in the large colon by the gut microbiota. Essentially, they provide a fuel source for the microbiota. Probiotics break down prebiotics to form certain types of fatty acids that help reduce gut inflammation. Foods known to contain a good amount of prebiotics include whole wheat, artichokes, garlic, leeks, onions, and asparagus.

Fiber

Foods high in dietary fiber may reduce the impact of anxiety and stress. When fiber is broken down by bacteria, it becomes fermentable and can promote the growth of good gut bacteria like *Lactobacillus* and *Bifidobacterium*, as mentioned above. This results in a positive effect on mood by activating brain pathways and nerves that can alleviate mental health issues. Dietary fiber also decreases inflammation in the body, which can be linked to increased anxiety. Therefore, dietary fiber can help by calming down the body's inflammatory response. If you are looking for foods high in fiber, choose beans, brown rice, berries, bran, pears, apples, bananas, broccoli, Brussels sprouts, carrots, artichokes, almonds, walnuts, and oats.[229]

Antioxidants

Studies suggest that a diet rich in antioxidants may help prevent stress and anxiety. Antioxidants can also help reduce inflammation, which is often found in people with chronic stress.[230] According to Scott C. Anderson in *The Psychobiotic Revolution: Mood, Food, and the New Science of the Gut-Brain Connection*, antioxidants can increase levels of healthy bacteria in the gut to help improve mental health. Foods and spices rich in antioxidants include garlic, turmeric, ginger, parsley, beans, walnuts, pecans, artichokes, kale, spinach, beets, broccoli, apples, prunes, cherries, plums, blackberries, strawberries, cranberries, raspberries, and blueberries.[231] In addition, polyphenols are a category of compounds naturally found in plant foods that act as an antioxidant. Polyphenols can be found in nuts, seeds, dark chocolate, olive oil, and berries.[232]

Water

As one of our most important natural resources, water is critical to our well-being. Although not a type of food, water is such a key element of our daily diet. Drinking enough water throughout the day can help minimize feelings of stress and anxiety for those already experiencing physical symptoms. Water plays a critical role in how our body functions. All our organs, including our brain, need water to work properly. If we are dehydrated, our body is strained and we can become edgy. Dehydration can lead to symptoms that feel like anxiety, such as dizziness, muscle fatigue, headache, feeling faint, increased heart rate, and nausea.

Dehydration has also been linked to higher cortisol levels.[233] According to the Calm Clinic, water appears to have natural calming properties. Drinking water can be soothing, and our body can benefit from the added hydration when we are stressed.[234] It is important that we encourage our children to drink enough water every day to help them stay balanced. The amount of water a child needs depends on several factors like activity level and local weather, but it is advised that children drink at least six to eight cups of water per day.

Adaptogens

Adaptogens are nontoxic plants that have been used for centuries in Chinese and Ayurvedic healing practices to help the body resist physical, chemical, and biological stressors. Some of these herbs can be eaten, while others are taken as supplements or brewed into tea. Although more scientific research needs to be completed, it is believed that adaptogens

impact stress hormone production. Some of the most popular herbs known to help reduce stress include chamomile, ashwagandha, Asian ginseng, holy basil, rosemary, lavender, and lemon balm.[235] (Please consult with a health professional before giving any of these herbs to your children. Your practitioner can determine the best dose for you or your child based on symptoms, weight, medical history, and other supplements or medications you may be taking.)

Foods to Avoid That Can Trigger Mental Health Issues

While there are foods known for their calming characteristics, others can trigger anxious feelings or changes in mood. These include fried foods, high glycemic carbohydrates (e.g., white bread, pretzels, potatoes), unrefined sugars, and caffeine. In *The Chemistry of Calm: A Powerful, Drug-Free Plan to Quiet Your Fears and Overcome Your Anxiety*, author Henry Emmons, MD recommends that individuals suffering from stress and anxiety eliminate stimulants such as coffee, caffeinated tea, and soft drinks. These beverages can make us feel on edge and interfere with sleep.

Next, he suggests that we minimize trans fats found in most fried foods, baked goods, and many processed foods. He also advises paying attention to food sensitivities since certain foods or food additives can cause unpleasant physical reactions in some people. These physical sensations may lead to shifts in mood, including irritability or anxiety.[236]

One of the most critical changes that anyone dealing with stress and anxiety can make to their diet is nixing caffeine. I gave up caffeine a long time ago because it made me feel so nervous and jittery. Caffeine is a stimulant, affecting the central nervous system by blocking adenosine throughout the body. This chemical is responsible for calming down neural activity. Caffeine enters the bloodstream through the stomach and small intestine, causing a stimulating effect within about fifteen minutes after being consumed. Once in the body, it can last for several hours. The boost our body gets from caffeine is caused by an increase in our heart and breathing rates. These are the same feelings we get during a stressful event when the fight-flight-freeze response kicks in. Consuming caffeine when we are already hyped up from stress only adds fuel to the fire, making it so much harder for the body to calm down and get back to a balanced state. While your children probably are not sipping cups of coffee, caffeine can sneak into their diets, so be sure to read labels carefully. Watch out for iced tea; energy drinks; and treats like cookies, candy, ice cream, and other desserts containing chocolate.

Another big culprit is sugar, including artificial sweeteners and high-fructose corn syrup. These sweeteners have been linked to mental health issues like anxiety and depression. Similar to how caffeine affects our nervous system, sugar highs can contribute to symptoms that mimic a panic attack. Our kids can experience fatigue, difficulty thinking, and increased heart rate just from eating sugar.[237] Unfortunately, these types of symptoms can exacerbate their anxiety.

The second way sugar can affect mental health is by contributing to depression and mood disorders due to the rise and crash of blood sugar levels. Too much sugar has been found to suppress brain-derived neurotrophic factor (BDNF), a protein linked to depression and anxiety.[238] One study looked at the connection between sugar and mood disorders.

Diets and medical conditions of eight thousand people over twenty-two years were assessed, and researchers found that patients without a mood disorder who consumed over sixty-seven grams of sugar per day (that is about six donuts or three candy bars) had a twenty-three percent increased risk of suffering from a mood disorder than those who ate forty grams or less.[239] Another study found that consuming high amounts of sugar is associated with depression.[240] Although the medical community is not quite ready to conclude that sugar *causes* depression, these studies and several others certainly raise concern.

While naturally occurring sugar may be perfectly healthy when found in fruits, vegetables, and milk, added sugar can be hidden in the foods you may serve your children. Did you know that bread, salad dressing, ketchup, yogurt, smoothies, and even "health" bars can be loaded with hidden added sugar? The best advice is to stick to the sugar intake recommendations and be mindful of the amount of sugar your children are consuming daily. According to the American Heart Association, children ages two to eighteen should not eat or drink more than twenty-five grams of added sugar daily, which is about six teaspoons.[241] For reference, that is equivalent to drinking an eight-ounce glass of apple juice.[242]

Can a Plant-Based Diet Improve Mental Health?

The simple answer is: we just do not know yet, but it cannot hurt.

Several studies have been completed in this area, but we see conflicting results. On one hand, some vegans and vegetarians report better moods than omnivores because of the possibility that animal fats could activate pathways in the brain responsible for stress and mood disorders. The link could also be related to other factors, such as vegans typically exercising more, spending more time outdoors, drinking less alcohol, eating fewer sweets, and eating more fruits and vegetables.[243] On the other hand, some studies show that a plant-based diet can cause more depression and anxiety. One possibility is that a vegan diet done improperly can result in nutritional deficiencies that can have a negative impact on mental health. Vitamin deficiencies of B12 and folate, omega-3 fatty acids, and amino acids, for example, have been linked to depression and poor mood regulation. Taking supplements containing these vitamins could resolve the issue.[244]

Melissa Mondala, MD, a double board-certified family medicine and lifestyle medicine physician and primary care director for the Institute of Plant-Based Medicine, encourages a plant-based diet to improve mental health. Because animal-based products contain a pro-inflammatory compound that can adversely impact mental health, she recommends that her patients minimize animal-based foods and instead choose whole plant foods. Plant-based foods contain fiber, vitamins, and minerals while animal-based products are deficient in these mood-regulating nutrients.[245]

Although we do not have a solid answer yet, I think this is an important question to consider since many of us often weigh how our diet choices impact our family's health and the planet. It is possible that we will never find a clear, consistent link between being a vegetarian or vegan and anxiety and depression. Many factors are involved that still need to be studied. Nonetheless, it is fascinating to monitor this aspect of the research, and another potential reason to cut back on eating animal products.

Pesticides and Mental Health

Could pesticides in our food cause mental health issues like anxiety and depression? This is a key question that scientists are currently exploring. Here is what we know. Pesticides are chemicals used to kill unwanted insects, plants, molds, and rodents. Multiple studies show how pesticide exposure in pregnancy and childhood can lead to serious health issues like cancer. Also, pesticides ingested on a regular basis can impair cognitive function and disrupt the endocrine system, which can contribute to depression.[246]

Several studies link pesticide use to increases in anxiety and/or depression experienced by farmers, which has raised concern. A *Scientific American* report cited epidemiologic studies that found that farmers who used organochlorine pesticides or fumigants had an eighty to ninety percent increase in risk of depression. The report also reviewed studies in France, which showed a two hundred percent rise in depression treatments sought by farmers who work at farms using herbicides.[247] Another study focused on adolescent exposure to pesticides measured levels of the enzyme acetylcholinesterase (AChE) in over five hundred individuals. Pesticides like organophosphates and carbamates inhibit AChE, and past studies show how this can be linked to mental health issues. They found that the teens who had low AChE levels, suggesting exposure to pesticides, had more symptoms of depression.[248]

So, what does this mean for your family? If farmers are being harmed from spraying pesticides on our produce, can our children also be affected when they bite into what otherwise would be considered healthy foods like fruits and vegetables? Since the research is inconclusive at this point, it is a good idea to monitor the situation. Given this information, you may choose organic food out of a sense of precaution. As Henry Emmons, MD writes in *The Chemistry of Calm*, "It also stands to reason that eating fruits and vegetables laced with pesticides, milk and meat filled with hormones, and foods processed with chemical additives and artificial sweeteners might not be good for the brain's health."[249]

Mindful Eating

It is not only what we eat, but how we eat that can affect how we feel. When we rush and inhale our food mindlessly in front of the television, we can feel anxious and experience some physical health issues like upset stomach. On the other hand, eating mindfully as a family can help us reduce stress, maintain healthy diet habits, and improve our relationships.

So, what is mindful eating? According to the Center for Mindful Eating, this practice allows us to become aware of the positive and nurturing opportunities that can come from preparing and eating food.[250] Instead of shoving food into our mouths and never really thinking about it, mindful eating awakens us to an entirely new experience with food. We can take a moment to savor and truly enjoy what we are eating.

During the Mrs. Mindfulness Summit, Dr. Susan Albers of the Cleveland Clinic, an expert on mindful eating, suggested a five-step program for changing the way we eat. She gave a clever quote for each step so we can easily remember them.

- Sit down: "Only eat off your feet"
- Chew slowly: "Pace, don't race"
- Savor food and take mindful bites: "We eat . . . just eat"
- Simplify and place healthy foods in accessible places: "In sight in mind, out of sight out of mind"
- Smile between each bite and take a pause: "Take a breath to manage stress"[251]

We can introduce some simple activities at mealtime so that our children can begin to slow down and eat mindfully.

- Invite your children to help prepare a meal. Focus on the range of colors of ingredients and how they smell and feel. Talk to them about the changes in foods when they are cooked, such as boiling vegetables to make them softer.
- Make sure to eat together as a family at the kitchen table and engage in positive, interactive conversation.
- Ask children to use their five senses to describe the food on their plates: color, texture, smell, taste, sounds as they chew.
- Talk about where the food comes from, such as farming, fishing, or your own garden.
- Consider taking a meal outdoors to soak in nature while you eat. This could be on your balcony, out on your back patio or deck, or at a local park for a picnic.
- Lead a mindful eating exercise, such as this one with an orange. You can adapt this process to any type of food.
  1. Start by holding an orange in your hand. Roll it around. Touch different parts of it. Notice how it feels. Is it hard or squishy? Is it smooth or rough?
  2. Inhale the fruit's scent. What does it smell like? Do different parts of the fruit have different smells?

3. Look at the fruit closely and from various angles. What colors do you see? Is the skin smooth or bumpy? What shape is it? What does it remind you of?

4. Slowly peel your orange, paying attention to how it feels in your fingers. Notice the juiciness, wetness, and any distinctions between how the inside and outside feel.

5. Take a whiff of the inside of the orange. Does it smell differently now that it is peeled?

6. Now it is time to taste the orange. Take a slow bite and notice how it feels on your tongue, on the inside of your cheeks, and against your teeth. How would you describe the flavor? Sweet, sour, bitter, etc.? Notice the texture of the piece of orange in your mouth and any juiciness as you chew it. Does it take much effort to chew it? Take your time and be mindful as you chew, taste, smell, and feel each bite of your orange.

7. Have fun reflecting on this experience together.

Benefits of Soil Bacteria
for Gut and Mental Health

Do you encourage your kids to play in the dirt? It is certainly no fun as a parent to have to clean up muddy children after they have been rolling around outside, but now scientists tell us that getting dirty can actually be good for our children's well-being. According to the National Wildlife Federation's *The Dirt on Dirt* pamphlet, "Making direct contact with soil, whether through gardening, digging for worms, or making mud pies, has been shown to improve mood, reduce anxiety, and facilitate learning."[252] The secret is in the microscopic bacteria found naturally in soil.

The discovery that soil could improve mental health was made by accident. In 2004, Dr. Mary O'Brien, an oncologist in London, published a paper with unexpected results. After injecting lung cancer patients with a common soil bacterium called *Mycobacterium vaccae* (not live) to see if it could prolong their life, she found that it significantly improved their mood and quality of life. Her patients reported feeling happier and more energetic.[253] This spurred additional research over the years.

A few years later, neuroscientist Dr. Christopher Lowry injected *Mycobacterium vaccae* into mice and observed them during a series of stress tests. The mice injected with the bacteria showed less stressed behavior than other mice. Lowry and his team explained that the bacteria activated neurons in the brain responsible for producing serotonin. This interaction is very similar to how antidepressants work and how we feel more positive emotions after physical exercise.[254] In addition, the neurons that lit up were related to the immune response, suggesting a connection between the immune system and emotional health. Lowry's research also found that eating the bacteria could result in the same benefits. He went on to conduct follow-up studies over the years that confirm the positive affect of the bacteria on mental health.

An intriguing study in 2020 found that playing in a forest-like environment can alter children's microbiome in a positive way. Daycares in Finland created such an environment by rolling out a lawn, planting forest undergrowth, and having the children care for crops in planter boxes.

As a result, the diversity of microbes in their guts and on their skin was healthier after about a month. Compared to other children in the city who play in standard urban daycares with schoolyards made of pavement, tile, and gravel, these children had more diversity in their microbiome, which is linked to a healthier immune system. Also, their intestinal microbiota was similar to children visiting a forest.[255]

As parents, we can easily use this information to help our children feel happier and calmer. Spending time digging in a garden, for example, can be emotionally beneficial to our children. In addition to all the advantages of being outside in nature, the *Mycobacterium vaccae* in the soil can boost their mood as well. It is believed that we can take in the bacteria by touching the soil, eating trace amounts of it on garden vegetables, and even breathing it in. This type of bacteria is known to thrive in typical backyard gardens or anywhere soil is enriched with organic matter. As much of society has moved away from an agricultural lifestyle to spend most time indoors, we have lost contact with the microorganisms we need in our gut to help regulate our immune system. This puts us at higher risk for inflammatory disease and stress-related issues.[256] By reconnecting to nature through activities like gardening, our children can benefit from the bacteria known to improve their overall health and well-being.

Gardening

I absolutely love it when we can pick fruits and vegetables grown in our own backyard and savor them at our dinner table. We are fortunate enough to have a lemon tree in our backyard, and we have enjoyed making our own lemon water, lemonade, and dishes like lemon chicken. We have also dabbled in growing our own tomatoes and peppers, which the children absolutely love doing. It is a wonderful experience for them to pick the produce and play a role in creating a healthy meal for our family that incorporates the food we grew ourselves. My children and I have also gotten a lot out of volunteering in a local community garden that serves a group of special-needs adults in our community. During our visits, we have helped by planting seeds, weeding, and picking vegetables. The best part is that the group uses what is grown in the garden to create healthy meals that they serve in their campus café.

Growing fruits and vegetables together as a family can be a fun, engaging, and calming activity. In addition to spending time outside in nature, gardening offers several other noteworthy benefits. First, it provides a healthy distraction. One study showed that engaging with a garden distracts us from our worries and stops us from obsessing about our problems. Over twelve weeks, participants saw an improvement in their mood during and immediately after gardening, and three months later they still reported significant improvements.[257] Another study showed that after thirty minutes of gardening, participants' cortisol levels dropped and they felt happier after the activity.[258]

Gardening is also similar to art in that it provides an opportunity to get lost in the moment. Whether we call it mindfulness or flow, focusing on something we love and losing track of time can dull our worries significantly. Shannon Brescher Shea knows this firsthand. In her book *Growing Sustainable Together: Practical Resources for Raising Kind, Engaged, Resilient Children*, she dedicates an entire chapter to the benefits of gardening. "My older son is an emotionally intense kid, often buzzing with pent-up energy. But when he goes outside, he simply relaxes. The very act of getting into nature—even if it is just our backyard—is transformational. The garden further reinforces this shift. As he is now quite knowledgeable about gardening, helping out gives him both a sense of control and pride in contributing to a family project."[259]

Next, gardening provides some light exercise (and possibly some more intense exercise if you do some lifting). When we move around and sweat a bit, our body produces feel-good endorphins. Exercise also reduces the level of stress hormones in our body like adrenaline and cortisol, helping us feel calmer.[260] So, do not be shy about giving your kids some physical work to do in the garden, such as digging, lifting, and bending up and down.

Gardening also motivates us to eat healthier foods that make us feel better. When kids are invested in growing their own fruits and vegetables, they feel more connected and want to enjoy the "fruit of their labor." Gardening instills in them an appreciation for where food comes from and the work involved in making every meal. When children are part of

growing their own food, they will want to taste it. By encouraging them to eat healthier through gardening, they will hopefully choose foods that nourish them instead of junk foods filled with sugar.

Another bonus of gardening is that it teaches children about acceptance, resilience, and how to get beyond perfectionism—all important traits to reduce stress and anxiety. Being a control freak is one of the major causes of unhappiness. Gardening teaches us how to embrace things as they are without trying to control or alter them. Through the process of gardening, children can learn that the unexpected happens even if they do everything by the book. Sometimes factors take over that are not in our control, like weather or critters that decide to enjoy the produce before we get to it. Also, sometimes a tomato or cucumber will not turn out as perfect as we imagined, but we can still enjoy the delicious vegetables—flaws and all.

Finally, social interaction and building community are positive aspects of gardening. Whether it is just you bonding with your children in the garden, sharing your produce and gardening stories with friends and neighbors, or volunteering in a community garden, that social interaction plays a major role in making us feel better. Experts tell us that the most important way to feel happier is through positive relationships, so gardening can provide a vehicle for our children to connect with others over a healthy hobby.

We can also look to the collection of research around the mental health benefits of gardening. A breakthrough study in the *Journal of Environmental Psychology* found that a healing garden at a children's hospital in California had positive effects on users—about eighty-five percent reported feeling more relaxed, refreshed, or better able to cope after spending only five minutes in the garden.[261] A collection of studies from around the world found a wide range of positive health outcomes from gardening, such as reductions in anxiety and depression and increases in life satisfaction, quality of life, and sense of community.[262] Finally, a key experiment explored the relationship between home gardening and dietary behaviors, physical activity, mental health, and social relationships among adolescents. The findings suggest that home gardening may contribute in a positive way to the health and well-being of adolescents and that it may promote stronger family connections.[263]

Because of these findings regarding the positive aspects of gardening, some doctors are now prescribing gardening to patients. Doctors at the Cornbrook Medical Practice in Manchester, England, for example, prescribe gardening to patients struggling with anxiety and depression. Each patient is given a "dosage" of plants to care for and then return to the medical center after a set amount of time. Patients carefully transfer their plants into the center's community garden.

This activity gives them meaning as they tend to the plants and an opportunity to engage with others in the community garden, which results in boosting their mood.[264]

How can you add gardening to your child's life?

- Teach them about gardening by reading books like *Growing Vegetable Soup*, *Up in the Garden and Down in the Dirt*, *Planting a Rainbow*, and *The Tiny Seed*; watch videos about gardening; and listen to fun music like "The Garden Song" and songs by the band Formidable Vegetable.
- Create a family garden in your backyard. You can engage your children in gardening by buying them their own gardening tools, asking them to pick out the seeds they want to plant, and using the produce you grow to cook meals together.
- If digging an entire garden in your backyard sounds intimidating, consider starting slow by growing a few herbs on your windowsill or one vegetable at a time in a large flowerpot.
- If you do not have the room or desire to create a garden in your backyard, collaborate with a neighbor or purchase a plot at a local community garden to tend.
- Look for opportunities to volunteer in a local community garden. Community gardens increase the amount of green space and build positive community interaction, and many also provide to those in need.
- Use gardening as a chance for mindfulness. When it is time to weed, plant, and till, slow down and disconnect from all distractions. Encourage your children to notice the birds chirping, the

gentle breeze, the feel of the plants and soil, and the aromas emanating from the garden.

- Lobby for a gardening program at your children's school.
- Register your children for a gardening club or start one in your community.

Discovering Peace in a Children's Peace Garden

Permaculture entails caring for people and nature and taking only a fair share of resources. As a mixture of both old and new methods to live sustainably, this philosophy is about working *with* rather than against nature. It is applied around the world in a number of contexts, including agriculture and education.

The Children in Permaculture (CiP) project supports educators to engage children in permaculture. The organization brings together parents and teachers from different schools, nurseries, and practices in several European countries to share and synthesize ideas around permaculture.

One of the projects of CiP cofounder Lusi Alderslowe was to construct a Peace Garden at an elementary school in Scotland. The goal was to design a biodiverse, sensory, and edible garden to help children be at peace with themselves, each other, and other living things like birds, insects, flowers, and trees. A group of twelve children learned various steps in the permaculture design process, including surveying the area; mapping out the elements of the garden; and grouping ideas into categories such as plants, animals, and structures. They also worked in the garden by testing the soil, collecting seeds, digging, planting trees and flowers, and picking produce. When they harvested enough food, all the children in the school got to take a bag of mixed produce home with them to enjoy with their family.

Besides the typical gardening activities, the children also engaged in writing poetry to reflect on their time in the garden, making signs, building benches, and researching about the garden. Of course, one of the most important skills they learned was to sit quietly in the garden and find peace. Lusi recalls, "While we were designing and creating the peace garden, we made sure that we regularly took the time to sit in the garden area to observe all that was around us. Some children were amazed at the wonderful opportunity to just sit in silence and not have to do anything." This was a novel experience for these children since they did not have the chance to relax much in school or at home given their hectic schedules filled with school-related activities and screen time. "The importance of finding peace in yourself can enable children to engage more calmly with others and with nature. Children reported feeling calm, relaxed, happy, awesome, and energized."

When the Peace Garden was ready, the group held an opening ceremony to reveal it to the whole school community. During the event, the children planted a peace pole with the quote "May peace prevail on Earth" written in four languages. The children were filled with pride and joy from being part of this special garden. This will certainly be an experience they will hold in their hearts forever. As one student declared on a video highlighting the project, "We were often given the opportunity to sit still, listen to the birds, find peace in ourselves, and imagine what the peace garden would be like in the years to come."[265]

Horticultural Therapy

Horticultural therapy formalizes gardening as a type of therapy. This practice uses plants, horticultural activities, and the garden environment to promote well-being. Shown to be effective in improving mental health issues, horticultural therapy has been used since the early nineteenth century. A therapeutic garden is a plant-dominated environment designed to facilitate interaction with the healing elements of nature. The basic features of a therapeutic garden include calming entrances and paths; raised plant beds and containers; and a variety of plants selected for their color, texture, and fragrance for clients to explore with their senses.[266]

Therapy sessions are administered by professionally trained horticultural therapists. The therapist works with and guides clients in activities in a garden setting, such as planting seeds, watering, weeding, picking fruits and vegetables, making flower arrangements, composting, participating in meditation practices, and journaling about their time in the garden.

Horticultural therapy offers many benefits to children related to well-being:

- **Improves confidence and self-esteem.** By learning new skills and accomplishing tasks in the garden, children can build their confidence and self-esteem. It can be especially rewarding when they see the result of their work and are able to pick and take home produce they helped grow.
- **Stimulates creativity.** Gardens provide an opportunity to be artistic, whether it be how plants are placed in the soil, flower arranging, or displaying freshly harvested produce.
- **Piques curiosity.** The garden provides a place for children to feel a sense of awe, wonder, and curiosity about plants and how they grow, which can boost their happiness.
- **Provides lessons through nature.** Therapists often use nature-related metaphors, such as the life cycle, to help children heal and reflect on what is going on in their lives.

- **Promotes socialization.** During horticultural therapy sessions, therapists work with their clients on garden projects, which helps the children communicate, cooperate, and share in responsibilities.
- **Offers a place to express tough emotions.** The soothing garden environment may relax children enough to open up to their therapist about their emotions. They also may relieve tension and aggression in a safe and healthy way while gardening, whether they are digging dirt or pulling weeds.[267]

A growing number of studies provide evidence linking horticultural therapy to improvements in mental health. A group of researchers set up a twelve-week therapeutic horticulture intervention that involved participants planting, cultivating, and cutting vegetables and flowers. The participants, who struggled with moderate depression, gardened twice a week for three hours each session. Following the activities in the garden, their depression scores improved significantly.[268] An additional study found that horticultural activities—including flower arranging, planting, and pressing—reduced stress and cortisol levels of elementary school children with emotional and behavioral issues.[269]

If you are interested in finding a horticultural therapist for your child, try reaching out to the nearest botanical garden or public garden in your area to inquire about trained horticultural therapists in your community. You can also check with local universities; many have departments dedicated to this area of research. Finally, you can contact the American Horticultural Therapy Association and Horticultural Therapy Institute for recommendations.

Finding Common Ground in the Garden

Amy Brightwood is a horticultural therapist who opened a therapeutic gardening facility she calls Common Ground in Chapel Hill, North Carolina. The mission of Common Ground is to connect people with

---

plants, garden activities, and nature to promote health and well-being. Amy provides her clients with opportunities to engage in gardening activities to awaken their senses; increase physical, social, emotional, cognitive, and spiritual well-being; participate in hands-on, meaningful individual or group work that supports their goals; and learn basic horticultural skills. She has worked with elementary school garden groups, mental health groups, and long-term care facilities. Also trained as a mindfulness-based stress reduction leader, she incorporates elements of mindfulness and meditation into her horticultural therapy sessions.

Groups and individual clients come out to the garden for horticultural therapy. She also visits schools to lead horticultural therapy sessions for students. She typically works with special/exceptional-needs children and those who have behavioral issues. They meet on a weekly basis usually for an hour to engage in activities related to growing seasonal vegetables and flowers. She also has a sensory garden for the children to explore filled with colorful plants and flowers to observe, taste, smell, and touch, and farm bells and chimes for sound.

Amy prefers to stick to a general routine during her therapy sessions with children in the garden. "It is really about sensory stimulation. I work hard to create ways for the kids to get in touch with all of their senses." She typically intertwines mindfulness into her practice. "I start with a mindful meditation to help them settle in. I ask them to close their eyes and to feel the ground. I then pose a set of questions and teach them to take deep breaths. What do you hear? What do you feel? What do you smell?" This mindfulness exercise helps them connect to their surroundings and build a better sense of their bodies.

After the initial mindfulness exercise, they work on assigned tasks in the garden. "I tend to set a framework with predictable routines because that brings comfort to the kids." This engaging time involves planting seeds, digging in the soil, watering plants, raking, building garden beds, harvesting food, and enjoying the breeze and sunshine. The children complete their session by writing in their garden journals. The journal is a record of their gardening time and a way for them to practice communication skills and reflect on their experience that day.

The garden offers a calming environment for them to relax and open up if they are ready. Therefore, some children may speak to her about their thoughts and feelings, similar to a talk therapy session.

Amy loves to reflect on the positive changes in the children who spend time with her in the garden. "I get to see the growth of the children who come to garden, along with the growth of the plants." She has seen how their social skills and confidence develop, as well as horticultural knowledge and gross and fine motor skills. "There was a third-grade girl who could not settle down. During her time in the garden, I watched her gain tremendous leadership skills as she helped the other children with plantings." Amy often works with kids who have behavioral issues like impulse control and anger. "The routine of the garden helps them. They are assigned tasks and responsibilities in the garden. Their cooperation and sense of teamwork grows, and they start feeling pride about what they built with their own hands." She also watches how they relax during their time outdoors. When she asked one of the boys what he liked most about being in the garden, he replied, "I like being in the country. I like the quiet, and I love flowers. They make me happy." Simple, yet so powerful.[270]

Other Ways to Connect with Nature Through Food

In addition to gardening, other options to enjoy food with our children are to visit a u-pick farm, shop at farmer's markets, and cook healthy meals together. One of my favorite memories of autumn as a child is going apple picking with my family. I was so enthralled by all the hidden treasures hanging in the orchard. I loved tasting the different varieties of apples and deciding which was the sweetest and juiciest. I especially cherished the warm apple cider samples that the farm gave out after we finished collecting our apples. Over the years, our family has gone to local farms to pick apples, strawberries, blueberries, raspberries, and peppers. We have also enjoyed a few pumpkin patches to pick out that perfect

orange treasure for Halloween. The kids loved each one of these experiences as much as I did.

U-pick farms are a terrific way for kids to experience fresh produce of the season. By taking children on a u-pick adventure, you will help them learn a tremendous amount about food and the environment, and you will build family memories that will last a lifetime. One of the best ways to get kids excited about eating healthier foods is to let them go out and touch and feel the fruits and vegetables for themselves. When you take your children to pick their own produce, you expose them to healthier options and make it fun for them to discover delicious whole foods.

They also have a chance to meet the actual farmers who grow the food and learn about the role the farmers play in food production. If possible, encourage your children to ask the farmers questions about the seasons, the land, different produce being grown, and the specific work they do daily. Visiting a u-pick farm also gives you a chance to talk to your children about the changing seasons, cycles of nature, and where certain crops grow during the year.

Farmer's markets offer a unique way to shop outdoors and to connect more closely with those who are growing the food we buy. When you purchase produce from a local farm or farmer's market, you are supporting your local community and protecting the environment. You help farmers succeed through your patronage, ensuring that there will be farms in your community in the future. Plus, locally grown food tastes better, is more nutritious, and stays fresher longer. It is picked at peak harvest time, transported shorter distances, and sold directly to consumers. The less time that passes between farm and table, the more nutrients remain.

Once you pick your own at the farm or choose fresh locally grown produce at the farmer's market, you can spend quality time together in the kitchen cooking or baking scrumptious meals. There are so many healthy kid-friendly recipes to discover that call for the fresh produce you brought home. Your children playing this much of a role in gathering and preparing their food will have a huge impact on them and influence the food decisions they make in the future. This is also the perfect time to incorporate all the calming foods listed earlier in this chapter into your family's meals.

Community Greening: Bringing the Magic of Urban Orchards to Communities in Florida

At one point, we had lemons, limes, grapefruit, and coconuts growing in our Florida backyard. It was delightful to be able to walk just a few steps and pull a piece of fresh fruit from a tree and enjoy it during our next meal. Over the years, we have made our own coconut water, lemonade, salad with grapefruit, lemon chicken, and guacamole with freshly squeezed lime juice.

Many people take trees for granted. Yet, there are communities that do not have any trees lining their streets or yards. In fact, tree cover is correlated to the economics of a neighborhood. This is unfortunate since trees provide so many health and emotional benefits. According to a study by the University of Wollongong in Australia, residents in urban areas have better overall health and a lower risk of developing stress if they have more trees within a walkable distance from their home. In neighborhoods with a tree canopy of thirty percent or more, adults have a thirty-one percent lower chance of developing psychological distress and a thirty-three percent lower chance of rating their general health as fair or poor.[271] Without trees, communities miss out on these critical health benefits.

Image courtesy of Community Greening.

That is where Community Greening steps in. Cofounders Mark Cassini and Matt Shipley started Community Greening in 2016 to address a need they saw to bring more green space to urban areas and to people who traditionally have not had resources to green their neighborhood. This urban forestry nonprofit based in Delray Beach, Florida, has quickly expanded throughout the region. The group works with local residents and organizations to improve the environment and community by planting trees. Since its founding, the organization has planted over 7,500 trees in parks, schoolyards, residential yards, and urban orchards with the help of over 4,000 volunteers of all ages. Through tree planting, they bring people together to create a healthy, sustainable environment.

Community Greening's urban orchard program is making a difference by helping communities thrive with fresh, healthy fruit that they can pick themselves at no cost. The program has transformed once neglected city-owned lots into vibrant green spaces that address food accessibility, healthy eating, and environmental stewardship. Some of the fruit trees planted in these urban orchards include avocado, breadfruit, fig, guava, jackfruit, Jamaican cherry, mango, mulberry, persimmon, starfruit, and sugar apple. Community Greening currently has three urban orchards in south Florida with plans to add more.

Image courtesy of Green Chimneys.

These orchards have brought so much positivity into these struggling communities. Where there was once a trash dump there is now a gorgeous grove of fruit trees blossoming throughout the year. The older members of the community from countries like Haiti and the Bahamas are so grateful to be able to enjoy some of the fruit they grew up eating, and it brings them pleasure to share it with their children and grandchildren. "Grandparents teach the harvesting techniques from their home countries to their grandkids. It is wonderful when the older residents tell the kids to go check and see what is ripe and ready to pick," Mark Cassini explains. In an area that is food insecure without access to a nearby grocery store or fresh fruit, residents can now walk to pick their own juicy fruit to enjoy.

Mark is thrilled with the impact Community Greening is having. "You can notice a change in how the residents view their neighborhood now that they have the orchard. All the children say they want to live by the grove and are proud it is in their neighborhood. It has been awesome to see that it has been working and making a difference," he says. The grove has also been a special learning tool for the children who have never been exposed to nature in this way. Throughout the process, the children have learned where food comes from and how to take care of the fruit trees. They learn so much from seeing the grove up close.[272]

Activity Checklist

Ü Try adding more calming foods to your family's meals.

Ü Limit foods like caffeine, sugar, and fried foods that can trigger mental health issues.

Ü Experiment with a plant-based diet and try to choose more organic foods.

Ü Invite your children to practice mindful eating during your next meal.

Ü Start a family garden in your backyard.

Ü If you do not have the space for a garden, consider starting slow by growing a few herbs on your windowsill or one vegetable at a time in a large flowerpot.

Ü Volunteer at a local community garden.

Ü Lobby for a gardening program at your children's school.

Ü Register your children for a gardening club or start your own in your community.

Ü Visit a u-pick farm or shop at a farmer's market for fresh produce.

Ü Consider horticultural therapy for your children if they are struggling.

Resources

Organizations

American Horticultural Therapy Association: https://www.ahta.org
Ample Harvest: https://ampleharvest.org
Center for Mindful Eating: https://www.thecenterformindfuleating.org
Center for Nutritional Psychology:
  https://www.nutritional-psychology.org
Children in Permaculture: https://childreninpermaculture.com
Eating Mindfully: https://eatingmindfully.com
Horticultural Therapy Institute: https://www.htinstitute.org
KidsGardening.org: https://kidsgardening.org
Local Harvest: https://www.localharvest.org
PickYourOwn.org: https://www.pickyourown.org
U-Pick Farm Locater: https://upickfarmlocator.com

Books

The Chemistry of Calm: A Powerful, Drug-Free Plan to Quiet Your Fears and Overcome Your Anxiety by Henry Emmons, MD

Earth Care, People Care and Fair Share in Education: The Children in Permaculture Manual by Lusi Alderslowe, Gaye Amus, and Didi Devapriya

Growing Sustainable Together: Practical Resources for Raising Kind, Engaged, Resilient Children by Shannon Brescher Shea

The Little Gardener: Helping Children Connect with the Natural World by Julie Cerny

The Psychobiotic Revolution: Mood, Food, and the New Science of the Gut-Brain Connection by Scott C. Anderson

This Is Your Brain on Food: An Indispensable Guide to the Surprising Foods That Fight Depression, Anxiety, PTSD, OCD, ADHD, and More by Uma Naidoo, MD

Wits Guts Grit: All-Natural Biohacks for Raising Smart, Resilient Kids by Jena Pincott

Children's Books

A Child's Garden: 60 Ideas to Make Any Garden Come Alive for Children by Molly Dannenmaier

Easy Peasy: Gardening for Kids by Kirsten Bradley

Garden to Table: A Kid's Guide to Planting, Growing, and Preparing Food by Katherine Hengel

Green Green: A Community Gardening Story by Marie Lamba and Baldev Lamba

Growing Vegetable Soup by Lois Ehlert

Inch by Inch: The Garden Song by David Mallett

The Nitty-Gritty Gardening Book: Fun Projects for All Seasons by Kari Cornell

Plant, Cook, Eat! A Children's Cookbook by Joe Archer and Caroline Craig

Planting a Rainbow by Lois Ehlert

The Tiny Seed by Eric Carle

Up in the Garden and Down in the Dirt by Kate Messner and Christopher Silas Neal

❦ **8** ❦

Volunteering

Unless someone like you cares a whole awful lot, nothing is going to get better. It's not.

Dr. Seuss

When my husband and I first moved from Washington, DC, to Florida in 2006, I turned to volunteering at a nature center to fill my soul with something positive during a major transition in my life. We had moved south for his company, leaving my steady, structured nine-to-five job behind me. I did not know anyone and had to start fresh. This was before we had kids and just a few months after we got married. Although I was ready for a change, being alone in the suburbs while my husband was working hard all day to build up a new office was definitely a lonely experience. I worked part-time from home, holding on to my DC job as long as I could.

But I needed something else to fill the gaps in my day, and for the first time in my life I really had the freedom to volunteer. Until that point, I had been either studying hard in college and graduate school or working a full-time job in the big city. I discovered the Green Cay Nature Center about ten minutes from our apartment and signed up to volunteer. The gig was to lead nature walks for visitors along a boardwalk snaking through wetlands. In order to identify various types of native birds, I stocked up on a few birding guides and worked hard to memorize key facts to share with visitors on the tour.

Being a volunteer at Green Cay seems like a hundred years ago now, since it was pre-kids. During that special time, I challenged myself to learn more about nature and educate others about the area, and I experienced the wonder of getting lost in the moment while trying to find and identify all the unique creatures in the habitat. I watched as photographers captured special moments from the boardwalk and mothers pointed out beautiful birds and other animals to their young children. I look back on that time fondly and recall how happy and relaxed it made me feel in my new environment, and how it helped me connect to others during a lonely time.

Doing good makes us feel good. Whether it is sending a donation, holding a door for a stranger, or volunteering on a weekly basis as I did at Green Cay, study after study proves that acts of kindness make us feel happier and healthier. Children have the foundation to be kind, and our job as parents is to nurture this part of them as they grow. We can spark our children's love for community service, especially activities that expose them to nature and its endless benefits. You can plant the seed (yes, both literally and figuratively) to help your children grow up wanting to spread love and kindness. In fact, children who volunteer are more likely to give back as adults, according to Youth Helping America. After analyzing the volunteering habits of youth between the ages of twelve and eighteen, the organization found that children with at least one parent who volunteers are almost twice as likely to volunteer as those with no family members who volunteer—and nearly three times as likely to volunteer regularly.[273]

It is not always easy to find the time, energy, motivation, or right venue to volunteer with our children, but with some research and creativity we can all give back in a way that the entire family will benefit from and enjoy. There are endless types of volunteer opportunities, but this book is about nature, so we will look at the specific benefits of environmental volunteering and volunteering outdoors. By combining community service and nature, we can experience a double dose of stress-busting bliss.

How Volunteering Helps Us Feel Happier and Calmer

We are all born with an instinct to give. Humans have evolved over time to be compassionate, and our brains are now wired to respond to those who are suffering. Essentially, kindness has become a "survival of the fittest" trait, as Charles Darwin advised that "communities which included the greatest number of the most sympathetic members would flourish best, and rear the greatest number of offspring."[274] In other words, the better we get along and help each other out, the more successful our society will be.

Scientists discovered that infants as young as eighteen months old who are not even talking yet help others, even though they are too young to have learned to be kind and polite. Researchers Felix Warneken and Michael Tomasello studied the behavior of twenty-four eighteen-month-old toddlers. They placed the children in situations in which an adult stranger was having trouble meeting a goal, such as trying to grab an out-of-reach object. In most cases, the children understood when the adult needed help and took action on their own initiative. It was not because they expected a reward. This study shows how young children have a natural tendency to help others, even when the other person is a total stranger and they do not receive any reciprocal benefit.[275] There is also evidence that children continue to show compassion as they grow. Toddlers who were asked to give away their own treats expressed greater happiness when they shared with others.[276] Therefore, taking part in pro-social behavior like volunteering can help people feel happier.

Our brain is wired to respond to those who are suffering, and it changes when we do something nice for someone else. Helping others through activities like community service makes us feel good and triggers a fascinating biological phenomenon called a "helper's high." This distinct physical sensation—sometimes described as euphoric—is associated with performing acts of kindness. It results from our brain releasing endorphins such as dopamine, giving us a rush and making us feel elated. This positive energy in our body is similar to how we feel after we exercise. According to *Psychology Today*, the helper's high is a literal "high," similar to a drug-induced sensation. In fact, this natural and automatic response has allowed humans to survive throughout history.[277]

Several studies confirm the positive relationship between acts of kindness and experiencing a natural chemical high. Happiness expert Sonja Lyubomirsky observed a helper's high in study participants when she asked them to perform five acts of kindness each week for six weeks.[278] Another study examined the relationships between volunteer work in the community and the following six aspects of personal well-being: happiness, life satisfaction, self-esteem, a sense of control over life, physical health, and depression. Volunteer work enhanced all six aspects of well-being.[279]

Volunteering can also reduce stress levels, which is often reflected in lower blood pressure.[280] It is believed that kindness may improve physical health and longevity since it helps decrease stress and accompanying physical symptoms.

The simple act of doing something for another can change our brain activity and trigger positive emotions. Kindness ends up being a win-win for both the giver and the receiver. The positive feelings that our kids can experience from volunteer work help make them happier and healthier by reducing stress and anxiety and feelings of sadness, loneliness, or depression.

DoSomething.org, an organization that promotes social change and volunteering in youth, conducted a national survey of teens and volunteering that evaluated over 4,300 individuals ranging in age from thirteen to twenty-two years old. They found that young people who volunteer are happier than those who do not volunteer. Another study observed about one hundred tenth-grade students who were split into two groups: the first group volunteered regularly for ten weeks while the other did not. The students who volunteered reported the greatest improvements in empathy, altruistic behavior, and mental health.[281] Finally, data from over one thousand high school students in the late 1980s and early 1990s was reviewed for trends in volunteering. Ultimately, researchers found that those who volunteered experienced beneficial health and well-being.[282]

Several aspects of volunteering make us feel better:

Connecting with Others

Volunteering helps us feel connected to others while we work on positive projects. Getting to know new people and experiencing a meaningful activity together can have a profound effect on our psychological well-being. This may be from building trust, learning to cooperate, and securing a special bond from that experience. When we volunteer with a group or give back to help others, we build connection and eliminate feelings of isolation. It is also important to choose volunteer projects we are passionate about so we can meet like-minded individuals who care about similar interests.

Providing a Healthy Distraction

Volunteering keeps our mind distracted to minimize negative thinking that can impact our emotional health. Whether we are working with adults, children, or pets, a meaningful connection can take our mind off our worries when we put our attention on someone or something else. The more enriching the experience, the more we will feel satisfied volunteering our time and talents.

Building Confidence

Some community service projects entail novel experiences and learning new skills. When we are challenged in a positive way, we can build up our confidence and boost our mood. If our children learn how to master a new skill, they will be so proud of themselves that they will not have time to worry.

Creating an Attitude of Gratitude

When we give to those in need, we become humbled and thankful because giving puts our life in perspective. Volunteer work is a marvelous opportunity for our children to appreciate what they have and gives them a glimpse of the broader world. When we venture out to an unfamiliar neighborhood or environment to give back, our child's character grows by leaps and bounds.

Delivering Inspiration

When children realize how incredible they feel after volunteering, they will want to keep doing more. They may even want to get others involved like friends or grandparents. Indeed, just one act of kindness can inspire several more acts of kindness by others.[283] Children can eventually serve as mentors to others, helping them build leadership skills and stimulating a chain of kindness and compassion.

Finding a Sense of Purpose and Meaning

Positive psychology researchers have discovered that people who have a clear purpose in life experience less pain and anxiety. Feeling good about the future is important for our emotional well-being, and having a purpose gives us direction and something to look forward to.

Volunteering can help us carry out our sense of purpose because it requires making a sacrifice (time or otherwise) for others. Our kids feel fulfilled when they see the smiles of the people they helped or realize the difference they made by planting more trees in the local park. By giving our children these types of volunteer experiences throughout their childhood, we can help them discover their passion and purpose so they can ultimately find happiness by pursuing their interests.

Benefits of Volunteering Outdoors

Besides spending more time outside enjoying nature, your children can play a role in improving and protecting it through a number of hands-on volunteer projects. Several incredible organizations show how volunteering outdoors can help both children and adults benefit emotionally.

Conservation Group Volunteers

A Deakin University program determined that volunteering in a conservation group focused on nature-based activities helps improve health and well-being for people experiencing anxiety and/or depression. Researchers looked at participants of a community development project who may have experienced stress, anxiety, depression, or social isolation. They completed at least ten hours of nature-based activities over two months, such as nature walks, weeding, planting, plant identification, wildlife watching, and wildlife counting. Following volunteer work, participants' stress decreased because of sharing an enjoyable experience with others, feeling positive about improving the environment, and relaxing from nature sounds like chirping birds and trickling water. Volunteers acknowledged that contact with nature has a calming, therapeutic effect and helps them forget about their worries.[284]

The Girl Scouts

The Girl Scouts of the United States of America collects information about the benefits of volunteering outdoors. They surveyed nearly three thousand girls ranging in age from eight to fourteen about their Girl Scouting experience and how it made them feel. Nearly two-thirds of the girls said they enjoyed the outdoor activities, and environmental volunteering was listed as a top ten favorite activity. Additionally, results showed that environmental volunteering through Girl Scouts was the strongest and most significant predictor of their environmental stewardship, while also providing them with a rewarding and inspiring activity that gives them a sense of purpose.[285]

The Wildlife Trusts

The Wildlife Trusts in the United Kingdom has been working hard to assess the link between environmental volunteering and improved mental health. They reviewed the health impacts of their volunteering programs and determined that mental well-being improved significantly. Half the people improved after twelve weeks and two-thirds

improved within six weeks.[286] More recently, The Wildlife Trusts released groundbreaking news that engaging in nature through volunteer work can save money by preventing avoidable health issues from developing or getting worse.[287]

Beach Cleanups

With increased awareness of the abundance of trash in the oceans being ingested by marine life and washing up along the shore, beach cleanups have become more frequent in coastal communities. My family has participated in a number of beach cleanups over the last several years, and I have taken an interest in discovering whether beach cleanups can make us feel calmer and happier. A Marine Conservation Society assessment found that beach cleanup volunteers had a more meaningful experience than other coastal activities, like simply walking on the beach. They felt refreshed, a stronger connection to the natural world, and a sense of satisfaction that the beach was visibly cleaner.[288]

I also conducted my own research to see if there was a connection between emotions and beach cleanups. I surveyed one hundred people

who participated in one or more beach cleanups. For a third of the respondents, it was their first or second time doing a beach cleanup, while another third had done ten or more cleanups. I provided them with a list of emotions and asked them to indicate how they felt during the beach cleanup. Joy was the most popular emotion felt. I then asked them if their stress level changed during the cleanup, and forty-two percent said their stress level decreased. The majority (seventy-four percent) said they would definitely clean up the beach again. Here are some of the comments provided by survey participants about how the beach cleanup made them feel:

- "A very 'Zen' calming feel!"
- "Stronger connection to nature through the ocean—peaceful, reflective, and enjoy the exercise at the same time."
- "Time being outside always makes me happy."
- "The beach is such a serene place. It was great to have our toes in the sand and do something good for our area at the same time."
- "The ocean is immense and endlessly awe inspiring—can't get that indoors!"
- "I enjoy being outdoors whenever I can. Being in nature makes me feel happier and calm."
- "Walking barefoot on the beach is the most relaxing thing for me. It gives me a peace of mind. Searching for ocean debris also grounds me. It's my treasure hunt, which is one reason it is a great family event and a challenge for your kids. Getting outside clears your head!"

Green Gyms

Green Gyms, a nationwide program with over one hundred locations in the United Kingdom, combines physical activity with local environmental projects, including gardening, planting trees, digging ponds, and managing trails. By creating opportunities for people to work together in meaningful outdoor projects, the program improves and maintains physical and mental health of volunteers. After participating in a Green Gym for two months, volunteers reported higher levels of well-being and lower levels of stress, anxiety, and depression from connecting with other participants, feeling a sense of achievement, and being passionate about protecting the environment.

Green Gyms also piloted a school program for elementary students. Children with anxiety or low self-esteem attended weekly outdoor activities such as fruits and vegetable gardening, wildlife walks, and food tastings. The program resulted in positive behavior and well-being for the children; some said they looked forward to the activity since it helped them cope with stress.[289]

We do not need scientific studies to tell us that volunteering makes us feel better. We can experience that incredible feeling on our own. Sarah Aadland, director of Big-Hearted Families Program at Doing Good Together, creates resources for families who want to develop a kindness practice at home and strives to make family volunteering a meaningful habit for her three children. "I can attest to my own family's sense of connection and calm when we make time to volunteer. I've been doing this work since my girls were two and four (they are now teenagers), and I believe the work we have done together has shaped them and our family life in a very meaningful way. We have fostered kittens, participated in a pet walk to support our local humane society, helped clear buckthorn [a type of shrub] locally, and advocated for the protection of the boundary waters."[290]

My family has participated in many outdoor volunteer experiences, and we always leave feeling happy and proud of how we did our part to make the world a better place. Cleaning up the beach, weeding in a community garden that serves adults with disabilities, and picking vegetables at a farm to donate to a local food bank have been such meaningful projects for my family to accomplish together. You walk away with a smile on your face, knowing that you are helping others—and then you start planning the next amazing outdoor volunteer adventure.

Finding the Right Volunteer Projects for Your Family

Teaching our children how to pay it forward is easier than you may think. There are endless opportunities to volunteer as a family and to give our children meaningful experiences that will both enhance their lives and help people, animals, and the natural environment.

The first step is to introduce the idea of volunteering to your children in a positive, collaborative way so they are engaged, excited, and involved in choosing the projects you work on. First, talk about the various projects they can do by offering some concrete choices like gardening, planting trees, cleaning up a local park, or helping animals. For some inspiration, read books about kindness to your children. Next, help your children discover their passions. It is important that their passions drive how they give because when they are excited about a project, they can embrace it, get more out of it, and feel happier. You can start by talking to them about their talents, skills, and interests that they can harness in a positive way to help the world.

Once you identify the kinds of projects to try, choose some specific opportunities that fit your family's goals and interests. Finding the right family volunteer activities can be overwhelming. You may feel uncertain about what is expected and question whether your children can participate. It is critical that your children feel comfortable where you volunteer, get inspired by the work, and enjoy themselves. Without these three components, our children will not reap all the amazing benefits of volunteering. Plus, we want them to love helping others and the planet so they continue to do so for a lifetime.

When searching for the right activities, consider the following priorities:

Organization's Mission

Do your research before you sign up with a specific organization. Find out the group's history and how it got started, the goals and mission, who the leaders are, and how it is funded. Check the website, search online for press coverage, and visit sites like https://www.charitywatch.org and https://www.charitynavigator.org. If possible, ask a current or past volunteer about the pros and cons of the organization. Getting a referral from someone you know and trust is the best option.

Location

Search for projects close to home so you do not have to drag your kids far to volunteer. In addition, it is generally most effective to volunteer locally, where you can observe the results of your efforts with your own eyes.

Cost

Although rare, there could be a fee to volunteer. Make sure to check with each organization if you will have to pay to volunteer. You may also want to consider any other costs involved like travel, equipment, required clothing, requested products, or expected monetary donations.

Time Commitment

Decide how much time you would like to commit to volunteer work. It could be once a week, once a month, or once a year. Start slow and gradually increase your involvement if the project works out well. Or you may choose to volunteer with different organizations each time to expose your children to a wide variety of experiences.

Age Range Guidelines

Look for activities that your entire family can participate in. Before you commit to a project, check to see if there are any age requirements. It may take some hunting around, but you should be able to find age-appropriate options. Even infants can take part in charity walks and cleanups.

Activity Expectations

Before you show up, find out exactly what you will be doing. Will you have to lift heavy objects? Will you have to get down and dirty? Will the project be a boring and repetitive task that will annoy your kids? Make sure the activity is something that your children will actually enjoy before you invest your time and energy.

Safety

No matter what, safety needs to come first when children are involved. You may want to avoid locations that make you uncomfortable. Be sure to ask about heavy equipment or other materials that could be a concern with young ones around. Also, your kids may be scared to talk to strangers, so consider starting with familiar people and places. As they get older, you can venture out and expose them to more mature situations. In her book *Simple Acts: The Busy Family's Guide to Giving Back*, Natalie Silverstein also suggests that families make sure the organization maintains insurance and that all volunteer activities are supervised appropriately.[291]

Fun Factor

If it is not an enjoyable experience for your kids, then what is the point? Choose projects that involve your children in a fun way but also teach and inspire them. Consider doing volunteer projects with another family or an organized group, since volunteering with others accentuates the happiness boost as you build social connections. Finally, avoid topics and activities that are too serious and sad for young children. Be sure to engage with them afterward and ask what they thought about the experience, and if they would be willing to do it again.

How to Address Stressful Environmental Topics

As we volunteer to help protect the environment, sensitive topics may come up. Some activities might involve helping to reduce the impact from threats like climate change and pollution. For children who are just learning about these issues, they may feel vulnerable and powerless, and worry that something bad could happen to them. It is never a good idea to shelter our children, but we can approach these topics carefully so they do not form a major case of eco-anxiety.

Here are some tips:

- **Have an informative, well-thought-out discussion with them about climate change and its potential effects.** Ask them what they already know and how they feel about it. Explaining that climate change is a lengthy process and we have some time to fix it can be reassuring to children. Point out positive examples of how scientists and others are finding solutions like electric cars and solar panels.
- **Make learning about climate change and weather fun for your kids.** Look for creative kid-friendly resources to teach about climate change on a level they can grasp, such as National Geographic Kids, NASA's Climate Kids, and Our Climate Our Future. Read books, attend science education events, and visit museum exhibits to learn more. Do your own experiments at home and encourage them to choose school science projects related to addressing climate change.
- **Show your children that they can play a role in helping the planet by reducing your family's carbon footprint.** Some ideas include replacing incandescent lightbulbs with fluorescent or LED bulbs, turning off lights and other electronics when you are no longer using them, eating less meat, and carpooling to school and extracurricular activities. Just be sure to instill the message that the goal is not perfection; they should do what they can and not stress about it.
- **Avoid watching excessive television coverage of extreme weather events.** The dramatic, intense images of tornadoes, flooding, and other harsh weather associated with climate change can petrify children.
- **Reassure and comfort your children every day so they feel loved and protected no matter what challenges they face.** Build a strong relationship in which they can talk to you about their fears so they will ultimately be more resilient. Remind your children that they are helping to make a difference by volunteering!

The best remedy to feeling anxious about the environment is to get out and volunteer.

Plant a Seed, Don't Force It

As parents, we can introduce our children to the idea of volunteering at any age. The earlier we start, the more ingrained it will be in our children's lives. However, it is important not to put pressure on our kids or force them to get involved in community service. There has actually been some controversy about school programs that require students to do a certain number of volunteer hours and to track everything closely. One study found that children and teens who volunteer have increased well-being as adults. However, this only occurs if the community service was voluntary and not forced on them.[292]

Jinho Kim, PhD, who worked on the study, clarifies, "According to my findings, it is encouraged to help kids experience a variety of civic and community service work. It is crucial, however, not to force them to engage in those activities. Only when they feel that they are doing them voluntarily, [will] they internalize civic identity and cultivate volunteerism that will lead to future voluntary work."[293]

Try to keep volunteering light and fun for your kids without having to drag them to activities. Give them more control by letting them decide which volunteer work they prefer to do. Keep the dialogue open with them no matter what age they are to get feedback from them about their experiences and how it makes them feel.

Environmental Volunteerism Ideas

Environmental volunteering is more than hugging trees. There are so many intriguing ways for your family to engage in helping people, animals, and the environment while also enjoying all that nature has to offer. Try one or try them all.

Parks and Nature Centers

Local, state, and national parks and wildlife preserves often need help with projects like hiking trail maintenance, cleanups, planting trees, and removing invasive plant species. The National Park Service offers youth programs for children to volunteer their time at a park. The Resource Stewardship Scout Ranger program, for example, invites Girl Scouts and Boy Scouts to participate in volunteer service projects at national parks to provide them with the opportunity to explore and learn more about protecting our natural resources. Some parks also have nature centers where you can volunteer as a docent or help with maintenance. As I mentioned earlier, I volunteered at a nature center when I first moved to Florida to help get acquainted with the area. My role was to take visitors on guided tours and point out the wildlife during our nature walk.

This would also be fun to do with children. Check with your town, county, or state department of natural resources or department of environmental protection to find outdoor volunteer opportunities for your family. My county puts out a call for volunteer projects on a monthly basis.

Cleanups

Nature offers so much beauty; it is critical that it stays pristine and garbage-free. One way that we can help to ensure this is by participating in a trash cleanup at a park, beach, lake, river, or other location. As I mentioned earlier, volunteers can feel more connected to nature and less stressed after spending time outside cleaning up a natural area. This is a simple activity to do with your kids, either on your own or through an organized group.

Hank Barnet of Florida has made cleaning up the beach his passion hobby by using some of the materials he finds to create intriguing artwork. "The sights, sounds, and smells of our beaches have always been special to me, so I started picking up trash during my walks along the shoreline. When our triplet grandchildren started spending weekends with us as toddlers, I naturally made trips to the beach a feature of their time with Pop Pop. They are teenagers now, and although they do not come as often, the trip to the beach to clean it up is still an important part of our time together."[294]

Tree and Flower Plantings

A lovely way to beautify our world and reduce the impact of climate change is to volunteer to plant trees, flowers, or other vegetation in your community. This is such a positive, hands-on activity for children because they will get to see for themselves the impact they can have. Many towns host planting events and have goals to plant a certain number of trees annually. My daughter participated in a field trip in which her class planted trees in honor of Arbor Day. The event was held at a nearby park and organized by a local garden club.

Sasha Olsen Wants Her Ocean Back

Sasha Olsen is a girl with a drive for global awareness of current issues that need improvement. She has traveled around the world to share her passion for the educational future of children growing up in today's society, especially when it comes to climate change and the health of our oceans.

She became concerned about the ocean after seeing lots of trash left on the sand every time she visited the beach in her Florida town. Sadly, she was unable to swim or enjoy going to the beach because of how dirty and polluted the ocean was, which really bothered her. "I started looking for ways that I could help and feel better about our natural surroundings," says Sasha. "I definitely wasn't okay with letting people leave our beautiful beaches unclean. I told my mom we had to help, so we started small. Since we live so close to the beach, I would go out there with my mom and sister as much as possible. We took bins and tools and started picking up pieces of trash. There is always so much plastic!"

Image courtesy of Sasha Olsen.

Although Sasha was worried about the condition of the beach and ocean because of all the garbage, the actions she took helped boost her mood. "I really feel like we are making a difference, and it started to make me feel way happier. I am also teaching my little sister how to take care of the ocean. We have a wonderful time when we go out and clean the beach, laughing and breathing in the refreshing ocean air. It makes all of us so happy to work together to improve our beaches and the ocean. We feel so calm when we clean and listen to the waves."

She became so dedicated to this environmental cause that she started her own ocean conservation movement, #iwantmyoceanback. "Now I'm working on spreading awareness through social media and my website: https://www.iwantmyoceanback.org. This way, more people can go out and support loving our environment. So many animals have to deal with plastic waste, so I want to make a change! I want people to understand that this is urgent." She hopes to influence other children to help older generations (their parents, especially) change their habits that are damaging the ocean.[295]

Community Gardens

Community gardens increase the amount of green space and build positive community interaction, and many also provide fresh produce to those in need. Look for opportunities to volunteer in a local community garden. Your children will enjoy planting seeds, weeding, and picking fruits and vegetables. The American Community Garden Association created a handy map to help you discover the community gardens in your area that you can find on their website. They will even walk you through the steps to create your own community garden if there is not one nearby.

Local Farms

Local farms are another place to give back while enjoying the outdoors. Contact a local farm to see if they need help with activities like weeding, planting seeds, sifting compost, digging, or watering. You can also ask about or organize your own gleaning project, which involves picking leftover crops from a farmer's field after they have been commercially

harvested and donating the produce locally. My children and I partic-ipated in a gleaning project a couple of years ago in which we enjoyed picking green peppers to donate to our local food bank to help those in need.

Work with Animals

There are many ways to volunteer your time as a family to help animals, whether it be at a nature center, zoo, horse ranch, or animal shelter. Many animal shelters, for example, need volunteers to walk the dogs at their facility. You can also consider fostering a dog or cat that has been rescued. If you own a pet cat, dog, guinea pig, rabbit, or bird, you can volunteer as a human-pet team to provide animal therapy to those in need and spread joy and kindness by visiting hospitals, hospices, nursing homes or assisted care facilities, rehabilitation centers, group homes, schools, libraries, air-ports, and workplaces. The purpose of visits can vary: social visits where you make conversation with individuals to cheer them up, stress breaks, therapy sessions where patients brush the animal as a soothing exercise, read-with-me sessions, and going on walks outside. Be sure to check age requirements for these activities.

Mother-Daughter Pet Therapy Team Spreads Joy

Jen Krasnow and her teenage daughter Simone have built a special bond through their Pet Partners volunteer work together. Simone joined her mother in the pet handler training class at age eleven, and both were so excited when they passed the test and became registered as pet handlers. Jen explained, "Doing the class together was so amazing. I was so proud of Simone."

Once registered for visits with their dog, Kako, a white and fluffy golden doodle, Jen and Simone connected with a nearby health and rehabilitation facility and started visiting clients twice a month. Clients of all ages are in the rehab to recover from issues like strokes, memory lapse, or falls. Jen was so impressed with how volunteering shaped her daughter. "I will never forget when the three of us went together for the first time and Simone was so happy when she walked out. It was like she was floating on a cloud. She totally connected with the experience of Kako bringing so much joy to people. It's a really wonderful feeling."

A typical visit involves walking around the facility with Kako and going up to each person to ask if they want to meet the dog. Jen and Simone introduce themselves and try to drum up a conversation, mostly about Kako. If the person seems interested, the mother-daughter team then encourages the patient to pet Kako because it can be very soothing. They also carry around a brush in case anyone wants to brush him; this is particularly beneficial to stroke victims who have issues with mobility. They might throw in some fun commands and tricks as well to engage their audience. One time the dog put his paws up and the patient who was bedridden laughed a ton.

Simone reflected on her volunteering experience. "It makes me happy because I know that if I was in the hospital I would want someone to come visit me with a dog because dogs make me happy. I try to get people's minds off of things. I love helping to cheer them up."[296]

How a Father Is Cleaning Up His Community One Family Jog at a Time

Who would have thought picking up trash could be so inspiring? Like many Americans, Andy Thomson, City Council member in Boca Raton, Florida, made a New Year's resolution to exercise more. But what he discovered turned into a much larger endeavor to help clean up his community with his children.

"This was going to be the year that I jogged the beautiful streets of our city more often," Andy explained. "On my very first jog to the local gym, early in the morning on January 2, I noticed something: trash on our streets. Lots of it. And it really bugged me." So, he asked the staff at the gym for a small trash bag, and on the jog home he picked up as much trash as he could carry. "The next morning I ran to the gym again, but this time I brought a trash bag with me and the same thing happened—lots of trash, enough to fill up the bag. At that point, I revised my New Year's resolution: jog more AND pick up a bag of trash from my neighborhood streets each day."

After a few days of collecting all sorts of discarded items, he began bringing along his children. His two daughters rode their bikes while his son sat in the jogging stroller. They all kept their eyes peeled for trash. Working together, they picked up three or four bags filled with trash each time they went outside on their family trip around the neighborhood.

This new habit served as a positive in their lives. Andy stated, "The kids absolutely love this daily routine. They enjoy being in nature, being active, and serving our community even in this small way. My son wakes up most mornings asking 'Can we go on a trash run today?' When we were at a recent school event, he walked around the school's courtyard picking up trash." Cleaning up their city has become a way of life for this active family.

Andy began telling friends, family, and colleagues about his family's exciting new mission: cleaning up his city one jog at a time. He posted pictures on social media and challenged others to join him. The response to the family's service to the community was overwhelming. "Lots of people had suggestions for where we could clean next, but better yet, some started cleaning their own neighborhoods as they jogged or walked." This self-initiated environmental volunteering project led by one man with a simple New Year's resolution first spread to his family and then to other residents in the town that he represents and cares so deeply about. A local television news station got wind of the Thomson family's mission and featured them in a story about the impact they were having in the community. Not only were they cleaning up the streets, but they were motivating others to do the same.

Andy's efforts have been so successful that he continues to challenge himself and his community to do even more. In 2021, he committed to run every street in the city—all 475 miles—to pick up trash and to get to know the residents he serves. Through his Run the City initiative, Andy has helped remove over one thousand one hundred pounds of trash from city streets, and he has inspired about 300 volunteers to get involved.

It really is incredible what you can do as just one individual or family to make an enormous difference. Andy hopes that more people will join him wherever they are to help clean up communities one jog (or walk or bike ride) at a time.[297]

Image courtesy of Andy Thomson.

Fitness for a Cause

Imagine the benefits of combining fitness, volunteerism, and spending time in nature. Look for charitable walks or runs that support environmental causes like Humane Society's pet walk. The Sierra Club offers a program called Team Sierra in which you can set up your own goals to raise money for the organization through activities like hikes, runs, or swimming laps. There are also opportunities to play sports and take part in other outdoor activities with children in need. My children played kickball with the boys and girls at SOS Children's Villages Florida on a couple of occasions. Everyone had a lovely time running around outside together.

Nature Clubs

An excellent way for children to get involved in ongoing nature volunteer projects is to join a nature club or to start your own. The goal of nature clubs is to connect children to nature through educational, recreational, and volunteer experiences. As mentioned before, Girl Scouts does work in this area and could be an option for your daughter, as well as Boy Scouts for your son. Roots & Shoots is another wonderful option. It was created by the renowned environmentalist Dr. Jane Goodall to empower and encourage youth of all ages to pursue their passion, mobilize their peers, and become compassionate citizens and leaders to ensure a better future for people, animals, and the environment. There are over 2,100 registered groups in all fifty states, so you are bound to find one in your neighborhood.

Wildlife biologist and mom Rachel Mazur loves volunteering with her children and decided to write a children's book series called *The Nature Club Books* to encourage more children to get involved with environmental volunteering. "I have found that kids enjoy volunteering if you tie it into wildlife or nature," she explains. "As a wildlife biologist, I want every child to grow up and know that part of life is to volunteer and help nature. Volunteering makes you feel good and that you are really doing something to make a difference." Her books focus on school-aged

characters in a nature club of their own, and she has received feedback from many readers that the stories inspired them to start their own nature clubs.[298] If you are looking to start your own nature club with your kids, the Children & Nature Network provides a Nature Clubs for Families Tool Kit: Do It Yourself! Do It Now! to provide inspiration, information, tips, and resources to help you get started. [299]

Citizen Science

Citizen science, which involves volunteering to collect scientific data, is a way for children to gain science experience and help the scientific community. It has also been found to benefit both the physical and mental development of children.[300] There are citizen science opportunities for kids of all ages and levels. Your family can get involved in your own backyard or through a more organized group like a school nature or science club. You can use apps to input data and images, including the geographic location of specific species. For example, elementary school students who participate in Global Learning and Observations to Benefit the Environment (GLOBE) Program observe clouds, measure rain, track bird activity, and take note of tree diversity.[301]

Where to Find Citizen Science Opportunities

There are many citizen science programs ready for your family to help. Besides the national programs included below, you can check with your county or state department of natural resources for ways to get involved.

Databases
- **CitizenScience.gov.** This searchable database provides a government-wide listing of citizen science projects.
- **SciStarter.** This database contains more than three thousand vetted projects and events searchable by location, topic, interest, and more.
- **Zooniverse.** This is the world's largest and most popular platform for people-powered volunteer research.

Projects
- **Audubon Christmas Bird Count.** Initiated in 1900, this is the nation's longest-running citizen science bird project. The bird count runs from December 14 through January 5 each year.
- **Cornell Lab of Ornithology.** The lab has several bird-related citizen science programs, including NestWatch, Project FeederWatch, and Great Backyard Bird Count.
- **FrogWatch USA.** This is part of the Association of Zoos and Aquariums in which participants report the mating calls of local frogs and toads.
- **Monarch Watch from University of Kansas.** This program involves tagging and tracking monarch butterflies during their annual North American migration.
- **National Geographic BioBlitz.** This event focuses on finding and identifying as many species as possible in a specific area over a short period to get a snapshot of biodiversity.
- **Project Budburst.** With climate change being its focus, this project involves monitoring the leafing, flowering, and fruiting of plants.

Random Acts of Kindness

Finally, your children can partake in many small acts of kindness on any given day. Actually, there are some special days designated for spreading kindness to mark on your family calendar: February 17 is National Random Acts of Kindness Day, World Kindness Day is November 13, and Make A Difference Day takes place annually on the fourth Saturday in October. And, of course, during the month of April when Earth Day takes place, there are always so many environmental projects and events to join. Here are some ideas to spread kindness that involve nature:

- Walk a neighbor's dog.
- Rake or weed a neighbor's yard.
- Grow your own flowers and give them out at a nursing home.
- Compost and then give the rich soil you created to a local community garden.
- Grow your own vegetables in your garden and donate them to a local food bank or soup kitchen.
- Give out seeds, plants, or tree saplings to neighbors or people who live in areas lacking greenery.

- Take your kids on a nature walk to collect items like sticks, fallen leaves and flower petals, pebbles, and so on, and ask them to use what they find to create get-well cards to distribute.

Where to Find Environmental Volunteer Opportunities

- Contact your city or county's sustainability or environmental director.
- Search for environmental organizations in your area.
- Check out Tree City USA, Garden Club of America, and the American Community Garden Association to discover opportunities related to plantings and community gardens.
- Find beach cleanups through Ocean Conservancy, Surfrider Foundation, 4ocean, and volunteercleanup.org.
- Check these service websites:
  - https://www.allforgood.org
  - https://www.doinggoodtogether.org
  - https://www.eventbrite.com
  - https://www.idealist.org
  - https://www.justserve.org
  - https://www.meetup.com
  - https://www.volunteermatch.org

Activity Checklist

ü Introduce the idea of volunteering to your children by reading books about kindness and sharing stories about your own volunteer experiences.

ü Present environmental volunteering options to your kids, such as gardening, planting trees, cleaning up the beach, or helping animals.

ü Choose the type of project—maybe have your family vote on it. If your kids have different ideas, consider rotating projects monthly.

ü Look for local organizations or events offering the type of projects your family is interested in doing.

ü Once you identify some possibilities, research the organization's mission and the location, cost, time commitment, age guidelines, and expectations of the project. This may involve checking websites, calling the organization, and asking friends about their experience volunteering with that group.

ü Prepare your children for the volunteer activity by discussing what you will be doing and why it is important.

ü Enjoy the experience!

ü Touch base with your children after the volunteer activity to find out what they liked about it and how the experience made them feel.

ü Capture your volunteer activities by asking your children to write about them in a giving journal or create a scrapbook or slide show of your family's volunteer activities.

ü Choose your next activity and invite friends along.

Resources

Organizations

All for Good: https://www.allforgood.org

American Community Garden Association: https://www
.communitygarden.org

CitizenScience.gov: https://www.citizenscience.gov

Doing Good Together: https://www.doinggoodtogether.org/volunteer-together-local

4ocean: https://www.4ocean.com

Garden Club of America: https://www.gcamerica.org

Idealist: https://www.idealist.org

JustServe: https://www.justserve.org

NASA's Climate Kids: https://climatekids.nasa.gov

National Geographic Kids: https://kids.nationalgeographic.com

Ocean Conservancy: https://oceanconservancy.org/trash-free-seas/international-coastal-cleanup/volunteer

Our Climate Our Future: https://ourclimateourfuture.org
Roots & Shoots: https://www.rootsandshoots.org
SciStarter: https://scistarter.org
Surfrider Foundation: https://www.surfrider.org/programs/
    beach-cleanups
Tree City USA: https://www.arborday.org/programs/treecityusa
VolunteerCleanup.org: https://www.volunteercleanup.org
VolunteerMatch: https://www.volunteermatch.org
Zooniverse: https://www.zooniverse.org

Books

Citizen Science Guide for Families: Taking Part in Real Science by Greg Landgraf

Doing Good Together: 101 Easy, Meaningful Service Projects for Families, Schools, and Communities by Jenny Friedman, PhD

The Field Guide to Citizen Science: How You Can Contribute to Scientific Research and Make a Difference by Darlene Cavalier, Catherine Hoffman, and Caren Cooper

Growing Sustainable Together: Practical Resources for Raising Kind, Engaged, Resilient Children by Shannon Brescher Shea

How to Talk to Your Kids about Climate Change: Turning Angst into Action by Harriet Shugarman

Simple Acts: The Busy Family's Guide to Giving Back by Natalie Silverstein, MPH

Children's Books

Bella Saves the Beach by Nancy Stewart

Can We Help?: Kids Volunteering to Help Their Communities by George Ancona

The Everything Kids' Environment Book by Sheri Amsel

Kids Can Help the Environment by Emily Raij

The Kid's Guide to Service Projects: Over 500 Service Ideas for Young People Who Want to Make a Difference by Barbara A. Lewis
The Nature Club Books series by Rachel Mazur

❧ CONCLUSION ❧

How Your Nature Habit Can Heal Your Family . . . and the Planet

THANK YOU for sticking with me. If you have found just one new nature-related activity for your family to enjoy together, then I have done my job. Whether you decide to start a family garden in your backyard, practice nature meditation with your kids before bedtime, or do something huge like booking an ecotourism trip in another country, you have found ecohappiness. Nature has so much to offer us if we open up all our senses to receive these extraordinary gifts.

I hope that your family's nature habit helps you all feel happier, healthier, and calmer. I invite you to return to this book often as your tool kit to spark fresh ideas and to find support on your ecohappiness journey.

The details of the numerous nature activities highlighted throughout this book are simply stepping-stones to reach the ultimate result, however. This nature habit you have started to build for your family does so much for you, your children, and beyond. By turning to nature, we can improve our mental health, our communities, and our planet. My goal is to open your eyes to the tremendous ways that nature helps us thrive.

Now that you know how beneficial nature is to your family's well-being, will you try to save it?

It is ironic that nature is ready and willing to provide us with the solution to help us feel more joyful, positive, and energetic, but we do not always treat our natural environment with the admiration and respect that it deserves. We are facing multiple threats to our environment from climate change to plastic pollution to overdevelopment, among other catastrophes. While this book focuses on how nature improves our children's mental health, there is a much larger picture to consider.

The next step beyond recognizing nature's healing power is to protect it for the future. If the local park turns into a shopping center, where will your children play? If the nearby lake or river fills with garbage, how will your kids swim and fish? If habitats are ruined, how will our children ever experience the awe and pleasure of watching various species of birds fly in the sky? In essence, how we treat our natural environment is a reflection of how we treat ourselves, our children, and all living things. And this impacts *all* our happiness.

In addition to helping families find a natural solution to stress, I wrote this book to shine a light on why mental health should be part of the environmental movement. This has been a missing piece for far too long. The bottom line is that we need to protect our environment for many critical reasons, including our mental health.

I also deeply believe that happy, balanced people do not hurt others. If more people utilize these happiness tools and learn to cherish nature's treasures, then our world will ultimately be safer and more peaceful. Isn't that what we all want anyway?

Keep challenging yourself to do more, go a little bit deeper, and experience something out of the ordinary. Try new activities, visit different places you have never explored, and experiment with what brings ecohappiness to your family. Then share your experiences and the tremendous benefits of nature with friends and strangers alike, and pay it forward by volunteering your time to help others and the planet. That is how we will see our world progress and transform for the better.

I believe that books enter our lives at the right moment, when we need to hear the message. No matter how you discovered this book or what background and experience you brought with you, I hope your time connecting to these pages brings you and your family immense joy and peace for many years to come.

Our adventure together does not end here. I cannot wait to learn all about the new, thrilling nature activities that your family discovers along the way. Please stay connected, share your stories, and unlock more eco-happiness tips and ideas on my website, www.ecohappinessproject.com.

Notes

1. Child Mind Institute, *Children's Mental Health Report*, 2017, https://childmind.org/downloads/2017-CMHR- PDF.pdf.

2. Centers for Disease Control and Prevention, "Data and Statistics on Children's Mental Health," June 15, 2020, https://www.cdc.gov/childrens-mentalhealth/data.html.

3. C.M. Mott Children's Hospital, Michigan Medicine, *Mott Poll Report: Top Health Concerns for Kids in 2020 During the Pandemic*, December 21, 2020, https://mottpoll.org/reports/top-health-concerns-kids-2020-during-pandemic.

4. Mathew White et al., "Spending at Least 120 Minutes a Week in Nature Is Associated with Good Health and Wellbeing," *Scientific Reports* 9 (2019).

5. Stephen R. Kellert et al., *The Nature of Americans: Disconnection and Recommendations for Reconnection National Report*, The Nature of Americans, April 2017, https://natureofamericans.org/sites/default/files/reports/Nature-of-Americans_National_Report_1.3_4-26-17.pdf.

6. George MacKerron and Susana Mourato, "Happiness Is Greater in Natural Environments," *Global Environmental Change: Human and Policy Dimensions* 23, no. 5 (2013): 992–1000.

7. Kristine Engemann et al., "Residential Green Space in Childhood Is Associated with Lower Risk of Psychiatric Disorders from Adolescence into Adulthood," *Proceedings of the National Academy of Sciences of the United States of America* 116 (2019): 5188–93.

8. Won Kim et al., "The Effect of Cognitive Behavior Therapy-Based Psychotherapy Applied in a Forest Environment on Physiological Changes and Remission of Major Depressive Disorder," *Psychiatry Investigation* 6, no. 4 (2009): 245–54.

9. Take Care Campaign, "Nature: No App Required," https://take-care.org/films/nature-no-app-required, accessed November 30, 2020.

10. Eva M. Selhub and Alan C. Logan, *Your Brain on Nature* (Toronto: Collins, 2012).

11 Stephen R. Kellert, *Nature by Design: The Practice of Biophilic Design* (New Haven, CT: Yale University Press, 2018).

12. Adam Alter, *Drunk Tank Pink* (New York: Penguin Books, 2013).

13. Courtney E. Ackerman, "What Is Kaplan's Attention Restoration Theory (ART)?," PositivePsychology.com, November 9, 2020, https://positivepsychology.com/attention-restoration-theory.

14. Florence Williams, *The Nature Fix* (New York: Norton, 2018).

15. Hyunju Jo, Chorong Song, and Yoshifumi Miyazaki, "Physiological Benefits of Viewing Nature: A Systematic Review of Indoor Experiments," *International Journal of Environmental Research and Public Health* 16, no. 23 (2019).

16. Natalie Angier, "True Blue Stands Out in an Earthly Crowd," *New York Times*, October 12, 2012.

17. Qing Li, *Forest Bathing: How Trees Can Help You Find Health and Happiness* (New York: Viking, 2018).

18. Kelly E. Robles et al., "A Shared Fractal Aesthetic across Development," *Humanities and Social Sciences Communications* 7 (2020): 1–8.

19. Alistair Griffiths et al., *Your Well-Being Garden: How to Make Your Garden Good for You* (London: DK, 2020).

20. Healthy Food House, "The Smell of the Rain Reduces Stress and 7 Other Benefits of Walking in the Rain," July 22, 2019, https://www.healthyfoodhouse.com/the-smell-of-the-rain-reduces-stress-and-7-other-benefits-of-walking-in-the-rain.

21. Sara Altshul, "The Healing Power of Pine," *Health*, December 5, 2012. http://www.health.com/health/article/0,,20428734,00.html.

22. Jereme Spiers, Hsiao Chen, and Nikolas Lavidis, "Stress Alleviating Plant-Derived 'Green Odors': Behavioral, Neurochemical and Neuroendocrine Perspectives in Laboratory Animals," *Phytochemistry Reviews* 14, no. 5 (2014): 713–25.

23. Tapanee Hongratanaworakit, "Stimulating Effect of Aromatherapy Massage with Jasmine Oil," *Natural Product Communications* 5, no. 1 (2010): 157–62.

24. Cassandra Gould van Praag et al., "Mind-Wandering and Alterations to Default Mode Network Connectivity When Listening to Naturalistic versus Artificial Sounds," *Scientific Reports* 7 (2017).

25. Jesper Alvarsson, Stefan Wiens, and Mats Nilsson, "Stress Recovery during Exposure to Nature Sound and Environmental Noise," *International Journal of Environmental Research and Public Health* 7, no. 3 (2010): 1036–46.

26. Selhub and Logan, *Your Brain on Nature*.

27. "The Meditative Power of Swimming," *Psychologies*, April 25, 2013, https://www.psychologies.co.uk/self/the-meditative-power-of-swimming.html.

28. Ashley Blacow and Wallace J. Nichols, "The Ocean's Effects on the Mind," *San Francisco Chronicle*, May 29, 2016, http://www.sfchronicle.com/opinion/openforum/article/The-ocean-s-effects-on-the-mind-7952579.php?t=01f2675c91cefdcb88&cmpid=twitter-premium.

29. Mireia Gascon et al., "Outdoor Blue Spaces, Human Health and Well-being: A Systematic Review of Quantitative Studies," *International Journal of Hygiene and Environmental Health* 220, no. 8 (2017): 1207–21.

30. Wallace J. Nichols, *Blue Mind: The Surprising Science That Shows How Being Near, In, On, or Under Water Can Make You Happier, Healthier, More Connected, and Better at What You Do* (New York: Little, Brown, 2014).

31. Adam Hadhazy, "Why Does the Sound of Water Help You Sleep?," *Live Science*, January 18, 2016, http://www.livescience.com/53403-why-sound-of-water-helps-you-sleep.html.

32. Kellert, *Nature by Design*.

33. Healthychildren.org, "Winter Blues and Seasonal Affective Disorder," American Academy of Pediatrics, https://www.healthychildren.org/English/health-issues/conditions/emotional-problems/Pages/Winter-Blues-Seasonal-Affective-Disorder-and-Depression.aspx, accessed November 30, 2020.

34. Qing Li, *Forest Bathing: How Trees Can Help You Find Health and Happiness* (New York: Viking, 2018).

35. Li, *Forest Bathing*.

36. Chorong Song et al., "Psychological Benefits of Walking through Forest Areas," *International Journal of Environmental Research and Public Health* 15, no. 12 (2018).

37. Ernest Bielinis et al., "The Effect of Winter Forest Bathing on Psychological Relaxation of Young Polish Adults," *Urban Forestry & Urban Greening* 29 (2018): 276–83.

38. Selhub and Logan, *Your Brain on Nature*.

39. Ben Long, "Urban Trees Found to Improve Mental and General Health," Phys.org, July 26, 2019, https://phys.org/news/2019-07-urban-trees-mental-health.html/

40. Melissa Breyer, "5 Health Benefits of Houseplants," Treehugger, November 23, 2020, http://www.treehugger.com/health/5-health-benefits-houseplants.html.

41. Yun-Ah Oh, Seon-Ok Kim, and Sin-Ae Park, "Real Foliage Plants as Visual Stimuli to Improve Concentration and Attention in Elementary Students," *International Journal of Environmental Research and Public Health* 16, no. 5 (2019).

42. Li, *Forest Bathing*.

43. Williams, *The Nature Fix*.

44. Williams, *The Nature Fix*.

45. Vanessa Perez, Dominik Alexander, and William Bailey, "Air Ions and Mood Outcomes: A Review and Meta-analysis," *BMC Psychiatry* 13 (2013): 29.

46. Selhub and Logan, *Your Brain on Nature*.

47. Peter Dockrill, "Just Looking at Photos of Nature Could Be Enough to Lower Your Work Stress Levels," *ScienceAlert*, March 23, 2016, http://www.sciencealert.com/just-looking-at-photos-of-nature-could-be-enough-to-lower-your-work-stress-levels.

48. Selhub and Logan, *Your Brain on Nature*.

49. I found the following: Ethan A. McMahan and David Estes, "The Effect of Contact with Natural Environments on Positive and Negative Affect: A Met-Analysis," *Journal of Positive Psychology 10*, no. 6 (2015): 507–19, https://doi.org/10.1080/17439760.2014.994224.

50. Nicola Yeo et al., "What Is the Best Way of Delivering Virtual Nature for Improving Mood?: An Experimental Comparison of High Definition TV, 360º Video, and Computer Generated Virtual Reality," *Journal of Environmental Psychology* 72 (2020): 101500.

51. Jon Katat-Zinn, Mindfulness.com, http://www.mindfulnesscds.com/pages/about-the-author.

52. Emily Campbell, "Mindfulness in Education Research Highlights," *Greater Good Magazine*, September 16, 2014, http://greatergood.berkeley.edu/article/item/mindfulnessineducationresearchhighlights

53. Daniel J. Siegel and Tina Payne Bryson, *The Whole-Brain Child: 12 Revolutionary Strategies to Nurture Your Child's Developing Mind* (New York: Bantam Books, 2011).

54. Cortney Cameron and Natalia Clarke, *Nature Therapy Walks: 22 Sensory Activities to Enjoy in Nature for Wellbeing* (Cortney Cameron, 2020).

55. Mark Coleman, Mindful Living Summit, March 19–22, 2020, https://www.mindfullivingsummit.com.

56. Zemirah Jazwierska, "Over the Rainbow Breathing," *Kids Relaxation* (blog), November 30, 2013, https://kidsrelaxation.com/deep-breathing/over-the-rainbow-breathing.

57. Mellisa Dormoy, phone interview with author, July 17, 2020.

58. Ariel Kusby, "An Intro to Flower Gazing Meditation," *Garden Collage Magazine*, February 13, 2017, https://gardencollage.com/heal/mind-spirit/intro-flower-gazing-meditation.

59. Mellisa Dormoy, phone interview with author, July 17, 2020.

60. Gretchen Cuda, "Just Breathe: Body Has a Built-In Stress Reliever," NPR, December 6, 2010, http://www.npr.org/2010/12/06/131734718/just-breathe-body-has-a-built-in-stress-reliever.

61. Rachael Link, "13 Benefits of Yoga That Are Supported by Science," *Healthline*, August 30, 2017, https://www.healthline.com/ nutrition/13-benefits-of-yoga.

62. Giselle Shardlow, phone interview with author, August 13, 2020.

63. Simon Meechan and Marthe de Ferrer, "You Now Can Take Yoga Classes with Lemurs—No, We're Not Joking!," *Leicestershire Live*, April 3, 2019, https://www.leicestermercury.co.uk/news/uk-world-news/you-now-can-take-yoga-2718147.

64. Jenn Jones Nienaber, email correspondence with author, August 12, 2020.

65. Sandra Whitehouse et al., "Evaluating a Children's Hospital Garden Environment: Utilization and Consumer Satisfaction," *Journal of Environmental Psychology* 21, no. 3 (2001): 301–14.

66. Kristine Arbolario, "What's Earthing and Why Is It Healthy for the Body?," *Medical Daily*, August 27, 2019, https://www.medicaldaily.com/whats-earthing-and-why-it-healthy-body-441567.

67. Sophie Qureshi, "Can Spending More Time Outside Really Have a Significant Impact on Your Health?," *Grazia*, July 21, 2019, https://grazia-daily.co.uk/life/health-fitness/benefits-of-being-outside.

68. Li, *Forest Bathing*.

69. Kyng-Sook Bang et al., "The Effects of a Health Promotion Program Using Urban Forests and Nursing Student Mentors on the Perceived and Psychological Health of Elementary School Children in Vulnerable Populations," *International Journal of Envi ronmental Research and Public Health* 15, no. 8 (2018).

70. Stone Kraushaar, phone interview with author, June 25, 2019.

71. Cameron and Clarke, *Nature Therapy Walks*.

72. Nichols, *Blue Mind*.

73. Justin Feinstein et al., "Examining the Short-Term Anxiolytic and Antidepres sant Effect of Floatation-REST," *PLoS ONE 13*, no. 2 (2018).

74. Nichols, *Blue Mind*.

75. David Delgado, Greater Good Science Center's The Art and Science of Awe conference, June 4, 2016, http://greatergood.berkeley.edu/newsevents/event/the_art_and_science_of awe.

76. Dacher Keltner and Jonathan Haidt, "Approaching Awe, a Moral, Spiritual, and Aesthetic Emotion," *Cognition and Emotion* 17 (2003): 297–314.

77. Hari Srinivasan, "Toward a Life of Meaning: In Conversation with UC Berkeley Professor Dacher Keltner," *Daily Californian,* January 24, 2020, https://www.dailycal.org/2020/01/24/toward-a-life-of-meaning-uc- berkeley-professor- dacher-keltner/.

78. Paul K. Piff et al., "Awe, the Small Self, and Prosocial Behavior," *Journal of Personality and Social Psychology* 108, no. 6 (2015): 883–99.

79. Michelle Shiota, Dacher Keltner, and Amanda Mossman, "The Nature of Awe: Elicitors, Appraisals, and Effects *on Self-Concept,"* Cognition *and Emotion* 21, no. 5 (2007): 944–63.

80. EurekAlert!, "Teaching Creativity to Children from a Galaxy Away," American Association for the Advancement of Science, May 17, 2012, http://www.eurekalert.org/pubreleases/2012-05/afottct051712.php.

81. Paul Piff, "Awe and the Greater Good: How Awe Can Inspire—and Be Inspired by—Acts of Altruism and Moral Courage," Greater Good Science Center's The Art and Science of Awe conference, June 4, 2016, http://greatergood.berkeley.edu/news_events/event/the_art_and_science_of_awe.

82. Adam Hoffman, "*How Awe Makes Us Generous," Greater Good Magazine,* August 3, 2015, http://greatergood.berkeley.edu/article/item/how_awe_makes_us_generous.

83. Melanie Rudd, Kathleen Vohs, and Jennifer Aaker, "Awe Expands People's Perception of Time, Alters Decision Making, and Enhances Well-Being," *Psychological Science* 23, no. 10 (2012): 1130–36.

84. Michael F. Steger, Laboratory for the Study of Meaning and Quality of Life, http://www.michaelfsteger.com/?page_id=113.

85. Louie Schwartzberg, *Wonder and Awe,* filmed December 3, 2016, Los Angeles, TEDx video, https://movingart.com/wonder-awe-tedxla/.

86. Heidi Wachter, "Awestruck," *Experience Life,* December 2015, https://experiencelife.com/article/awestruck/.

87. Yasmin Anwar, "Can Awe Boost Health?," *Greater Good Magazine,* February 12, 2015, https://greater-good.berkeley.edu/article/item/awe_boosts_health.

88. Michiel van Elk et al., "The Neural Correlates of the Awe Experience: Reduced Default Mode Network Activity during Feelings of Awe," *Human Brain Mapping* 40, no. 12 (2019): 3561–74.

89. Keltner and Haidt, "Approaching Awe."

90. Craig L. Anderson, Maria Monroy, and Dacher Keltner, "Awe in Nature Heals: Evidence from Military Veterans, At-Risk Youth, and College Students," *Emotion* 18, no. 8 (2018): 1195–1202.

91. Jonah Paquette, *Awestruck: How Embracing Wonder Can Make You Happier, Healthier, and More Connected?* (Boulder, CO: Shambala Publications, 2020).

92. Robert A. Emmons, *Thanks! How the New Science of Gratitude Can Make You Happier* (New York: Houghton Mifflin, 2007).

93. Goldie Hawn, *10 Mindful Minutes* (New York: Penguin Group, 2011).

94. Kassy Eichele, phone interview with author, March 23, 2020.

95. Andy Tix, "Nurturing Awe in Kids," *Reflections on Mystery and Awe* (blog), September 26, 2015, https://mysteryandawe.wordpress.com/2015/09/26/nurturing-awe-in-kids/.

96. Louie Schwartzberg, Earth Day Live 2020 interview, April 22, 2020, https://www.earthday.org/earth-day-2020/earth- day-live/.

97. Alice Chirico, Francesco Ferrise, Lorenzo Cordella, and Andrea Gaggioli, "Designing Awe in Virtual Reality: An Experimental Study," *Frontiers in Psychology* (2018), https://doi.org/10.3389/fpsyg.2017.02351.

98. Richard Louv, *Last Child in the Woods: Saving Our Children From Nature-Deficit Disorder* (Chapel Hill, NC: Algonquin Books of Chapel Hill, 2008).

99. Business Wire, "Survey Finds Today's Children Are Spending 35% Less Time Playing Freely Outside," press release, September 20, 2018, https://www.businesswire.com/news/home/20180920005526/en/Survey-Finds-Today%E2%80%99s-Children-Are-Spending-35-Less-Time-Playing-Freely-Outside.

100. Stephen Moss, *Natural Childhood*, National Trust, 2012, https://nt.global.ssl.fastly.net/documents/read-our-natural- childhood-report.pdf.

101. Victoria Rideout and Michael B. Robb, T*he Common Sense Census: Media Use by Tweens and Teens* (San Francisco: Common Sense Media, 2019).

102. Peter Gray, "Free Play Is Essential for Normal Emotional Development," *Psychology Today*, June, 21, 2012, https://www.psychologytoday.com/blog/freedom-learn/201206/free-play-is-essential-normal-emotional-development.

103. Alan Mozes, "City Parks Are a Mood Booster," *WedMD*, August 20, 2019, https://www.webmd.com/balance/news/20190820/city-parks-are- a-mood-booster#1.

104. Dawn Coe et al., "Children's Physical Activity Levels and Utilization of a Traditional versus Natural Playground," Chi*ldren, Youth and Environments* 24, no. 3 (2014): 1.

105. Children & Nature Network, "Green Schoolyards Can Provide Mental Healthy Benefits," (infographic), 2016, https://www.childrenandnature.org/wp-content/uploads/2015/03/CNN_2016GSY_MentalHlth_d5.pdf.

106. Ken Finch, *A Parents' Guide to Nature Play: How to Give Your Children More Outdoor Play . . . and Why You Should!*, Green Hearts Institute for Nature in Childhood, 2009, http://www.greenheartsinc.org/uploads/A_Parents Guide_to_Nature_Play.pdf.

107. Linda Åkeson McGurk, *There's No Such Thing as Bad Weather: A Scandinavian Mom's Secrets for Raising Healthy, Resilient, and Confident Kids* (from *Friluftsliv to Hygge*) (New York: Touchstone, 2017).

108. Angela J. Hanscom, *Balanced and Barefoot: How Unrestricted Outdoor Play Makes for Strong, Confident, and Capable Children* (Oakland: New Harbinger Publications, 2016).

109. Hanscom, *Balanced and Barefoot*.

110. Finch, A *Parents' Guide to Nature Play*.

111. National Wildlife Federation, "Connecting Kids and Nature," https://www.nwf.org/Kids-and-Family/Connecting-Kids-and-Nature.

112. Finch, *A Parents' Guide to Nature Play*.

113. Louv, *Last Child in the Woods*.

114. Lorien Nesbitt et al., "Who Has Access to Urban Vegetation? A Spatial Analysis of Distributional Green Equity in 10 US Cities," *Landscape and Urban Planning* 181 (2019): 5179.

115. "Impact: How We Started the Green Exercise Revolution," University of Essex, https://www.essex.ac.uk/research/showcase/how-we-started-the-green-exercise-revolution.

116. Harvard Health Publishing, "Exercising to Relax: How Does Exercise Reduce Stress? Surprising Answers to This Question and More," Harvard Medical School, July 7, 2020, http://www.health.harvard.edu/staying-healthy/exercising-to-relax.

117. Robin Madell, "Exercise as Stress Relief," *Healthline*, March 26, 2020, http://www.healthline.com/health/heart-disease/exercise-stress-relief#2.

118. Gregory N. Bratman et al., "The Benefits of Nature Experience: Improved Affect and Cognition," *Landscape and Urban Planning* 138 (2015): 41–50.

119. Tytti P. Pasanen et al., "Can Nature Walks with Psychological Tasks Improve Mood, Self-Reported Restoration, and Sustained Attention? Results from Two Experimental Field Studies," *Frontiers in Psychology* 9 (2018).

120. Jennifer Pharr Davis and Brew Davis, *Families on Foot: Urban Hikes to Backyard Treks and National Park Adventures* (Falcon Guides, 2017).

121. Petr Šrámek et al., "Human Physiological Responses to Immersion into Water of Different Temperatures," *European Journal of Applied Physiology* 81 (2000): 436–42.

122. Julie Gilchrist and Erin M. Parker, "Racial/Ethnic Disparities in Fatal Unintentional Drowning Among Persons Aged ≤29 Years—United States, 1999–2010," *Morbidity and Mortality Weekly Report* 63, no. 19 (2014): 421–26.

123. Maui Goodbeer, phone interview with author, January 7, 2021.

124. *The Green Parent*, "5 Ways to Get Active with Kids," January 31, 2018, https://thegreenparent.co.uk/articles/read/5-ways-to-get-active-with-kids.

125. Amit Kumar, Matthew A. Killingsworth, and Thomas Gilovich, "Waiting for Merlot: Anticipatory Consumption of Experiential and Material Purchases," *Psychological Science* 25, no. 10 (October 2014): 1924–31.

126. Peter Gray, *Free to Learn* (New York: Basic Books, 2013).

127. Hanscom, *Balanced and Barefoot*.

128. The International Ecotourism Society (TIES), https://eco-tourism.org.

129. Chris Fagan, phone interview with author, September 2, 2020.

130. Audrey Monke, *Happy Campers: 9 Summer Camp Secrets for Raising Kids Who Become Thriving Adults* (New York: Center Street, 2019).

131. Jamie Lynn Langley, "Nature-Deficit Disorder: Implications on Mental Health and How Nature Play Therapy Can Help" (presentation during Tennessee Conference on Social Welfare, August 28, 2020).

132. Jamie Lynn Langley, phone interview with author, November 9, 2020.

133. Cheryl Fisher, *Mindfulness and Nature-Based Therapeutic Techniques for Children: Creative Activities for Emotion Regulation, Resilience and Connectedness* (Eau Claire, WI: PESI Publishing & Media, 2019).

134. Cory Stieg, "What Is Wilderness Therapy & How Can It Help You," *Refinery* 29, July 5, 2019, https://www.refinery29.com/en-us/wilderness-therapy.

135. Louv, *Last Child in the Woods*.

136. Aspiro, "Wilderness Therapy Programs: A Comprehensive Guide for Parents," 2019, https://aspiroadventure.com/wp-content/uploads/2019/03/Wilderness-Therapy-Program.pdf.

137. Second Nature, "Why Wilderness Therapy Is Effective," May 22, 2019, https://www.second-nature.com/blog/why-wilderness-therapy-is-effective.

138. American Art Therapy Association, "Definition Document," June 2017, https://www.arttherapy.org/upload/2017DefinitionofProfession.pdf.

139. Daisy Fancourt and Saoirse Finn, *What Is the Evidence on the Role of the Arts in Improving Health and Well-being? A Scoping Review* (Copenhagen:

WHO Regional Office for Europe, 2019), https://apps.who.int/iris/bit-stream/handle/10665/329834/9789289054553- eng.pdf.

140. Girija Kaimal, Kendra D. Ray, and Juan Muniz, "Reduction of Cortisol Levels and Participants' Responses Following Art Making," *Art Therapy* 33, no. 2 (2016): 74–80.

141. Functional Diagnostic Nutrition, "Here's What Happens When You Color," http://functionaldiagnosticnutrition.com/stress-management-benefits-coloring-adults/.

142. Dana Dovey, "The Therapeutic Science of Adult Coloring Books: How This Childhood Pastime Helps Adults Relieve Stress," *Medical Daily*, October 8, 2015, http://www.medicaldaily.com/therapeutic-science-adult-coloring-books-how-childhood-pastime-helps- adults-356280.

143. Dovey, "The Therapeutic Science of Adult Coloring Books."

144. Ruth Atchley, David Strayer, and Paul Atchley, "Creativity in the Wild: Improving Creative Reasoning through Immersion in Natural Settings," *PLoS ONE* 7, no. 12 (2012).

145. Richard Louv, *Vitamin N: The Essential Guide to a Nature-Rich Life* (Chapel Hill, NC: Algonquin Books of Chapel Hill, 2016).

146. Lydia Anderson, email correspondence with author regarding Lee Foster-Wilson's new book, *The Grown-Up's Guide to Making Art with Kids: 25+ Fun and Easy Projects to Inspire You and the Little Ones in Your Life*, June 28, 2019.

147. Deborah Bazer and Lahri Bond, phone interview with author, July 31, 2020.

148. Kimberly Monaghan, *Organic Crafts: 75 Earth-Friendly Art Activities* (Chicago: Chicago Review Press, 2007).

149. Leave No Trace, "The 7 Principles," https://lnt.org/why/7-principles/.

150. Deborah Bazer and Lahri Bond, phone interview with author, July 31, 2020.

151. Kin Ming Chan and Karen Horneffer-Ginter, PhD, "Emotional Expression and Psychological Symptoms: A Comparison of Writing and Drawing," *Arts in Psychotherapy* 33, no.1 (2006): 26–36.

152. James W. Pennebaker, "Writing About Emotional Experiences as a Therapeutic Process," *Psychological Science* 8 (1997): 162–66.

153. Paula Peeters, *Make a Date with Nature: An Introduction to Nature Journaling* (Sandgate, Australia: Paula Peeters Productions, 2016).

154. John Muir Laws and Emilie Lygren, *How to Teach Nature Journaling: Curiosity, Wonder, Attention* (Berkeley, CA: Heyday, 2020).

155. Kelly Pfeiffer, email correspondence with author, August 7, 2020.

156. Peeters, *Make a Date with Nature*.

157. Harriet Levin, "Poetry Walk: Let Your Students Improve Their Writing as They Take a Walk," Poetry Foundation, https://www.poetryfoundation. org/articles/70286/poetry-walk.

158. Sound-Mind.org, Photography: A Fun Stress Management Skill" (blog), http://www.sound-mind.org/stress-management-skill.html#. V6yz1o-cEVM.

159. Meghan Kluth, "Riverwoods Program Helps Veterans Heal through Nature Photography," *ABC 7 Eyewitness News*, July 12, 2019, https://abc-7chicago.com/health/riverwoods-program-helps-veterans-heal-with-nature-photography/5391910/.

160. Ruth Davey, phone interview with author, October 5, 2020.

161. Rachel C. Sumner, Samantha Hughes, and Diane M. Crone, *Engage with Your Community with Fresh Eyes: Preliminary Evaluation of Mindful Photography as an Intervention to Support Wellbeing* (Cheltenham, UK: University of Gloucestershire, 2019).

162. Scott D. Sampson, *How to Raise a Wild Child: The Art and Science of Falling in Love with Nature* (New York: Mariner Books, 2016).

163. Suzi Eszterhas, phone interview with author, September 23, 2020.

164. Childhood by Nature, "Mandalas: A Practically Perfect Form of Nature Art" (blog), October 22, 2019, https://childhoodbynature.com/mandalas-a-practically-perfect-form-of-nature-art/.

165. M. Petterson, "Music for Healing: The Creative Arts Program at the Ireland Cancer Center," *Alternative Therapies in Health and Medicine* 7, no. 1 (2001): 88–9.

166. Mona Lisa Chanda and Daniel J. Levitin, "The Neurochemistry of Music," *Trends in Cognitive Sciences* 17 (2013): 179–93.

167. Heather Stuckey and Jeremy Nobel, "The Connection between Art, Healing, and Public Health: A Review of Current Literature," *American journal of Public Health* 100, no. 2 (2010): 254–63.

168. MindTravel, https://www.mindtravel.com.

169. Murray Hidary and Megan Bennett, email correspondence with author, August 20, 2020.

170. American Pet Products Association, "Pet Industry Market Size & Ownership Statistics," https://www.americanpetproducts.org/pressindustrytrends.asp.

171. American Veterinary Medical Association, "U.S. Pet Ownership Sta- tistics," https://www.avma.org/resources-tools/reports-statistics/us-pet-ownership- statistics.

172. Rebecca Purewal et al., "Companion Animals and Child/Adolescent Development: A Systematic Review of the Evidence," *International Journal Environmental Research and Public Health* 14, no. 3 (2017): 234.

173. Lindsey Melfi, email correspondence with author, November 7, 2019.

174. Human Animal Bond Research Institute, "Interactions with Animals to Reduce Children's Stress," https://habri.org/grants/projects/interactions-with-animals-to-reduce-childrens-stress.

175. Lisa Walden, "Staffies and Westies Have Been Revealed as the Most Affectionate Dog Breeds," *Country Living*, May 1, 2019, https://www.countryliving.com/uk/wildlife/dog-breeds/a27328818/affectionate-dog-breeds-staffies-westies/.

176. Deborah Cracknell et al., "Marine Biota and Psychological Well-Being: A Preliminary Examination of Dose–Response Effects in an Aquarium Setting," *Environment and Behavior* 48, no. 10 (December 2016): 1242–69, https://doi.org/10.1177/0013916515597512.

177. Purewal et al., "Companion Animals and Child/Adolescent Development."

178. Allen R. McConnell et al., "Friends with Benefits: On the Positive Consequences of Pet Ownership," *Journal of Personality and Social Psychology* 101, no. 6 (2011): 1239–52, https://doi.org/10.1037/a0024506.

179. Dr. Adam Strassberg, phone interview with author, June 23, 2020.

180. Darlene Kertes et al., "Effect of Pet Dogs on Children's Perceived Stress and Cortisol Stress Response," *Social Development* 26, no. 2 (2017): 382–401.

181. Anne Gadomski et al., "Pet Dogs and Children's Health: Opportunities for Chronic Disease Prevention?," *Preventing Chronic Disease* 12 (2015).

182. Tara Parker-Pope, "The Best Walking Partner: Man vs. Dog," *New York Times Well Blog*, December 14, 2009, https://well.blogs.nytimes.com/2009/12/14/the-best-walking-partner-man-vs-dog/?mtrref=undefined&gwh=3619D9122481FD6617D6F4ECC6C542C3&gwt=regi&assetType=REGIWALL.

183. Human Animal Bond Research Institute, "Publication of Largest-Ever Study on Pets in the Classroom Indicates Positive Impact on Aca- demic and Social Behavior," https://habri.org/pressroom/20190826.

184. Andrea Beetz et al., "Psychosocial and Psychophysiological Effects of Human-Animal Interactions: The Possible Role of Oxytocin," *Frontiers in Psychology* 3 (2012).

185. Charlotte Brouwer, "Top 10 Family Friendly Dog Breeds," *Good Housekeeping*, February 6, 2016, https://www.goodhousekeeping.com/uk/lifestyle/a561691/the-top-10-family-friendly-dog-breeds-for-families-with-small-children/.

186. *The Telegraph*, "Reading Can Help Reduce Stress," March 30, 2019, https://www.telegraph.co.uk/news/health/news/5070874/Reading-can-help-reduce-stress.html.

187. Janice Lloyd and Reesa Sorin, "Engaging the Imagination: The Effect of the Classroom Canines™ Program on Reading and Social/Emotional Skills of Selected Primary School Students," 2015.

188. Lynne Perrigo, phone interview with author, July 10, 2020.

189. Samantha Joseph, email correspondence with author, October 6, 2020.

190. Marie Carter, "How Pets Improve Mental Health Issues, from Depression to PTSD," *Independent*, December 3, 2018, https://www.independent.co.uk/news/long_reads/pets-improve-mental-health-depression-loneliness-ptsd-alcohol-drugs-a8656096.html, accessed 6/15/2020.

191. Elisabeth Van Every, "More Than Dogs: The Pet Partners Therapy Animal Program Takes Pride in Having Multiple Species of Therapy Animals," *Pet Partners Interactions Magazine*, Spring 2019, https://petpartners.org/wp-content/uploads/2019/04/PP-Spring2019-Web.pdf.

192. Moosh, "Why Reptiles Make Surprisingly Good Emotional Support Animals," https://mooshme.com/reptiles-make-surprisingly-good-emotional-support-animals/#:~:text=While%20they're%20not%20a, emotional%20support%20to%20their%20owners.

193. Kaitlyn Wilson et al., "Equine-Assisted Psychotherapy for Adolescents Experiencing Depression and/or Anxiety: A Therapist's Perspective," *Clinical Child Psychology and Psychiatry* 22 (2017): 16–33.

194. Patricia E. Kelly, phone interview with author, June 22, 2020.

195. Kevin N. Morris et al. *Documentation of Nature-Based Programs at Green Chimneys* (Denver, CO: University of Denver, Institute for Human-Animal Connection, 2019).

196. Kristin Sutch, phone interview with author, October 10, 2019.

197. Haley Hansen, "How Spending Time with Cows Helped Michigan State Students De-stress before Finals," *Lansing State Journal*, December 11, 2018, https://www.lansingstatejournal.com/story/news/2018/12/10/msu-students-finals-stress-brushing-cows/2213232002.

198. Rachel Martin, "Feeling Blue? Might Be Time to Cuddle a Cow," *Morning Edition*, NPR, July 1, 2019, https://www.npr.org/2019/07/01/737535407/feeling-blue-might-be-time-to-cuddle-a-cow.

199. A. Pawlowski, "Cow Cuddling Lets People Relax with Help of Friendly Bovines," *Today*, September 23, 2019, https://www.today.com/health/cow-cuddling-lets-people-relax-help-friendly-bovines-t163117.

200. Gerald P. Mallon, "Cow as Co-therapist: Utilization of Farm Animals as Therapeutic Aides with Children in Residential Treatment," *Child and Adolescent Social Work Journal* 11 (1994): 455–74.

201. Bente Berget et al., "Animal-Assisted Therapy with Farm Animals for Persons with Psychiatric Disorders: Effects on Anxiety and Depression, a Randomized Controlled Trial," *Occupational Therapy in Mental Health* 27 (2011): 50–64.

202. Horse and Petting Pal Interaction, Inc. (HAPPI Farm), http://www.happifarm.org/.

203. Green Chimneys, "More Than Chores: Weekly Sessions on the Farm Help Foster a Child's Interests While Supporting Therapeutic Growth" (blog), November, 30, 2016, https://www.greenchimneys.org/news-events/more-than-chores-weekly-sessions-on-the-farm-help-foster-a-childs-interests-while-supporting-therapeutic-growth/.

204. Susanne Curtin, "Wildlife Tourism: The Intangible, Psychological Benefits of Human–Wildlife Encounters," *Current Issues in Tourism* 12 (2009): 451–74.

205. Richard Louv, *Our Wild Calling: How Connecting with Animals Can Transform Our Lives—and Save Theirs* (Chapel Hill, NC: Algonquin Books, 2019).

206. *ScienceDaily*, "Watching Birds Near Your Home Is Good for Your Mental Health," February 25, 2017, https://www.sciencedaily.com/releases/2017/02/170225102113.htm.

207. Eleanor Ratcliffe, Birgitta Gatersleben, and Paul T. Sowden, "Bird Sounds and Their Contributions to Perceived Attention Restoration and Stress Recovery," *Journal of Environmental Psychology* 36 (2013): 221–28.

208. National Trust, "Woodland Sounds Boost Wellbeing, According to New Study," September 12, 2019, https://www.nationaltrust.org.uk/press-release/woodland-sounds-boost-wellbeing-according-to-new-study.

209. Joe Harkness, *Bird Therapy* (London, Unbound, 2019).

210. Shannon Brescher Shea, email correspondence with author, August 10, 2020.

211. Aleanna Siacon, "It's Science: Viewing Zoo Animals Reduces Your Stress Levels," *Detroit Free Press*, April 15, 2019, https://www. freep. com/story/news/local/michigan/oakland/2019/04/15/detroit-zoo-animals-membership/ 3471882002/, accessed 6/15/2020.

212. Richard Louv, "Summer of COVID-19: Teens and Screens?," Children and Screens webinar presentation, June 10, 2020, https://www.youtube.com/ watch?v=0PgsTvGwoo&feature=youtu.be&mc_cid=187be29c34&mc_ eid=c72e0ca883.

213. Sweet Farm, https://www.sweetfarm.org/goat-2-meeting.

214. Kellie B. Gormly, "Kids Are Reading to Therapy Dogs on Zoom: They Can't Pet the Pooches, but Sessions Still Book Up Fast," *Washington Post*, May 13, 2020, https://www.washingtonpost.com/lifestyle/2020/05/13/ kids-are-reading-therapy-dogs-zoom-they-cant-pet-pooches-sessions-still-book-up-fast/.

215. Center for Nutritional Psychology, https://www.nutri- tional-psy-chology.org.

216. Felice Jacka et al., "A Randomised Controlled Trial of Dietary Improvement for Adults with Major Depression (the 'SMILES' Trial)," *BMC Medicine* 15 (2017).

217. Uma Naidoo, *This Is Your Brain on Food: An Indispensable Guide to the Surprising Foods That Fight Depression, Anxiety, PTSD, OCD, ADHD, and More* (New York: Hachette Book Group, 2020).

218. Deakin University and Food & Mood Centre, "Food and Mood: Improving Mental Health Through Diet and Nutrition," (online course), https://www.futurelearn.com/courses/food-and-mood.

219. John Cryan, "A Gut Feeling About Happiness," World Government Summit, February 13, 2018, https://www.youtube.com/ watch?v=UP-0ohxo_7w.

220. Naidoo, *This Is Your Brain on Food*.

221. Uma Naidoo, "Nutritional Strategies to Ease Anxiety," Harvard Health (blog), August 29, 2019, https://www.health.harvard.edu/blog/ nutritional-strategies-to-ease-anxiety-201604139441.

222. Jillian Kubala, "18 Foods to Help Relieve Stress," *EcoWatch*, June 13, 2020, https://www.ecowatch.com/stress-relieving-foods-2646171995. html?rebelltitem= 2#rebelltitem2.

223. William W. Li, "Using Food to Combat Anxiety in Kids," *U.S. News & World Report*, December 12, 2019, https://health.usnews.com/ wellness/for-parents/articles/foods-for-anxiety-lower-kids-stress-levels-with-these-healthy-choices.

224. Naidoo, *This Is Your Brain on Food*.

225. Naidoo, "Nutritional Strategies to Ease Anxiety."

226. Naidoo, T*his Is Your Brain on Food*.

227. Jena Pincott, *Wits Guts Grit: All-Natural Biohacks for Raising Smart, Resilient Kids* (Chicago: Chicago Review Press, 2018).

228. Henry Emmons, *The Chemistry of Calm* (New York: Atria Paperback, 2010).

229. Naidoo, *This Is Your Brain on Food.*

230. Ryan Raman, "12 Healthy Foods High in Antioxidants," *Healthline*, March 12, 2018, https://www.healthline.com/nutrition/foods-high-in-antioxidants.

231. Scott C. Anderson, *The Psychobiotic Revolution: Mood, Food, and the New Science of the Gut-Brain Connection* (Washington, DC: National Geographic Partners, 2017).

232. Naidoo, "Nutritional Strategies to Ease Anxiety."

233. Mahmoud Ali et al., "Effects of Dehydration and Blockade of Angiotensin II AT1 Receptor on Stress Hormones and Anti-oxidants in the One-humped Camel," *BMC Veterinary Research* 9 (2013): 232.

234. Micha Abraham, "Can Anxiety Be Caused by Dehydration?," Calm Clinic,. October 10, 2020, http:// www.calmclinic.com/anxiety/causes/water-dehydration.

235. Jamie Ducharme, "What Are Adaptogens and Why Are People Taking Them?," *Time*, February 28, 2018, https://time.com/5025278/adaptogens-herbs-stress-anxiety.

236. Emmons, *The Chemistry of Calm.*

237. David Sack, "4 Ways Sugar Could Be Harming Your Mental Health," *Psychology Today*, September 2, 2013, https://www.psychologytoday.com/blog/where-science-meets-the-steps/201309/4-ways-sugar-could-be-harming-your-mental-health.

238. R. Molteni et al., "A High-Fat, Refined Sugar Diet Reduces Hippocampal Brain-derived Neurotrophic Factor, Neuronal Plasticity, and Learning," *Neuroscience* 112 (2002): 803–14.

239. Anika Knüppel et al., "Sugar Intake from Sweet Food and Beverages, Common Mental Disorder and Depression: Prospective Findings from the Whitehall II Study," *Scientific Reports* 7 (2017).

240. Arthur N. Westover and Lauren Marangell, "A Cross-national Relationship between Sugar Consumption and Major Depression?," *Depression and Anxiety* 16, no. 3 (2002).

241. American Heart Association, "Sugar Recommendation Healthy Kids and Teens Infographic," https://www.heart.org/en/healthy-living/healthy-eating/eat-smart/sugar/sugar-recommendation-healthy-kids-and-teens-infographic.

242. "How Many Teaspoons of Sugar Is Your Child Drinking?," Michigan State University, College of Nursing, http://www.kansaswic.org/

download/cooksmarteatsmart/Reduce%20Sugar%20Sweetened%20Beverages[1].pdf.

243. Bonnie Beezhold, "Vegans Report Less Stress and Anxiety Than Omnivores," *Nutritional Neuroscience* 18, no. 7 (2015): 289–96.

244. McGill University, "Can a Vegan Diet Have a Negative Impact on Your Mental Health?," April 2018, https://www.mcgill.ca/manulife-prize/ideas-move-you/april-2018-edition/can-vegan-diet-have-negative-impact-your-mental-health.

245. Melissa Mondala, "Going Plant-Based for Your Mental Health? Here Are Some Things to Keep in Mind," Forks Over Knives, October 9, 2020,https://www.forksoverknives.com/wellness/mental-health-plant-based-doctors-tips.

246. Anna Johansson, "The Chemicals in Your Food Can Affect Your Mood," *Thrive Global*, October 19, 2017, https://thriveglobal.com/stories/the-chemicals-in-your-food-can-affect-your-mood.

247. Peter Bongiorno, "Is There a Link Between Lawn Care and Mental Health?," *Psychology Today*, May 4, 2019, https://www.psychologytoday.com/us/blog/inner-source/201905/is-there-link-between-lawn-care-and-mental-health.

248. José R. Suarez-Lopez et al., "Associations of Acetyl-cholinesterase Activity with Depression and Anxiety Symptoms among Adolescents Growing Up near Pesticide Spray Sites," *International Journal of Hygiene and Environmental Health*, 222, no. 7 (2019).

249. Emmons, *The Chemistry of Calm.*

250. Center for Mindful Eating, http://www.thecenterformindfuleating.org.

251. Susan Albers, "How to Practice Mindful Eating," Mindfulness Summit, https://themindfulnesssummit.com/sessions/susan-albers.

252. National Wildlife Federation, The Dirt on Dirt: *How Getting Dirty Outdoors Benefits Kids*, 2012, https://www.nwf.org/~/media/PDFs/Be%20Out%20There/Dirt_Report_2012.ashx.

253. Mary O'Brien et al., "SRL172 (killed Mycobacterium vaccae) in Addition to Standard Chemotherapy Improves Quality of Life without Affecting Survival, in Patients with Advanced Non-small-cell Lung Cancer: Phase III Results," *Annals of Oncology: Official Journal of the European Society for Medical Oncology* 15, no. 6 (2004): 906–14.

254. Christopher Lowry et al., "Identification of an Immune-Responsive Mesolimbocortical Serotonergic System: Potential Role in Regulation of Emotional Behavior," *Neuroscience* 146, no. 2 (2007): 756–72.

255. Carly Cassella, "Daycares in Finland Built a 'Forest Floor', and It Changed Children's Immune Systems," *Science Alert*, October 22, 2020, https://www.sciencealert.com/daycares-in-finland-built-a-backyard-forest-and-it-changed-children-s-immune-systems.

256. Peter Dockrill, "This Odd Bacterium Appears to Protect Its Host from the Damaging Effects of Stress," *ScienceAlert*, June 17, 2019, https://www.sciencealert.com/this-dirt-loving-bacteria-may-hold-the-secrets-to-a-real-life-stress-vaccine.

257. Marianne Gonzalez et al., "Therapeutic Horticulture in Clinical Depression: A Prospective Study," *Research and Theory for Nursing Practice* 23, no 4 (2009): 312–28.

258. Holly Harris, "The Social Dimensions of Therapeutic Horticulture," *Health & Social Care in the Community* 25, no. 6 (2017): 1328–36.

259. Shannon Brescher Shea, email correspondence with author, November 23, 2020.

260. Harvard Health Publishing, "Exercising to Relax," Harvard Medical School, July 7, 2020, http://www.health.harvard.edu/staying-healthy/exercising-to-relax.

261. Sandra Whitehouse et al., "Evaluating a Children's Hospital Garden Environment Utilization and Consumer Satisfaction," *Journal of Environmental Psychology* 21, no. 3 (2001): 301–14.

262. Masashi Soga, Kevin Gaston, and Yuichi Yamaura, "Gardening Is Beneficial for Health: A Meta-analysis," *Preventive Medicine Reports* 5 (2017): 92–99.

263. Laila Lier et al., "Home Gardening and the Health and Well-Being of Adolescents," *Health Promotion Practice* 18 (2017): 34–43.

264. Mariecor Agravante, "Doctors Are Prescribing Gardening to Improve Patients' Health," *Inhabitat*, October 1, 2019, https://inhabitat.com/doctors-are-prescribing-gardening-to-improve-patients-health.

265. Lusi Alderslowe, email correspondence with author, October 27, 2020, http://childreninpermaculture.com/resources/case-studies/; http://childreninpermaculture.com/resources/videos/.

266. American Horticultural Therapy Association, https://www.ahta.org.

267. Hillside Atlanta, https://hside.org/unique-therapies/horticulture-therapy.

268. Gonzalez et al., "Therapeutic Horticulture in Clinical Depression."

269. Min Jung Lee et al., "A Pilot Study: Horticulture-related Activities Significantly Reduce Stress Levels and Salivary Cortisol Concentration of Maladjusted Elementary School Children," *Complementary Therapies in Medicine* 37 (2018): 172–77.

270. Amy Brightwood, phone interview with author, October 15, 2020.

271. T. Astell-Burt and X. Feng, "Association of Urban Green Space with Mental Health and General Health Among Adults in Australia," *JAMA Network Open* 2, no. 2 (2019).

272. Mark Cassini, phone interview with author, October 12, 2020.

273. Robert Grimm et al., *Building Active Citizens: The Role of Social Institutions in Teen Volunteering,* Brief 1 in the Youth Helping America series (Washington, DC: Corporation for National and Community Service, November 2005).

274. Dacher Keltner, "The Compassionate Species," *Greater Good Magazine,* July 31, 2012, http://www.mindful.org/cooperate/.

275. Max Planck Society, "Baby's Helping Hands: First Evidence for Altruistic Behaviours in Human Infants and Chimpanzees," Sci- enceDaily, March 5, 2006, www.sciencedaily.com/releases/ 2006/03/060303205611.htm.

276. Lara Aknin, J. Kiley Hamlin, and Elizabeth Dunn, "Giving Leads to Happiness in Young Children," *PLoS ONE* 7, no. 6 (2012).

277. Christine L. Carter, "What We Get When We Give," *Psychology Today,* February 19, 2010, https:// www.psychologytoday.com/blog/raising-happiness/201002/what-we-get-when-we-give.

278. Sonja Lyubomirsky, Kenneth Sheldon, and David Schkade, "Pursuing Happiness: The Architecture of Sustainable Change," *Review of General Psychology* 9, no. 2 (2005): 111–31.

279. Peggy Thoits and Lyndi Hewitt. "Volunteer Work and Well-being," *Journal of Health and Social Behavior* 42, no. 2 (2001): 115–31.

280. Rachel Piferi and Kathleen Lawler, "Social Support and Ambulatory Blood Pressure: An Examination of Both Receiving and Giving," *International Journal of Psychophysiology: Official Journal of the International Organization of Psychophysiology* 62, no. 2 (2006): 328–36.

281. Hannah M. C. Schreier, Kimberly Schonert-Reichl, and Edith Chen, "Effect of Volunteering on Risk Factors for Cardiovascular Disease in Adolescents: A Randomized Controlled Trial," *JAMA Pediatrics* 167, no. 4 (2013): 327–32.

282. Brenda Tran, "An Overview of Volunteering in Adolescence: Predictors, Outcomes, and Time Trends,"(2016).

283. Jessica Cassity, "The Science of Giving: Why One Act of Kindness Is Usually Followed by Another," *Happify Daily,* accessed November 28, 2020, http://my.happify.com/hd/the-power-of-a-single-act-of-kindness/.

284. Matthew Ebden and Mardie Townsend, *Feel Blue, Touch Green,* Deakin University, December 2006.

285. Girl Scout Research Institute, *More Than S'mores: Successes and Surprises in Girl Scouts' Outdoor Experiences*, 2014, https://www.girlscouts.org.

286. Mike Rogerson et al., *The Health and Wellbeing Impacts of Volunteering with The Wildlife Trusts*, June 2017, https://www.wildlifetrusts.org/sites/default/files/2018-05/r3thehealthandwellbeingimpactsofvolunteering withthewildlifetrusts-university_of_essex_report_3_0.pdf.

287. Anne-Marie Bagnall et al., *Social Return on Investment Analysis of the Health and Wellbeing Impacts of Wildlife Trust Programmes*, September 2019, https://www.wildlifetrusts.org/ sites/default/files/2019-09/SROI Report FINAL - DIGITAL.pdf.

288. Kayleigh Wyles et al., "Can Beach Cleans Do More Than Clean-Up Litter? Comparing Beach Cleans to Other Coastal Activities," *Environment and Behavior* 49, no. 5 (2017): 509–35.

289. The Conservation Volunteers (TCV), "Trust Me I'm a Doctor– Green Gyms Proven to Reduce Stress," https://www.tcv.org.uk/greengym/trust-me-im-a-doctor.

290. Sarah Aadland, email correspondence with author, November 18, 2019.

291. Natalie Silverstein, Simple Acts: *The Busy Family's Guide to Giving Back* (Lewisville, NC: Gryphon House, 2019).

292. Jinho Kim and Kerem Morgül, "Long-Term Consequences of Youth Volunteering: Voluntary versus Involuntary Service," *Social Science Research* 67 (2017): 160–75.

293. Jinho Kim, email correspondence with author, October 21, 2019.

294. Hank Barnet, phone interview with author, May 21, 2019.

295. Alyona Olsen, email correspondence with author, August 22, 2019.

296. Jen Krasnow and Simone Snow, phone interview with author, November 18, 2019.

297. Andy Thomson, email correspondence with author, October 30, 2019.

298. Rachel Mazur, phone interview with author, July 10, 2019.

299. Family Nature Club: Step-by-Step Guide and Resources, https://www.childrenandnature.org/wp-content/uploads/CNN_FNC_stepby stepguideFULL_20-10-20.pdf

300. Karen E. Makuch and Miriam R. Aczel, *Environmental Citizen Science for Social Good: Engaging Children and Promoting Justice, Diversity, Health and Inclusion*, January 2019, https://www.researchgate.net/publication/333746541 Environmental_citizen_science_for_social_good_Engaging_ children_and_promoting_justice_diversity_health_and_inclusion.

301. The GLOBE Program, https://www.globe.gov.

Index

A

Aadland, Sarah, 243
Adams, Ansel, 23, 127
adventure
    outdoor, 110-112
    therapy, 92, 120-124
Aetna's Champions for Change, 179
Albers, Susan, 210
aldehydes, 14
Alderfer, Lauren, 61
Alderslowe, Lusi, 218-219, 230
aliphatic alcohols, 14
All for Good, 262
Alliance of Therapy Dogs, 177, 192
Alter, Adam, 8
American Academy of Pediatrics, 97
American Art Therapy Association, 161
American Birding Association, 192
American Camp Association, 116, 124
American Community Garden Association, 252, 261-262
American Heart Association, 206
American Horticultural Therapy Association, 222, 230
American Kennel Club, 177, 192
Ample Harvest, 230
Amsel, Sheri, 263
Amus, Gaye, 230
Ancona, George, 263
Anderson, Scott C., 201-202, 230
Andrews, Kim, 126
animal(s), 163-192
    awe and, 79
    care farms, 182-183
    dances, 158

    emotional support, 171-177
    farm, 177-178
    fear of, 190-191
    metaphors, 3
    online encounters, 189
    pets, 163, 165-166, 168-170
    support programs, 176-177
    teaching children to respect, 166
    therapeutic farms, 177-178
    volunteering with, 253
    wild, 166, 184-188
    yoga, 30, 42-47, 59
    zoos, 163, 187
Animal-Assisted Therapy (AAT), 177
Animal Poems (Worth), 162
Animals Helping With Healing (Squire), 192
Apple Cake: A Gratitude (Casey), 89
aquariums, 23, 163, 165-166
Arbor Day, 250
Archeological Resources Protection Act, 139
Archer, Joe, 231
Ard, Catherine, 126
Art and Science of Awe conference, 65
Association for Experiential Education, 123-124
Association for Play Therapy, 124
Association of Nature and Forest Therapy, 60
At Ease, 151
attention, four states of, 8
Attention Restoration Theory (ART), 7-9, 18, 132

Audubon Christmas Bird Count, 259

Audubon Medal, x

Austin, Alfred, 193

Awake in the Wild: Mindfulness in Nature as a Path to Self-Discovery (Coleman), 30, 60

awe, 63-89

    activities to help children experience, 75-80

    anxiety and, 70-71

    audio recordings about, 84

    benefits of, 68-71

    blogging about, 84, 88

    books, making books about, 83-84, 88

    broadening social connections through, 68

    collages about, 84

    core qualities of, 65

    creativity and, 69

    definition of, 63-67

    depression and, 70-71

    experiencing through our children's eyes, 73-74

    finding purpose in life through, 70

    health and, 70

    kindness and generosity and, 69

    gratitude and, 70-72, 83-86

    opportunities to feel, 64

    perception of time and, 69

    sounds and, 80

    stimulating curiosity through, 68-69

    triggering, 67

    videos about, 86, 88

    views, 78-79

    virtual experience, 80-82

Awe Factor: How a Little Bit of Wonder Can Make a Big Difference in Your Life, The (Klein), 88

awecations, 75-78, 88

Awestruck (Paquette), 67, 71, 89

B

"Baby Beluga" (Raffi), 157

Backpack Explorer: On the Nature Tail: What Will You Find?, 126

Backyard Adventure: Get Messy, Get Wild, Build Cool Things, and have Tone of Wild Fun! (Thomsen), 126

Balanced and Barefoot (Hanscom), 96, 111, 125

Barnet, Hank, 250

Barton, Jo, 102

Baylor, Byrd, 61

Bazer, Deborah, 136-140

BBC Wildlife, 153

beach cleanups, 240-242

Beer, Julie, 126

Bella Saves the Beach (Stewart), 263

Big-Hearted Families Program, 243

biking, 109-110

biophilia, 7

Bird Therapy (Harkness), 186

Birdology: 30 Activities and Observations for Exploring the World of Birds (Russo), 192

birdsong, 185, 188

birdwatching, 185-188, 266

    benefits of, 185-186

    mindfulness and, 185

Blue Mind (Nichols), 16, 58

Blue Planet, The, 88

Bond, Lahri, 136-138

Boy Scouts, 249

Boynton, Alice, 192

Bradley, Kirsten, 231

brain-derived neurotrophic factor (BDNF), 205

Braun, Lindsey, 165

breathing

    dandelion breath, 41

    exercises, 27

    flower breath, 41

    hand breath, 42

    mindful, 41-42, 59

    outdoors, 30-31

sunrise breath, 41-42

wave breath, 41

Brightwood, Amy, 222-224

Bryson, Tina Payne, 30

Butterfly Pavilion, 45

Butterfly World, 164

C

C. S. Mott Children's Hospital, ix

Calm, 60

Cameron, Cortney, 30, 60

camp, 124, 136-138, 160

benefits of, 116

scholarships, 116

sleepaway, 115-116

Can We Help? Kids Volunteering to Help Their Communities (Ancona), 263

care farms, 182-183

Carle, Eric, 231

Cornell, Kari, 231

Carson, Rachel, 89

Casey, Dawn, 89

Cassini, Mark, 227

Cavalier, Darlene, 263

Celebrate Urban Birds project, 81

Center for Mindful Eating, 209, 230

Center for Mindfulness in Medicine, Health Care, and Society, 29

Center for Nutritional Psychology (CNP), 195, 230

Centers for Disease Control and Prevention (CDC), ix, 97, 106

Cerny, Julie, 230

Challenger space shuttle, 67

Charitynavigator.org, 245

Charitywatch.org, 245

Chemistry of Calm, The (Emmons), 204, 209, 230

Child's Garden: 60 Ideas to Make Any Garden Come Alive for Children, A (Dannenmaier), 231

Children & Nature Network, x, xi, 101, 124

Green Schoolyards program, 94-95

Nature Clubs for Families Tool Kit: Do It Yourself!, 258

Children in Permaculture, 230

China Conservation and Research Center for the Giant Panda, 112

Citizen Science Guide for Families: Taking Part in Real Science (Landgraf), 263

citizen science projects, 188, 258-259

CitizenScience.gov, 259, 262

Clarke, Natalia, 30, 60

Cleveland Clinic, 210

climate change, discussing, 246-247

CNN Top 10 Hero award, 179

cognitive behavior therapy, 29

Coleman, Mark, 30-31, 60

color(s), 9-11

cool, 11

mapping, 146

meditation, 35-37

neutral, 11

coloring books, 141-142

Common Ground, 222-223

Common Sense Media, 93

Community Greening, 227-229

Cooper, Caren, 263

Cornbrook Medical Practice, 217

Cornell Lab of Ornithology, 81, 259

cortisol, x, 16, 130, 156, 172, 197, 222

Count by Nature, 174

Court, Rob, 162

COVID-19, 52, 80, 173, 189

cow cuddling, 181-182, 191

Craig, Caroline, 231

creativity/creative arts, 71, 127-162

awe and, 69

benefits of, 128-131

definition of, 128-129

as a distraction, 130

encouraging, 135

flow, 130

mental health and, 129, 130
mindfulness and, 130-131
nature and, 131-132
nature, building a connection to, 132-134
nature drawing, painting, and coloring, 140-142
play and, 96
reduced stimulation and, 131
self-care and, 131
stress and, 129, 130, 131
Cryan, John, 196
Curious Nature Guide, The (Leslie), 89
curiosity
awe and, 68-69
play and, 96
Curtin, Susanne, 185
cytokines, 70

D

dance and movement, nature-themed, 157-158
Dannenmaier, Molly, 231
Darwin, Charles, 65, 235
Davey, Ruth, 151
Davis, Brew, 103
Davis, Jennifer Phare, 103
Deakin University, Food & Mood Centre, 196
Delgado, David, 65
Delta Society Classroom Canines Program, 173
Detroit Zoo, 187
Detroit Zoological Society, 187
Devapriya, Didi, 230
DiOrio, Rana, 61
Dirt on Dirt, The, 212
Disney the Conservation Fund, 2
Doing Good Together, 243, 262
Doing Good Together (Friedman), 263
dopamine, 16, 106, 169, 195
Dormoy, Mellisa, 35, 40
DoSomething.org, 236-237

Down and Dirty Guide to Camping with Kids, The (Olsson), 125
drawing, 141
Drunk Tank Pink (Alter), 8
Dubbo School of Distance Education, 143, 145

E

Earth Care, People Care and Fair Share in Education (Alderslowe, Amus, Devapriya), 230
Earth Day Live 2020, 81
earthing, 51-52
Easy Peasy: Gardening for Kids (Bradley), 231
Eating Mindfully, 230
eBird, 192
Ebony Horsewomen, Inc., 178-180
Ecohappiness Project, viii
ecopsychology, 2-3
EcoPsychology Initiative, 3, 25
ecotherapy, 2, 3
ecotourism, 111-112, 124, 188
Eichele, Kassy, 73-74
Einstein, Albert, 65
Ehlert, Lois, 231
Emmons, Henry, 204, 209, 230
Emmons, Robert, 71-72, 89
emotional support animals (ESAs), 171-177
definition, 171
cats, 175
dogs, 171-174, 254
reptiles, 176
smallies, 176
endorphins, 102, 106
environmental psychology, 2
Equine-Assisted Psychotherapy (EAP), 177-180
Eszterhas, Suzi, 153-154
Everything Kids' Environment Book, The (Amsel), 263

Expedition: Two Parents Risk Life and Family in an Extraordinary Quest to the South Pole, The (Fagan), 112

Explore Nature Activity Book for Kids (Andrews), 126

Explore.org, 81

F

Fagan, Chris, 112-114

Fagan, Marty, 112-114

Families on Foot (Davis), 103

farmer's markets, 224, 226

Farrell, Holly, 60

Field Guide to Citizen Science, The (Cavalier, Hoffman, Cooper), 263

52 Hike Challenge, 105, 124

Finch, Ken, 97

Fisher, Cheryl, 120

Fishman, Jon M., 192

float therapy, 58-59, 60

Florian, Douglas, 162

flower(s), 20
    breath, 41
    creative projects involving, 38
    -gazing meditation, 37-38
    viewing after surgery, 21

food, 193-231
    antioxidants, 201-202
    to avoid, 204-206, 229
    caffeine, 204, 205, 229
    complex carbohydrates, 196-197
    fermented foods, 200-201
    fiber, 201
    growing your own, 214-218
    improving mental health, 196-204
    L-tryptophan, 197
    mindful eating, 209-211
    minerals, 197-199
    omega-3, 200
    plant-based diets, 207-208, 229
    stimulants, 204-205
    sugar, 205-206, 229

supplements, 207

trans fats, 204-205, 229

vitamins, 197-199, 207

water, 202-204

forest bathing, 54-56, 60

Forest Bathing Central, 60

Forest Bathing: How Tress Can Help You Find Health and Happiness (Li), 19, 54-55

Forest School for All, 92, 124

Formidable Vegetable, 217

Foster-Wilson, Lee, 133, 161

4ocean, 261, 262

Franklin Experience, 82

Free Forest School, 92, 124

free play, 92-94, 97

Free to Learn (Gray), 93, 111, 125

Friedman, Jenny, 263

"Friends With Benefits," 168

FrogWatch USA, 259

Frost, Robert, 80

G

gamma-animobutyric acid (GABA), 195, 199

garden(s)/gardening, 214-218
    benefits of, 215-216
    community, 252
    clubs, 218, 229
    horticultural therapy, 220-224, 229
    indoor, 23
    meditation, 47-49, 60
    metaphors, 3
    mindfulness and, 217-218, 223
    peace, 218-219
    planting seeds, 3
    therapeutic, 220

Garden Club of America, 261-262

"Garden Song, The," 217

Garden to Table (Hengel), 231

Gardening for Mindfulness (Farrell), 60

Gateway to the Great Outdoors, 101, 124

Get Out Stay Out/Vamos Afuera, 101, 125

Gilbert, Melissa, 91-92

Girl Scouts of the United States of America, The, 239, 249, 257

Girls Who Click, 153-154, 161

Giving Thanks (Swamp), 89

Global Learning and Observations to Benefit the Environment (GLOBE) Program, 258

Gold Arrow Camp, 115

Goodall, Jane, 257

GoodMorningAmerica.com, 153

Goodbeer, Maurice "Maui," 107-108

gratitude, 63, 140
    awe and, 70-72, 83-86
    definition of, 71-72

Gratitude Project (Smith), 89

Gratitude Revealed, 70

Gray, Peter, 93, 111, 125

Greater Good Science Center, 65, 88

Greatest Places, The, 88

Green Cay Nature Center, 234

Green Chimneys, 180, 183
    Farm Kid of the Month's Award, 184
    Teaching Barn, 183-184

green exercise, 92, 102-103

Green Green: A Community Gardening Story (Lamba), 231

Green Gyms, 242-243

Green Hearts Institute for Nature in Childhood, 96-97

"Green Hour," 97

Green Schoolyards program, 94, 95

greenhouses, 23

Growing Sustainable Together (Shea), 186, 214-215, 230, 263

Growing Vegetable Soup (Ehlert), 217

Grown-Up's Guide to Making Art with Kids, The (Foster-Wilson), 133, 161

guided imagery, 30, 35

Guinness Book of World Records, 112

gut microbiome, 195-196, 201, 212-213

H

Haidt, Jonathan, 65

Hamilton, John, 162

Handful of Quiet: Happiness in Four Pebbles, A (Hanh), 61

Handsprings: Poems & Paintings (Florian), 162

Hanh, Thich Nhat, 56, 60-61

Hanscom, Angela J., 96, 111, 125

Happy Campers: 9 Summer Camp Secrets for Raising Kids Who Become Thriving Adults (Monke), 115

Happy Science Mom, viii

Harkness, Joe, 186

Harris, Pearl, 170-171

Harvard Medical School, 196

Harvard University, 7

Hawn, Goldie, 72

Healthy US Collaborative, 6

helper's high, 235-236

Helping Dogs (Hoffman), 192

Hengel, Katherine, 231

Hero Therapy Dogs (Fishman), 192

Hidary, Murray, 159-160

Hike It Baby 30, 105, 125

Hobbies, 131, 140

Hoffman, Catherine, 263

Hoffman, Mary Ann, 192

Honovich, Nancy, 126

Horse and Petting Pal Interaction, Inc (HAPPI Farm), 183

horticultural therapy, 220-224, 229

Horticulture Therapy Institute, 222, 230

How to Draw Things in Nature (Court), 162

How to Raise a Wild Child: The Art and Science of Falling in Love With Nature (Sampson), 125

How to Raise a Wild Child (Sampson), 152

How to Talk to Your Kids About Climate Change (Shugarman), 263
How To Teach Nature Journaling (Laws, Lygren), 143, 161
Human Animal Bond Research Institute (HABRI), 165, 192
Humane Society of the United States, 192, 257
    Team Sierra, 257
hydrotherapy, 58

I

Idealist, 262
Inch by Inch: The Garden Song (Mallett), 231
Institute of Plant-Based Medicine, 208
International Ecotourism Society, 111-112
International Journal of Environmental Research and Public Health, 165
International Rose Test Garden, 77
Island Alpaca Farm, 45
Iwantmyoceanback.org/#iwantmyoceanback, 252

J

Jacka, Felice, 196
Jenny's Winter Walk (Shardlow), 44
Jones, Jenn, 45
Joseph, Samantha, 174
Journal of Environmental Psychology, 216
journaling, nature, 142-147, 161
    activities, 146-147
    benefits of, 142
    clubs, 145
    color mapping, 146
    deep listening, 146-147
    materials, 146
    word search, 147
Jung, Carl, 154
JustServe, 262

K

Kabat-Zinn, Jon, 28-29
Kaplan, Rachel, 7, 18, 132
Kaplan, Stephen, 7, 18, 132
Keats, John, 80
Kellert, Stephen R., 7, 18, 25
Kelly, Patricia E., 178-181
Keltner, Dacher, 65
Kids, Art & Nature, 136-138
Kids Can Help the Environment (Raij), 263
Kid's Guide to Service Projects, The (Lewis), 264
Kids Yoga Stories, 43, 60
    Calm Down Yoga Cards, 44
KidsGardening.org, 230
"Kidscape," 97
Kiley, Dennis, 3
Kim, Jinho, 248
kindness, 69, 235, 236
    random acts of, 260-261
Klein, Allen, 88
Krasnow, Jen, 254
Krasnow, Simone, 254
Kraushaar, Stone, 56

L

Lamba, Baldev, 231
Lamba, Marie, 231
Landgraf, Greg, 263
Langley, Jamie Lynn, 117-119
Larson, Laura, 61
Last Child in the Woods: Saving Our Children from Nature-Deficit Disorder (Louv), x, 92, 99, 120
Latino Outdoors, 101, 125
Lauri Berkner Band, 157
Laws, John Muir, 143, 161
Leave No Trace, 135, 138-140, 161, 166
Lebeuf, Darren, 162
Leslie, Clare Walker, 89
Let's Play Outdoors! Exploring Nature for Children (Ard), 126
Lewis, Barbara A., 264

Lewis, J. Patrick, 89
Li, Qing, 19, 20, 54-55
library dog reading programs, 172-174, 189
Life of Birds, 88
light, natural, 18-19
Little Bit of Dirt, A (Citro), 161
Little Gardener: Helping Children Connect with the Natural World (Cerny), 230
Little House on the Prairie, 91-92
Local Harvest, 230
Logan, Alan C., 15, 24-25
Look Again, 151, 161
Lopez, Ashley, 47
Louv, Richard, x, 67-68, 92, 99, 120, 133, 163, 185, 188, 192
Love on a Leash, 177
Lowry, Christopher, 212
Lygren, Emilie, 143, 161
Lyubomirsky, Sonja, 236

M
MacLean, Kerry, 61
Make a Date with Nature: An Introduction to Nature Journaling (Peeters), 142, 162
Make a Difference Day, 260
Mallett, David, 231
mandalas, nature, 154-156
    steps for building an outdoor, 155-156
Mappiness Study, 2
Maria Explores the Ocean (Shardlow), 44
Marine Conservation Society, 240
Martin, Laura C., 162
Massachusetts General Hospital, 196
Mazur, Rachel, 257-258, 264
McGurk, Linda Akeson, 96, 126
meditation, 27-30, 32, 71
    CDs/audios, 32, 35, 59
    color, 35-37
    compassion, 39

flower-gazing, 37-38
gardens, 47-49, 60
garden, common elements found in, 49-51
guided, 35, 40
loving-kindness, 39
nature, 34, 35, 59
Peaceful Butterfly, 40
silence and, 33
tree-hugging, 56-58
walking, 52-53
mental health issues, 2
Messner, Kate, 231
Metta, 39
Mia's Mountain Hike (Shardlow), 44
Michigan State University, 181, 187
Mindful Living Summit, 30
Mindful Monkey, Happy Panda (Alderfer), 61
Mindful Wonders: A Book About Mindfulness Using the Wonders of Nature (Zivkov), 61
mindfulness, 27-61, 159
    benefits of, 28
    birdwatching, 185
    breathing, 41-42, 59
    creativity and, 130-131
    definition, 28-30
    eating, 209-211
    float therapy, 58-60
    gardening and, 217-218, 223
    images and, 32
    nature-related, 28, 30-34
    nature walks, 52-54
    photography, 150-151
    practicing, 29-30
    sounds and, 32
    touch and, 32
    ways for kids to feel mindful from looking at nature, 31-32
Mindfulness and Nature-Based Therapeutic Techniques for Children (Fisher), 120
MindTravel, 159-160, 161
    SilentHike, 159

SilentWalk, 160

Mister G, 157

Monaghan, Kimberly, 138, 162

Monarch Watch, 259

Mondala, Melissa, 208

Monke, Audrey, 115

Morning Altars: A 7-Step Practice to Nourish Your Spirit through Nature, Art, and Ritual (Schild-kret), 162

Morning, Sunshine! (Parrack), 162

Mortali, Micah, 27, 60

Mother Natured Blog, 125

Mount St. Helens National Volcanic Monument, 78

Moving Art, 88

Ms. Mindfulness Summit, 210

Muir, John, 65

Mundo Verde/Green World (Mister G), 157

Museum of Awe, 65

music, nature-themed, 156-157
benefits of, 156-157

My Forest is Green (Lebeuf), 162

My Grateful Book (Smith), 89

Mycobacterium vaccae, 212-214

N

Naidoo, Uma, 196, 200, 230

NASA,
Climate Kids, 247, 262
Jet Propulsion Laboratory (JPL), 65

National Association of Therapeutic Schools and Programs, 123, 125

National Audubon Society, 192

National Conservation Training Center, 81

National Cowgirl Hall of Fame, 179

National Geographic Animal Encyclo-pedia (Spelman), 192

National Geographic BioBlitz, 259

National Geographic Book of Nature Poetry (Lewis), 89

National Geographic Kids, 153, 247, 262

National Geographic Kids' Get Outside Guide (Honovich, Beer), 126

National Park Service, 249

National ParkRx Initiative, 25

National Poll on Children's Health, ix

National Random Acts of Kindness Day, 260

National Wildlife Federation, xi, 97, 192, 212

nature
art, 135-138, 160
being raised in, 2
benefits of time spent in, 1-2
colors, 9-11, 23
connections to, building, 132-134
creativity and, 131-132
dance and movement, 157-158
healing power of, 1-25
hikes, 103-106
images of, 31, 142
indoors, 22-23
journaling, 142-145, 161
live cams, 81
mandalas, 154-156
media, 23, 24
meditation, 34, 35, 59
metaphors, 3-4
mindfulness and, 28, 30-34
music, 156-157
patterns, 11-12
photography, 150-154
play therapy, 92, 117-120
poetry, 80, 147-149, 161
prescriptions, 5-7
psychology of, 2-7
scents, 12, 13, 14
sensory benefits of, 9-15
sounds, 14-15, 23, 32
specific elements of, 16-24
textures, 15

theories on why nature heals, 7-9

tools, 97, 99

videos, 23-24, 88

viewing, stress reduction by, 9, 22

virtual, 23-24

ways for kids to feel mindful from looking at, 31-32

walks, 29, 52-54, 103-106

Nature by Design: The Practice of Bio- philic Design (Kellert), 7, 18, 25

Nature Club Books, The, 257-258, 264

nature-deficient disorder, 92-93

Nature Fix, The (Williams), 22, 25

nature gratitude journal, 83-84

video log, 86

Nature of Americans, The, 2

nature play, 94-99

specific attributes of, 94

unstructured, 118-119

Nature Play at Home (Striniste), 125

nature play therapy, 92, 117-120

definition of, 117

perfectionism and, 119-120

Nature Therapy Online, 25

Nature Therapy Walks: 22 Sensory Activities to Enjoy in Nature for Wellbeing, (Cameron, Clarke), 30, 60

nature tools, 97, 99, 124

Nature's Art Box (Martin), 162

Neal, Christopher Silas, 231

negative ions, 21-22

neuroplasticity, 30

Niagara Falls, 164

Nichols, Wallace J., 16, 58

Nitty-Gritty Gardening Book, The (Cornell), 231

Noise By Nature Podcast by ABC Kids, 60

O

O'Brien, Mary, 212

Ocean Conservancy, 261-262

Olsen, Sasha, 251-252

Olsson, Helen, 125

100 Parks, 5,000 Ideas: Where to Go, When to Go, What to See, What to Do (Yogerst), 125

1000 Hours Outside, 125

Oregon Zoo, 77-78

Organic Crafts: 75 Earth-Friendly Art Activities (Monaghan), 138, 162

Orienteering USA, 125

Our Climate Our Future, 247, 263

Other Way to Listen, The (Baylor), 61

Our Wild Calling: How Connecting with Animals Can Transform Our Lives—and Save Theirs (Louv), 67-68, 185, 192

Outdoor Afro, 101, 125

Outdoor Alliance for Kids, 101, 125

Outdoor Behavioral Healthcare Council, 123, 125

outdoor play, 91, 92-93

access to, 101, 106

biking, 109-110

common barriers to, 99-101

fear of, 99

as medicine, 97

team sports, 110

time and, 100

travel and adventure, 110-112

unstructured, 96-97

water sports, 105-106

weather, 100

outdoor labyrinths, 53-54

Outdoor Photography (Hamilton), 162

oxytocin, 16, 56, 181, 201

P

painting, 140-141

Paquette, Jonah, 63, 67, 71, 89

Parent, Joseph, 61

Parent, Nancy, 61

Parents' Guide to Nature Play, A (Finch), 97

Park Rx America, 6, 7, 25
Parr, Todd, 89
Parrack, Keely, 162
patterns, 11-12
Peaceful Piggy Meditation (MacLean), 61
Peeters, Paula, 142, 146, 162
Pennebaker, James W., 142
People. Animals. Love. (PAL), 189
permaculture, 218-219
Perrigo, Lynne, 173-174
pesticides, 208-209
pet(s), 163, 165-166, 170-171, 191
    as a healthy distraction, 168
    benefits of having, 165, 168-170
    birds, 174-176
    cats, 174
    classroom, 170, 191
    companionships of, 168
    dogs, 167, 169-174
    emotional support animals (ESAs), 171-177
    exercise, 169-170
    fish, 165-166
    fostering, 170
    guinea pigs, 166
    positive hormones, 169
    rabbits, 166
    social interaction and, 169
    stress and, 172
    therapy visits, 170, 254
    volunteering to care for, 170, 191
Pet Partners, 177, 192, 254
PetFinder, 192
Pfeiffer, Kelly, 143, 145
photography, nature, 150-154
    benefits of, 151
    clubs, 153-154
    decorating with, 23
    mindfulness, 150, 151
phytoncides, 19-20
PickYourOwn.org, 230
Piff, Paul, 67, 69
Piku Calm Kids App, 60

Pincott, Jena, 230
plane rides, 75-76
Plant, Cook, Eat! A Children's Cookbook (Archer, Craig), 231
Planting a Rainbow (Ehlert), 217, 231
Planting Seeds: Practicing Mindfulness with Children (Hanh), 60
playgrounds, 94
poetry
    haiku, 147-148
    nature, 147-149, 161
    walks, 128, 148-149, 161
    walks, instructions, 149-150
    walks, materials, 149
Poetry Foundation, 149
pollution, discussing, 246-247
positive psychology, viii, 70
post-traumatic stress disorder (PTSD), 151
Pretty, Jules, 102
Project Budburst, 259
Psychobiotic Revolution: Mood, Food, and the new Science of the Gut-Brain Connection, The (Anderson), 201-202, 230
Psychology Today, 93, 236
Pulitzer Prize, 7

R

Rachel's Day in the Garden (Shardlow), 44
racism, 106, 178
Raffi, 157
Raij, Emily, 263
Rails to Trails, 113
Ranger Rick, 153
Rasine, Birgitte, 190
Rasine, Aria Luna, 190-191
Reading to Rover (R2R) program, 173-174
Reflections on Mystery and Awe (Tix), 75
Resource Stewardship Scout Ranger program, 249

Rewilding (Mortali), 60
risks, allowing children to take, 122
Rodsky, Stan, 130
Roots & Shoots, 257, 263
Rousso, June, 89

S

Sampson, Scott D., 125, 152
sand tray play therapy, 118
Sayre, April Pulley, 89
scent, anxiety and stress reduction and, 12-14
Schildkret, Day, 162
Schwartzberg, Louie, 70, 81, 88
Science, 9
science museums, 23, 163
Scientific America, 208
Scientific Reports, 1
SciStarter, 259, 263
Scobie, Lorna, 162
Seasonal Affective Disorder (SAD), 18-19
Second Nature, 122
Selhub, Eva M., 15, 24, 25
Sense of Wonder, The (Carson), 89
serotonin, 16, 106, 169, 195-196
Seuss, Dr., 233
ShambalaKids, 35, 60
Shardlow, Giselle, 43-44
Shea, Shannon Brescher, 186-187, 214-215, 230, 263
Shelley, Percy Bysshe, 80
shinrin-yoku, 54
Shipley, Matt, 227
Shugarman, Harriet, 263
Siegel, Daniel J., 30
Silverstein, Natalie, 246, 263
Simple Acts: The Busy Family's Guide to Giving Back (Silverstein), 246, 263
sit spots, 33-34, 124
Smith, Diana, 89
Smith, Jeremy Adam, 89
Smith Lake Farm, 47
Smithsonian, 153

"soft fascination," 132
soil bacteria, 212-214
SOS Children's Villages Florida, 257
Soul Trak Outdoors, 101, 125
sounds, natural, 14-15
    awe and, 80
    mindfulness and, 32
    music, nature-themed, 156-157
    recording nature, 32
    stress reduction and, 15
Spelman, Lucy, 192
Squire, Ann O., 192
Story Dogs, 174
StoryWalk programs, 104-105, 125
Strassberg, Adam, 168
Strayer, David, 132
StreetWaves Inc., 106-108
    Aquatics Enrichment Program, 107-108
Stress Reduction Clinic, 29
Stress Reduction Theory (SRT), 9
Stewart, Nancy, 263
Striniste, Nancy, 125
Sullivan, Catriona, 47
Supporting the Modification of Lifestyle in Lowered Emotional States (SMILES), 195
Surfrider Foundation, 261, 263
Sutch, Kristin, 180-181
Swamp, Jake, 89
Sweet Farm, 189
    Goat-2-Meetings, 189

T

Taylor, Richard, 11
team sports, 110
10 Mindful Minutes (Hawn), 72
Tennyson, Alfred Lord, 80
textures, 15, 32
365 Days of Art in Nature: Find Inspiration Every Day in the Natural World (Scobie), 162
365 Gratitude, 88
Thank You, Earth (Sayre), 89

Thankful Book, The (Parr), 89
Thanks! How the New Science of Gratitude Can Make You Happier (Emmons)
therapeutic farms and farm animals, 177-178
    cows, 181-182, 191
    donkeys, 180
    goats, 180-181, 191
    horses, 177-180
Therapy Animals (Animals That Help Us) (Boynton), 192
There's No Such Thing as Bad Weather (McGurk), 96, 126
This Is Your Brain on Food (Naidoo), 196, 200, 230
Thomsen, Amanda, 126
Thomson, Andy, 255-256
Time, 153
Tiny Seed, The (Carle), 217, 231
Tix, Andy, 75
TodayShow.com, 153
Tomasello, Michael, 235
Towler, Paige, 61
travel and adventure, 92, 110-112
tree(s), 19-21
    defense system, 19-20
    happiness and, 19
    hugging, 56-58
    Japan study on, 19, 20
    metaphors, 3
    pine, 13
    Poland study on, 19
    scent, 19, 20
    stress and, 20-21
    United Kingdom study on, 19
Tree City USA, 261, 263
Treehouse Learning, 158
Turtle: The Incredible Journey, 88
21-Day Journey to Embracing Yourself, Your Life, and Everyone Around You, A (Kraushaar), 56

U
u-pick farms, 224-225, 229
U.S. Fish and Wildlife Service, 2, 81
University of Essex, 102
University of California, Irvine, 67
University College Cork, Department of Anatomy & Neuroscience, 196
University of Gloucestershire, 151
University of Kansas, 259
University of Massachusetts Medical School, 29
University of Woolongong, 226
Ulrich, Roger, 9
Up in the Garden and Down in the Dirt Messner, Neal), 217, 231
urban orchards, 226, 228-229

V
virtual reality (VR), 23-24
    awe and, 80-82
Vitamin N (Louv), 133
VolunteerCleanup.org, 261, 263
volunteering, 233-263, 266
    activity expectations, 245-246
    age range guidelines, 245
    with animals, 253
    attitude of gratitude and, 238
    beach cleanups, 240-242, 250-252
    benefits of, 235-243
    building confidence during, 237
    citizen science, 258-259
    cleanups, 250-252, 255-256
    community gardens, 252
    connecting with others through, 237
    conservation group, 239
    cost, 245
    delivering inspiration, 238
    environmental, 249-250, 261
    finding a sense of purpose and meaning, 238, 239
    finding the right volunteer projects for your family, 244-249

fitness for a cause, 257
fun with, 246, 249
how to address stressful environmental topics, 246-247
internalizing civic duty, 248-249
local farms, 252-253
location of activities, 245
nature clubs, 257-258
organization's mission, 244-245
parks and nature centers, 249
providing a healthy distraction, 237
outside, 238-243
safety, 246
service websites, 261
time commitment, 245
tree and flower plantings, 250
VolunteerMatch, 263

W
Waldorf Education, 92, 125
walk and talk therapy, 5
Walk in the Wood: Medications on Mindfulness with a Bear Named Pooh (Parent), 61
Walk with a Doc, 25
Wampler, Linda, 86-87
Warneken, Felix, 235
water and waves, 16-18
"blue mind," 16
float therapy, 58-60
metaphors, 3
mindfulness and, 18
sounds, 18
sports, 105-106
We All Live on This Planet Together (Rousso), 89
What Does It Mean to Be Present? (DiOrio), 61
Whitehouse, Penny, 91
Whole-Brain Child, The (Siegel, Bryson), 30
Wild Diversity, 101, 125
Wild Mindfulness (Larson), 61

Wild Roots Mini Farm, 47
wilderness therapy, 92, 120-124
wildlife tourism, 184-188
Wildlife Trusts, The, 239-240
Williams, Florence, 22, 25
Wilson, Edward O., 1, 7
Wits Guts Grit: All-Natural Biohacks for Raising Smart, Resilient Kids (Pincott), 230
Wordsworth, William, 80
World Health Organization, 129
World Kindness Day, 260
Worth, Valerie, 162

Y
Yale University, 2, 165
yoga, 30, 42-47, 105
animal, 42, 44-47, 59
bunny, 45
goat, 45-47
"lemoga," 44
horse, 44-45
nature-themed, 42
origin of, 44
outdoor, 42, 43
restorative, 36
Yoga Animals: A Wild Introduction to Kid-Friendly Poses (Towler), 61
Yogerst, Joe, 125
Your Brain on Nature (Selhub, Logan), 15, 24, 25
Youth Helping America, 234

Z
Zarr, Robert, 6
Zivkov, Michelle, 61
Zooniverse, 259, 263

Acknowledgments

First and foremost, I would like to thank my family for their love and support throughout my journey to put this book out into the world. I could not have done it without them. To my dear children, Alec and Alana, you are my inspiration, and I am extremely blessed to have you in my life. This book is for you, and all children, with the hope that it will help make the world a better place. To my amazing husband Barry, thank you for being by my side through the ups and downs of both the writing process and life in general. Your editorial feedback was priceless, and I appreciate you challenging me to be the best writer I can be. I also want to thank you for giving me the encouragement and freedom to follow my dreams. To my parents, Elise and Craig Rudenstein, thanks for always cheering me on and for giving me the opportunity to spread my wings to follow my interests. To my brother, Jared Rudenstein, I am grateful for all your patience and help with my website over the years.

Thank you to Kent Sorsky and his incredible team at Linden Publishing for their guidance and expertise throughout the editorial and printing process. I truly appreciate how you have brought my words to life with engaging images and design. It has been a pleasure working with you.

I am also thankful to everyone I interviewed for this book. Your stories and insights were extremely enriching. My goal was to bring together all your extraordinary work in the nature and mental health space to create a one-of-a-kind tool kit to share with readers. In addition, I want to recognize the researchers whose work I quote in this book. Your scientific knowledge is an essential part of this project.

Next, I want to give a big shout out to my writing community, which has done so much to support me. Thanks for always answering my many questions and pointing me in the right direction. To my writing group—Cheryl Maguire, Shannon Brescher Shea, and Dawn Sherling—your mentorship, input, and friendship are so special to me. I am also grateful for everyone involved in the Nonfiction Authors Association, Women in Publishing Summit, American Society of Journalists and Authors, and Binders.

I am also indebted to the passionate environmental and mental health communities that I have been involved in over the years. So much of my knowledge and drive stems from experiences with your organizations, events, books, trainings, and more.

I extend my gratitude to everyone who reviewed my book. I also want to thank all the great authors who have come before me, particularly Richard Louv and Gretchen Rubin, whose work sparked my idea for *Finding Ecohappiness.*

Finally, thank you from the bottom of my heart to the many readers over the years of my blog, articles, and now book. Your positive feedback encouraged me to keep on writing. Thank you for helping to make a difference!

About the Author

Sandi Schwartz is a journalist specializing in parenting, wellness, and the environment. She has written for *Chicken Soup for the Soul*, *Scary Mommy*, and *Very Well Family*, among other publications. She founded the Eco-happiness Project to help families build a nature habit to feel happier and calmer by exploring positive psychology tools through engagement with nature. Previously, she held communications positions at the United States Environmental Protection Agency and National Academy of Sciences. Schwartz has a master's in government (environmental focus) from Johns Hopkins University and a Specialization Certificate in Foundations of Positive Psychology from the University of Pennsylvania. She is an active member in environmental and writing organizations, including Children & Nature Network, American Society of Journalists and Authors, Sierra Club, and more. Schwartz splits time between Florida and New Jersey with her husband and two children. Schwartz's website is www.ecohappinessproject.com.